PRAISE FOR
Beyond the Big Test

"With a fresh and integrated approach, Sedlacek's book seeks to improve the evaluation process for all students, especially nontraditional students in higher education."

—Norbert S. Hill, Jr., executive director, American Indian Graduate Center

"William E. Sedlacek has devoted his career to assessment of diverse populations using cognitive and noncognitive variables. He again provides the profession with important information based on his programmatic research and that of others. I recommend the book for assessment professionals."

—Patricia B. Elmore, associate dean for administrative services and professor, Department of Educational Psychology and Special Education, College of Education, Southern Illinois University, and editor, *Measurement and Evaluation in Counseling and Development*

"This book should be required reading for all college personnel involved with admissions, recruitment, retention, and assessment."

—John V. Fraire, dean of admissions, Western Michigan University

"This must-read, book emphasizes the use of noncognitive variables in admissions, teaching, advisement, and program evaluation, shifting the paradigm from an overdependency on the SAT and other big tests in higher education."

—Shirley Hune, professor and associate dean, Graduate Programs, Graduate Division, University of California, Los Angeles

"Sedlacek has made a very significant contribution to scholarship on noncognitive predictors of the admissibility and performance of students of color in postsecondary education and to higher education policy. Readers should pay special attention to the chapter on the conceptual and research foundations for these critical noncognitive measures."

—William T. Trent, professor of educational policy studies and sociology, University of Illinois

"In this thought-provoking book, William Sedlacek not only accentuates the point that noncognitive variables can and should be used by college admissions offices, as they are better predictors of success among nontraditional college students, but he suggests ways that they can be used in advising, counseling, designing and evaluating programs, and teaching. In my judgment, this book is a must-read for colleges and universities interested in diversifying their student bodies and improving the overall quality of campus life."

—Donald Brown, AHANA Program, Boston College

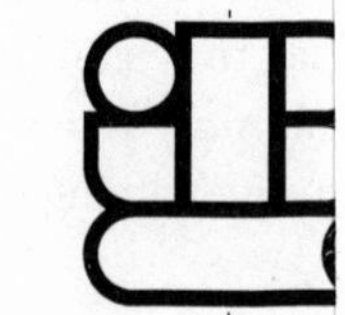

BEYOND THE BIG TEST

Noncognitive Assessment in Higher Education

William E. Sedlacek

JOSSEY-BASS
A Wiley Company
www.josseybass.com

Published by Jossey-Bass
A Wiley Imprint
989 Market Street, San Francisco, CA 94103-1741 www.josseybass.com

Jossey-Bass books and products are available through most bookstores. To contact Jossey-Bass directly call our Customer Care Department within the U.S. at 800-956-7739, outside the U.S. at 317-572-3986 or fax 317-572-4002.

Jossey-Bass also publishes its books in a variety of electronic formats. Some content that appears in print may not be available in electronic books.

Library of Congress Cataloging-in-Publication Data
Sedlacek, William E.
Beyond the big test : noncognitive assessment in higher education / William E. Sedlacek.—1st ed.
p. cm. —(The Jossey-Bass higher and adult education series)
Includes bibliographical references and index.
ISBN 0-7879-6020-9 (alk. paper)
1. Universities and colleges—United States—Entrance requirements. 2. Educational tests and measurements—United States. 3. Educational evaluation—United States. I. Title. II. Series.
LB2351.2.S43 2004
378.1'662—dc22 2003023208

Printed in the United States of America
FIRST EDITION
HB Printing 10 9 8 7 6 5 4 3 2 1

The Jossey-Bass

Higher and Adult Education Series

I would like to thank the many students and colleagues who have worked with me over the years for making this book possible. I would also like to acknowledge my wife, Alex, and our dogs, Beckett, Bradley, and Ruach (who is no longer with us), for their loving reminders that life is more than research and writing.

CONTENTS

Appendices

PREFACE

What Can This Book Do for You?

If you are a college or university administrator, this book offers you:

- Legal grounding for enrollment, financial aid, and support of diverse student groups
- Assessable approaches to admissions, retention, and financial aid
- Usable instruments you can copy or modify and distribute
- A set of heuristics as to which individuals and programs succeed and fail—and why
- Ways to make your institution more responsive to your entire student body
- Case studies of what has and has not worked in other situations
- Ways to evaluate faculty and staff programs
- Ways to present your program to students, faculty, parents, administrators, trustees, and others
- Ways to integrate academic and nonacademic programs
- Ways to integrate pre- and postmatriculation programs

If you are a faculty member, this book offers you:

- Assessable approaches to classroom success
- Usable instruments you can copy and distribute

- Ways to make your courses more useful to all your students, and to help your students get more out of (and be more receptive to) the material you teach—whether it is art or zoology
- A set of heuristics as to which individuals and programs succeed and fail—and why
- Case studies of what has and has not worked in other situations
- Ways to advise your students using a model related to their success
- Ways to approach diversity in and out of the classroom
- Approaches to researching culture, race, gender, and other diversity-related variables

If you are a college or university staff member, this book offers you:

- Assessable approaches to how your department can serve all members of the student body
- Particular attention to advising and counseling services
- Usable instruments you can copy or modify and distribute
- A set of heuristics as to which individuals and programs succeed and fail—and why
- Ways to incorporate principles of diversity in all your programs
- Case studies of what has and has not worked in other situations
- Ways to relate your program to student academic and nonacademic success

If you are an assessment professional, this book offers you:

- A pragmatic, success-focused form of assessment
- A built-in developmental capability to assess change over time and predict improvement strategies
- A solid grounding in peer-reviewed literature in a variety of disciplines
- Ways to assess diversity-related variables

If you develop and support students of color, women, or other individuals from a range of populations representing diversity in any context, this book offers you:

- A style of assessment that takes your population's specific needs into consideration
- Legal grounding for increasing diversity and responding to charges of reverse discrimination
- A level playing field where all forms of intelligence and skill are valued and considered

- Usable instruments you can copy or modify and distribute
- A set of heuristics as to which individuals and programs succeed and fail—and why
- A positive, proactive approach to working with your students

The issues listed here and more are addressed throughout the book. With an overall model that can be employed by all on a campus, there is a greater possibility of coordinating academic and nonacademic programs. This can lead to increased understanding and communication among all those working on the common goal of educating students in the best way possible.

What Is the Big Test?

Nicholas Lemann popularized the term in *The Big Test: The Secret History of the American Meritocracy.* The Scholastic Aptitude Test, or SAT, is the best example of a Big Test in that students, parents, and educators alike have made the exam an end in itself. SAT scores have become the ultimate symbol of ability and potential.

As every student who has ever taken a Big Test (as well as every administrator or educator who has ever reviewed the results) knows, Big Tests are generally divided into two sections: verbal and quantitative. These two dimensions form the basis for what is often called "cognitive" intelligence, the only measure of ability that Big Tests assess.

The Importance of Diversity

Higher education has seen a great increase in the diversity of its students in recent years. These students bring a wider range of abilities, interests, and backgrounds that are based on culture, race, gender, and other aspects of diversity to the academy than ever before. We need better ways of doing assessments that are useful and fair to these students. This book presents a model for producing assessments that are fairer to all students than those based on the Big Test.

Chapter Summaries

Chapter One consists of a brief history of the SAT and other Big Tests, an analysis of why they are so popular and entrenched, an overview of diversity issues, and a discussion of "nontraditionality" and racism. These issues are followed by a proposed alternative to the Big Test, the advantages of this new paradigm, and the tools necessary to implement the alternative.

Chapter Two reviews basic statistical concepts, including validity and reliability as well as measurement issues important in developing the proposed model of assessment.

Chapter Three reintroduces the issues of diversity and nontraditionality; it relates them to the requirements of useful assessment, using a list of five ways that these issues affect statistical validity and reliability.

Chapter Four contains a discussion of noncognitive variables, the research behind them, and how they can be measured. Here is the system of noncognitive variables that form the underlying core of the book:

- Positive self-concept
- Realistic self-appraisal
- Successfully handling the system
- Preference for long-term goals
- Availability of a strong support person
- Leadership experience
- Community involvement
- Knowledge acquired in a field

In Chapter Five, methods of selecting students for admission or financial aid awards are presented.

Noncognitive variables can be employed in a variety of settings involving teaching, as covered in Chapter Six.

Chapter Seven looks at advising, an important but complicated function in higher education. Where advising ends and counseling begins is a difficult line to draw, but noncognitive variables can help educators and service providers work with students productively and developmentally.

Noncognitive variables can be employed in evaluating programs, and services. In Chapter Eight, a number of examples are discussed, including some involving evaluation of faculty and staff.

Chapter Nine contains summary comments and suggestions for use of noncognitive variables in a number of areas involving students, faculty, and community members.

The hope is that anyone working in the education system, or concerned with educating all our students, should be able to find some useful idea or application in this book.

ABOUT THE AUTHOR

William E. Sedlacek is a professor of education and assistant director of the Counseling Center at the University of Maryland, College Park. He is also an adjunct professor of pharmacy at the University of Maryland at Baltimore. He earned a B.S. degree in industrial administration and an M.S. degree in industrial psychology from Iowa State University and a Ph.D. degree in psychology and statistics from Kansas State University.

He is senior author of *Racism in American Education: A Model for Change* (with Brooks, published by Nelson Hall) and a measure of racial attitudes, *The Situational Attitude Scale* (SAS). In addition, he has published more than 300 articles in professional journals on a wide range of topics including multicultural issues, college admissions, advising, research methodology, and employee selection. Also, he has presented more than 200 research papers at professional conferences and conventions.

He has served as editor of *Measurement and Evaluation in Counseling and Development* and is currently on the editorial board of that journal. He is also on the editorial board of the *Journal of College Student Development* and does reviews for a number of other journals and publications. His advisory boards include the Gates Millennium Scholars Research Advisory Committee and the Washington State Achievers Research Advisory Committee.

He has consulted with more than 300 different organizations, colleges, and universities on interracial and intercultural issues and has served as an expert witness in race and sex discrimination cases. In 1993, he received the Ralph F. Berdie Memorial Research Award "for research affecting directional changes in the field of counseling and college student personnel work," which was presented by the American Counseling Association. Also in 1993, he received the John B. Muir Editor's Award from the National Association of College Admission Counselors for his article "Employing Noncognitive Variables in the Admission and Retention of Nontraditional Students."

In 1997, he received the research award from the American Counseling Association for his article "An Empirical Method of Determining Nontraditional Group Status" published in *Measurement and Evaluation in Counseling and Development.* In 1998, he was named a Senior Scholar by the American College Personnel Association and became a Diplomate in 2003. In 2002, he was recognized by the American College Personnel Association as a Diamond Honoree, for his service and research in student affairs.

"Sed" lives with his wife Alex and his two dogs, Beckett and Bradley, in Silver Spring, Maryland. His son Joe is a lawyer in California. Sed's activities include playing basketball, developing an electronic calendar of favorite comments and events (http://www.counseling.umd.edu/SedCal/), and listening to classical guitar and jazz. He also enjoys unusual films, reading biographies, following baseball, chopping firewood, and the solitude in his retreat in rural West Virginia. Information on his publications and other details can be found on his website at http://www.counseling.umd.edu/sedlacekresearch.html.

CHAPTER ONE

THE BIG TEST . . . AND AN ALTERNATIVE APPROACH

The first examination administered by the College Entrance Examination Board (now the College Board) was in 1901. More than a century later, standardized admission tests in higher education are more popular than ever (Linn, 1993). More than four million people took either the SAT (formerly known as the Scholastic Aptitude Test and Scholastic Assessment Tests) or the ACT (American College Test) in 2002. Standardized tests typically measure verbal and quantitative problem solving. Scores on these two components are commonly added to form a single score, but they are best considered as separate attributes. Along with the SAT and ACT, other standardized tests of note are the MAT (Miller Analogies Test) and the GRE (Graduate Record Examination).

The College Board has long felt that the SAT was limited in what it measured and should not be relied upon as the only tool with which to judge applicants to colleges and universities (Angoff, 1971; Sedlacek, 1998a). The board gave advice in 1926, as it developed its first test, that is as relevant today as it was then:

> The present state of all efforts of men [sic] to measure or in any way estimate the worth of other men, or to evaluate the results of their nurture, or to reckon their potential possibilities does not warrant any certainty of prediction. This additional test now made available through the instrumentality of the College Entrance Examination Board may resolve a few perplexing problems, but it should be regarded merely as a supplementary record. To place too great

> emphasis on test scores is as dangerous as the failure properly to evaluate any score or rank in conjunction with other measures and estimates which it supplements [Brigham, 1926, pp. 44–45].

In 1993, a reasoning exam was added to the SAT, and in 2003 the College Board announced that an essay would be added and the analogies item type removed as of 2005. Despite various changes and versions over the years, the SAT in essence measures what it did in 1926: verbal and math ability. It is basically still a general intelligence test (Sedlacek, 1998a, 1998b, 2003a, forthcoming).

The ACT, first administered in 1959, was intended to be an alternative to the SAT, emphasizing a wider range of abilities than simply verbal and math. The reality is that the two tests are highly correlated (Sedlacek, 1998a; Willingham, Lewis, Morgan, and Ramist, 1990). They measure many of the same things and have the same advantages and disadvantages.

Yet today the Big Test is the focal point in our schools (Lemann, 2000), the standard by which we judge ourselves and others. Many people assume that if an individual has high SAT scores, or if a school has high average SAT scores, the students must be learning something, and the school must be good.

Why Is the Big Test So Popular?

There are a number of reasons why tests are so popular. Some of these reasons are discussed below.

Level Playing Field

One reason that standardized tests are frequently used by college admissions personnel is that they constitute a common way to evaluate candidates with varied backgrounds and experiences. It seems fair to use the same test to compare an eighteen-year-old White student from a rural high school in Iowa to a twenty-four-year-old Puerto Rican applicant from New York City. In fact, although the first test was designed to distinguish among White students attending private schools in the eastern United States, the original idea behind the College Board test was nonetheless to provide just such a common yardstick.

Perhaps the most important implication of viewing standardized tests as a fair and leveling means of judging all students is that standardized tests are not prone to generate lawsuits. The reasoning goes that so long as one uses a single common measure, the letter of the law is being followed.

Ease of Use

Standardized tests can readily be required of applicants, and they are easy to acquire from the testing companies. Also, since they yield numerical scores, they are a convenient way to compare candidates, especially when sorting through large numbers of applicants. If one simply selects those students with higher test scores, admissions can be viewed as a relatively simple and equitable process, even though virtually every decision maker who uses standardized tests professes to use other variables as well. The test score is an easy thing to fall back on in defending admissions decisions to students, parents, faculty, alumni, and other potential critics. As computers have become more sophisticated, it has become easier and easier to process test scores electronically and to develop prediction equations and models.

Simple Assessment Standards

Standardized test scores also are used to assess the quality of a college or preparatory school. Everyone has seen the officials of an institution express excitement over an increase in test scores, or bemoan lower scores. Students, faculty, and others such as the publishers of college guides often join the chorus. Unfortunately, this was never one of the designated purposes of standardized tests, and confusing test scores with the quality of education at an institution likely serves no one well.

At the level of the individual rather than the institution, students with high scores are assumed to be smart, and they are presumed capable of learning on their own. Whether they actually learn anything or how they learn is seldom assessed. On the other hand, often those with low scores are presumed, without further verification, to need remedial instruction. Neither conclusion is based on the quality of the institution and how it educates students.

Low Expense

Standardized tests are also a relatively inexpensive way for college administrators to feel they are measuring student abilities. Students and their families bear the cost of the exams. As budgets tighten, keeping the costs of the admissions system down is seen as more important than ever before.

The Importance of Diversity

More than thirty major higher education organizations signed this advertisement that appeared in the *Chronicle of Higher Education* in July 2003:

> In a nearly unprecedented expression of consensus, virtually the entire higher education community urged the United States Supreme Court to recognize that racial diversity on campus is a compelling national interest. . . . [The organizations] applaud the Court's explicit recognition that diversity is indeed a compelling educational and civic value—essential to excellence as well as equity. . . . [We] now know, from experience and a growing body of research, that engaging diversity on campus deepens students' individual learning and reaps rich dividends—in both knowledge and values—for democracy ["Diversity and Democracy," 2003, p. A29].

Quite apart from the question of wider social benefit, diversity is also an important part of the student learning experience in college. In his book *Making the Most of College: Students Speak Their Minds,* Richard J. Light stated that "[r]acial and ethnic diversity can, and often does, enhance learning in the classroom and beyond," adding that "many students of all racial and ethnic backgrounds draw a sharp contrast between positive experiences they are having with diversity at college and negative experiences they had in high school" (Light, 2001, pp. 4–5).

Clearly, campus diversity creates both an immediate educational opportunity and a long-term benefit to students and to the society of which they form a part.

The Terminology of Diversity

There is often much confusion about how diversity is defined, which groups should be included, and what terms should be applied to those groups. Questions arise such as, Should we include gays and lesbians in our conceptualization? Should we use "*Black*" and "*African American*" interchangeably? Is the whole issue just a matter of being politically correct?

Labels and terminology are important and contain many symbolic and connotative elements, but those concerned with assessment can help cut through some of the ambiguity by helping to define terms operationally. Differences or similarities among groups can be demonstrated through measurement.

Nontraditionality. The labels used in the *Education Index* to describe what I call "nontraditional students" were studied over a forty-year period (Westbrook and Sedlacek, 1991). Terms have varied, from a focus on acculturation in the 1950s to disadvantaged in the 1960s, to culture-specific differences in the 1970s, to multicultural issues in the 1980s. Diversity could be called the "in" term for the 1990s. Although these terms may suggest a number of approaches to the groups discussed, operationally we may still be discussing the same people, that is, people with cultural experiences different from those of White, middle-class, heterosexual, males of European descent, those with less power to control their lives, and those who experience discrimination in the United States. But does it make sense to include such variables as gender, sexual orientation, or status as an athlete as aspects of cultural experience?

Results from applying the Situational Attitude Scale (SAS) and the Noncognitive Questionnaire (NCQ, described in detail in Chapter Three) lead to the conclusion that if a group experiences prejudice and demonstrates abilities in ways differing from those with traditional experiences, it is useful to define that group operationally as nontraditional.

The concern in this book is not that one concept or another is best, but that decisions based on measurement principles and empirical evidence be made wherever possible. The implication of the term *nontraditional* is that we need to think of the cultural context and experiences of some people differently from those of the group in power if we wish to be fair to them. Nontraditional people have some experiences that are not typical of those in traditional power groups. Those nontraditional experiences should be considered in evaluating the potential of people who have had them.

Even though groups as contrasting as athletes and older people may show their diversity in different ways, the variables underlying the problems in dealing with their development and in coping with a traditional system that was not designed for them may have some similarities (see Sedlacek, 1996a, 1996b). Similarly, groups as much a part of the current mainstream as women still show attributes that can affect their performance on Big Test–style scales (see Chapters Two and Three).

Many would disagree with the conclusions and definitions of nontraditional presented here. For example, Helms (1992) saw visible racial/ethnic groups (VREGs) as having some distinct problems and characteristics. Also, nontraditional has been used by some as referring only to older students. Sue, Arredondo, and McDavis (1992) expressed concern that the term cross-cultural can be defined as broadly as it is, that it allows counseling professionals to avoid dealing with what they see as the four main "minority" groups in our society: African Americans, American Indians, Asian Americans, and Latinos. Still others may feel that any term sounding negative, or including what is different from the norm, is ill-advised. However, I feel that relevant variation based on nontraditionality and more specific group memberships both can be measured.

Racism. Racism can take many forms. The word is used here to cover all types of -isms (sexism, ageism, even "athleteism"). Racism can be individual as well as institutional, but the primary concern in this book is the ability to deal with the policies, procedures, and barriers (intentional or otherwise) that interfere with the development of people.

Institutional racism is defined as the negative consequences that accrue to a member of a given group because of how a system or subsystem operates in the society (for instance, college admissions), regardless of any other attributes of the individual (Sedlacek, 1988, 1995b; Sedlacek and Brooks, 1976). Thus if we have an evaluation system that yields more useful results for people with traditional experiences than for those with less traditional experiences, we have an example of racism regardless of the motives involved.

Why Do We Need to Go Beyond the Big Test?

In light of a commitment to diversity and fairness to a diverse student body, Big Tests don't give us everything we need from a test. We may need to use a variety of measures to achieve equitable assessments for all. Sackett, Schmidt, Ellingson, and Kabin (2001) felt that to increase ethnic diversity one should not be limited to the cognitive measures on which Big Tests rely. They recommended "using selection materials that assess the full range of relevant attributes" (p. 302).

Test results should be useful to educators, student service workers, and administrators, by constituting the basis to help students learn better and analyze their needs. As currently designed, tests do not accomplish these objectives. Many teachers teach for their students to get the highest test scores; student service workers may ignore the tests; and too many administrators are satisfied if the average test scores rise in their school. We need tests that are fair to all and that give us a good assessment of the developmental and learning needs of students, while being useful in selecting outstanding applicants to colleges and universities.

Our current tests don't do that. They give us *some* information that is useful for *some* students in predicting what grades they will get in their first year in college, but they don't even do that well for people of color, women, or anyone who has not had a White, middle-class, Euro-centric, heterosexual, male experience in the United States.

If we want tests that are truly useful to a variety of students, parents, and educators, modifying the Big Tests is not enough. We need a fresh approach, one that is useful in evaluating candidates for admissions and scholarships, but also useful after students start college. We need a test or a system of tests that is fair to all; has legal authority; and helps students develop throughout their time in an undergraduate, graduate, or professional school. Instead of asking "How can we make the SAT and other such tests better?" we need to ask "What kinds of measures will meet our needs now and in the future?" We do not need to ignore our current tests; what we need is to add some new measures that expand the potential we can derive from assessment.

Where Can We Find Alternatives or Supplements to the Big Test?

Thirty years of development, testing, and legal challenges demonstrate that the use of noncognitive variables can provide what is missing from the Big Test approach. *Noncognitive* is used here to refer to variables relating to adjustment, motivation, and student perceptions, rather than relying solely on the traditional verbal and quantitative (often called cognitive) areas typically measured by standardized tests.

These are the eight noncognitive variables (NCVs) identified by extensive research in this area:

- Positive self-concept
- Realistic self-appraisal
- Successfully handling the system
- Preference for long-term goals
- Availability of strong support person
- Leadership experience
- Community involvement
- Knowledge acquired in a field

The goal of using noncognitive variables is not to *substitute* this approach for the cognitive focus more commonly employed in assessments, but to *add* to the range of attributes that we consider in making the many judgments required of us all.

What Tools Do Educators, Parents, and Students Need to Go Beyond the Big Test?

Everything you need to begin the process of replacing the Big Test with a system of testing based on noncognitive variables is available in this book. Anyone working in the education system or concerned with educating all our students should be able to find some useful idea or application here.

Guidelines for assessing individuals on each of the eight noncognitive variables, along with sample attitude scale questionnaires, are the building blocks for an entire NCV-oriented program in any area where you as an administrator, faculty member, staff member, parent, or student may see the need.

In addition, this book provides:

- A full explanation of the rationale behind the NCV approach
- A detailed survey and analysis of the research underpinnings that support the approach

- Practical guidelines in how to implement the approach in various contexts
- A rich assortment of quantitative and case study examples of successes and failures with the NCV approach, including analysis of the underlying dimensions that differentiate success from failure
- A model for evaluating programs and services for diverse or nontraditional students using a comprehensive approach that can include Big Test elements as well as a commitment to NCVs

Advantages of an Integrated, Legally Tested, Research-Based Assessment Paradigm

A number of the advantages of using the noncognitive variable system detailed in this book are discussed below.

Pragmatism

Many assessment approaches claim to be practical by virtue of recommending separate measures that they say fit every assessment situation. Want a measure to assess campus climate? Here is one you can use off the shelf. Need a measure of teaching efficacy, career interests, and admissions? No problem. We have something for everyone. Just plug in and crank.

Such strategies appear to offer practical solutions; however, they fall short because they set no overall context for the use of the measures they propose and make no effort to integrate the measures recommended into the academic environment in which they will be used. Each measure is presented as a separate stand-alone assessment device. In many cases, the proponents of these tools offer no information on the quality of the measures they recommend, and they rarely if ever provide references to the evidence of a measure's effectiveness as published in peer-reviewed professional journals. The higher education community needs practical assessment instruments that are readily available and easy to use, but today's commonly used tools do not give us a solid base of information that relates the recommended assessments to one another; nor do they yield empirical evidence of their value.

The noncognitive variable assessment paradigm is practical, and it has the additional value of being carefully and thoroughly researched, demonstrably applicable to a broad range of needs and circumstances, and capable of integrating all aspects of assessment in the college or university environment.

Basis in Theory

Theories of measurement, intelligence, and student development are critical to the achievement of good assessment instruments. However, these theories (and the books that describe them) rarely include concrete examples that educators and practitioners in higher education can follow or apply to their particular institution. To be truly useful, a book on assessment should propose measures the reader can apply without having to create his or her own instruments. This book presents example instruments that can be used in conducting many types of higher education assessment, along with a fully documented theoretical context for assessments.

Tested Legally

The argument that race could be used as one factor in admission was developed in the *Bakke* case (*Regents of the University of California* v. *Bakke,* 1978). However, rulings in more recent cases, including one of the two 2003 U.S. Supreme Court cases detailed here, have questioned the legality of using race in admissions. In several of these cases, noncognitive variables have been proposed as alternatives to traditional measures, or to using race in admissions (see *FairTest Examiner,* 1997; Yalof-Garfield, 1997; Michaelson, 1996). In *Adarand Constructors* v. *Peña* (1995) the Supreme Court of the United States ruled that firms could not award contracts on federal highway projects on the basis of race. The Fifth Circuit Court of Appeals (*Hopwood* v. *Texas,* 1994) struck down a University of Texas Law School plan to target a student body with certain percentages of Latino and Black students. Also in 1996, the voters of California passed Proposition 209, amending the state Constitution and making it illegal to consider race, sex, color, ethnicity, or national origin for preferential treatment in state organizations, including colleges and universities.

At this writing *Hopwood* applies only to the Fifth Circuit (Texas, Arkansas, and Louisiana) and Proposition 209 is limited to California. However, the reasoning in Proposition 209 has been challenged in *Castañeda* v. *The University of California Regents* (1999) and *Farmer* v. *Ramsay* (1998), both of which raise the question of noncognitive variables as an alternative approach. The *Farmer* court has ruled in favor of allowing the University of Maryland to employ noncognitive variables in admitting students to its medical school; the plaintiff has appealed this judgment.

Two cases decided by the Supreme Court of the United States further challenged the use of race in admissions. The cases involved the University of Michigan's policies to consider race in admissions to add diversity to its general undergraduate program and law school (*Gratz and Hamacher* v. *Bollinger et al.*, 2002; *Grutter* v. *Bollinger et al.*, 2002).

In the former case, the Court ruled that the university could not assign a specific weight to an applicant solely because of race. For example, Michigan awarded twenty points to each "underrepresented minority," which was one-fifth of the points necessary to guarantee admission.

However, in *Grutter v. Bollinger,* the Court ruled that the law school could consider race as one of many factors in admitting students. This logic is similar to that used by Justice Powell in his dissenting opinion in the *Bakke* case.

Whereas I supported the efforts of the University of Michigan to consider race directly in its admissions policies, I believe there is a better way to proceed. If the university were to use the noncognitive variables proposed here in its admissions systems, it would achieve diversity in its classes by virtue of considering variables that reflect race, culture, gender, and the other aspects of nontraditionality discussed earlier. Thus, by not directly selecting according to aspects of diversity, a school can achieve increased diversity in a more sophisticated way, on the basis of the research evidence available. The noncognitive variable method yields important attributes correlating with student success that appear to be legal and fair to all applicants.

Focus on Success

Most assessment theories present assessment results as ends in themselves. That is, the scores on a measure are not deemed to be related to other attributes. At best, some attempt is made to relate the results of the assessments they recommend to a single criterion (such as the SAT purporting to predict first-year grades). Most practitioners in higher education, however, would appreciate a great deal more from an assessment instrument. Educators and administrators would like to be able to relate measurement results to long-term outcome measures, such as student grades across the college career, retention at our institutions, and (ideally) graduation. Similarly, if we are measuring student reactions to a diversity program we have started on campus, we would like to be able to relate the results of that assessment to the long-term success of students on campus. We would like, in short, to have an *overall* assessment model: one that helps us interpret assessment results in terms of both present and future student success.

The integrated assessment model presented here allows administrators, educators, parents, and students to find answers to specific evaluation or assessment questions and to tie those answers to a larger plan whose fundamental principle is the facilitation of student success. The success focus of the integrated assessment model strengthens the value of the assessment to many audiences in higher education. For example, using this model to evaluate a program to enhance social justice in campus residence halls allows educators to evaluate not just the immediate impact of the new program but its relationship to student retention as well.

Developmental Capability

Assessment tools rarely attempt to provide measures that are useful in assessing how a person or program develops on the variables being measured. Typically, an assessment is seen as a static snapshot of a moment in time. Appropriate changes may be suggested by the assessment results, but the discussion of those results rarely includes any strategy for helping an examinee or service improve along specified dimensions.

The integrated assessment model is a plan for assessing variables that have both predictive and developmental implications. This model can be used for individuals and organizations alike, to promote positive change along the dimensions of the assessment.

The developmental nature of the variables used in the integrated assessment model encourages users to take a longitudinal view of students, faculty, and staff in higher education. This long-term view of student and employee development appears in many college catalogues, but it is rarely evaluated. The integrated assessment model not only allows such evaluation, it builds on the findings by suggesting programs to encourage positive change.

Relevance to Institutional Policy

A frequent criticism of assessment in higher education is that it does not help administrators struggling to make policy decisions. Many difficult questions face policy makers today: Should we change our admissions policies? Do we need to provide more support for students of color? What information should we give parents? How can we evaluate our efforts to recruit faculty and staff of color? The noncognitive variable assessment model sets a context for answering policy-relevant questions by helping decision makers develop practical measurement instruments tied to theory, outcomes, and specific strategies for implementing positive change.

As has been discussed here, some of the most complicated questions in higher education policy today are about the legality of certain types of assessment. Decision makers throughout higher education are confronted with questions such as these: Is it legal to award scholarships on the basis of anything other than grades and test scores? Can we be sued if we try to increase our enrollment of students from certain racial or cultural groups? What arguments can we give our attorneys to support our use of alternative evaluation methods? . Fortunately, the NCV assessment system can help answer these questions. The integrated assessment model has been tested in the courts and is a way for decision makers to be proactive in doing innovative evaluations in higher education.

Promotion of Equity

Most assessment approaches either shy away from mentioning issues of fairness or cover them superficially. To provide fair and useful assessment, especially assessment that takes the values of diversity into consideration, questions of this sort must be asked: Can an entire method of assessment be biased? Does a given test work better for some groups than for others? Do people from various racial or cultural groups show their abilities and accomplishments in different ways? Should we evaluate men and women differently? Unfortunately, these questions are rarely addressed systematically or from a statistically rigorous point of view.

The method of assessment presented in this book works well for all persons and is particularly sensitive to individual differences that reflect diversity of experience and socialization.

Broad Base in Academic Literature

Arguably, the greatest strength of the integrated assessment model presented in this book is that it has been studied and refined for more than thirty years. The integrated assessment model is rooted in cognitive science and measurement theory, and its usefulness has been demonstrated in a range of research studies. Assessment is frequently presented as a discipline that does not require reference to research, theory, and practice or to methodologies used in a variety of fields. Many books on evaluation and measurement do not include references to the research literature in content areas.

This book includes numerous references to research that supports the points being made about measurement instruments and assessment practices. In addition to documenting the development and evaluation of the integrated assessment model, these references represent extensive source material on a range of content and methodological issues in assessment.

CHAPTER TWO

GOING BEYOND THE BIG TEST

In the previous chapter, limitations in assessment approaches were discussed. This chapter covers an analysis of the difficulties with the measures currently available to do assessments.

The assessment model presented in this book takes us beyond the Big Test. It yields assessments that can be used in a variety of situations. This book focuses on some of the major kinds of assessment in higher education, among them assessment of academic potential, program evaluation, curricular evaluation, and campus climate. It presents a comprehensive model of assessment that is based on noncognitive variables, tied to student ability and performance. Assessment techniques—tests, interviews, focus groups, observational methods, portfolios, and so on—are discussed generically. The terms *test, measure,* and *assessment* or *evaluation* method or technique are used interchangeably throughout the book.

Before we can address the issues posed in Chapter One, we need to examine the limitations in current tests and measures—in other words, why we need another approach.

Current Tests Don't Work Well

Any effective assessment method should yield reliable and valid results. Validity is defined as how well scores from a test measure what they are supposed to measure.

Reliability refers to the consistency of measurement, or how varied we can expect repeated measures of the same thing to be time after time. Unfortunately, there is a lack of validity and reliability evidence for many of the commonly employed measures with particular samples or groups such as women or people of color. In some cases, validity and reliability information is lacking because the difficult and often time-consuming work of developing a measure has not been done. In other circumstances, there is some evidence of the lack of validity and reliability, but it is ignored. We often expect too much of our measures, and we go well beyond the limits of what a test can do.

Validity

Some discussion of validity may be useful here in helping to understand the limitations in current tests. Validity is determined by estimating if scores from a measure assess what they are supposed to assess. There are a number of ways that validity of the scores on a measure can be established, (see, for example, Anastasi & Urbina, 1997; Linn & Gronlund, 2000) and they are briefly summarized later, along with comments on their advantages and disadvantages. This summary may help in understanding why some methods have not been employed as much as they might have been, and why the newer measures that are needed may not have been developed.

Before beginning the discussion of particular types of validity, it is important to state that validity should be discussed in relation to some criterion. Validity should always be stated in terms of a specific purpose for a specific group; it is a characteristic of the results, or scores, on a measure, rather than the measure itself (*Standards for Educational and Psychological Testing,* 1999). For example, do the scores on a measure show validity and reliability in predicting grades for Asian American students at a certain college? Validity is not a general characteristic of an assessment method; it is a characteristic of the scores from a particular sample in a specific context.

Face Validity

The scores on a measure have face validity if they look as though they are measuring topics of interest, with no further evidence. Chances are you have been in a meeting where a group is evaluating a questionnaire, or other measure, by looking over the items. With nothing but your own hunch, you pick your measure. The obvious disadvantage of face validity is that it is not typically based on any empirical work, or even scholarship, of any kind. But it is quick, and it looks as if something has been done. It is helpful to have a measure that appears to be on target for soliciting cooperation from those to whom the measure will be applied, as well as cooperation from those sponsoring the assessment. For example, if there is interest in knowing how well students liked a course, questions dealing with the course would seem appropriate. This seems simple and easy enough, but content can be misjudged, and a very poor measure might result. In most cases, one would never know how good or bad a measure is, and some very inappropriate decisions may be made on the basis of the results.

Content Validity

Content validity requires more work than face validity, but it is worth the trouble. The logic here is that the content of items on a questionnaire, questions in an interview, themes in a focus group, and so on should contain the content that one is seeking. As opposed to face validity, content validity requires some empirical information and should have a scholarly foundation. For example, if one wishes to determine the effectiveness of a career counseling program, the first step would be to go to the literature on career counseling and identify some issues or themes that have been shown to be important in career counseling. In this example, eight issues might be found, things such as long-term goals, intrinsic interest in the work, and education required.

The next step would be to generate some items or questions that reflect those eight themes. The items could come from other studies reported, or they might be created by the developer of the measure. The items are then presented to a minimum of two judges in a random order where there is no indication of which items go with which themes. The judges then independently rate the items as to which theme each item seems to best represent. The items that are agreed upon by the judges can be said to have content validity. If more than two judges are employed, agreement among two-thirds (or three quarters, and so on) can be employed as a minimum standard. Cohen's Kappa (Bakeman & Gottman, 1986) can be calculated as a statistical test of the extent of the agreement.

Another technique that could be employed is to use Likert-type, or Summated Rating, statements in an agree-disagree format (Edwards, 1957; Isaac & Michael, 1995) and have judges indicate the extent to which each item represents an issue. Items rated the highest could be retained. Raters should judge the content of the item, not whether it is positively or negatively stated. For example, the item "I have long-term goals" would be judged as reflecting the same issue as the item "I do *not* have long-term goals." Both items deal with long-term goals.

Thurstone Equal Appearing Intervals (Edwards, 1957; Isaac & Michael, 1995) is an additional method that could be used in determining content validity.

This is a useful technique that has been overlooked in recent literature (Sedlacek, 2002). The first step in this procedure is to have a large group of judges (ten or more) rate the extent to which a large pool of items reflects a certain attribute. The item pool should be much larger than the number of items one wishes to use in the final scale. Thurstone used an eleven-point scale to have judges rate the extent to which the items were positive or negative in assessing a certain attitude, although any number of scale points from five to eleven is recommended. For example, the judges rated the extent to which the item reflected positive or negative feelings toward "Negroes" in the original work (Thurstone & Chave, 1929).

Items are then selected that judges have agreed upon in rating the items along the eleven-point scale (for example, low variability), and whose means, or average ratings, are spread along the eleven-point continuum. Therefore, if items are selected at half-point intervals (1, 1.5, 2, 2.5, and so on) one has a total of twenty-two items in the final scale. The instructions to respondents in the evaluation or study are to select the items with which they agree. The respondent's attitude, or score on the scale, is the mean or median of the items that he or she has chosen. Since the items are preweighted, there is little work required of the respondents or the evaluator at that point.

In this example, suppose the procedure results in a measure of campus climate containing twenty-two items. If a given person feels four of those statements seem to best represent his or her feelings about the environment, the mean or median of those four items is calculated, which would be the score for that person. The primary advantage of the Thurstone Equal Appearing Intervals method is that the item analysis is done before the items are administered to respondents, so a higher participation rate is often achieved than with other methods.

Determining content validity takes some time and effort beyond face validity. However, that drawback is minimal in exchange for some systematic evidence of validity that face validity does not produce.

Construct Validity. In construct validity, use is made of more sophisticated statistical techniques than are necessary with content validity. Typically, factor analysis or cluster analysis is employed (Merenda, 1997). A number of items are written to cover certain constructs or dimensions of interest, or the items are taken from the literature on a topic. They can be in a Likert format along some continuum (agree-disagree, most-least, good-bad), although Thurstone Equal Appearing Intervals scaling can also be employed. Responses to the items are obtained from a fairly large sample (one hundred or more) and the results factor- or cluster-analyzed. The analysis groups the items statistically, according to some rules set by the investigator, and is based on correlations among the items seen by the respondents. The groups of items are then labeled according to their apparent content.

The distinction from content validity is mainly that the items are grouped by a statistical procedure before they are judged. Many times, novel or useful themes emerge that were not anticipated by the test developer; conversely, many items that seem similar are not grouped together.

Factor analysis can be "exploratory" (the investigator has no preset ideas as to what factors may emerge) or "confirmatory" (if one wishes to test some groupings according to a theory or model). See Tracey and Sedlacek (1984a, 1984b, 1988), Woods and Sedlacek (1988), Fuertes, Miville, Mohr, Sedlacek, and Gretchen (2000), Majors and Sedlacek (2001), and Liang and Sedlacek (2003b) for examples of using factor analysis in instrument development.

Construct validity requires more effort and more participants than content validity does, but the statistical grouping of items can be useful, and it yields different (and usually better) evidence for validity than does content validity.

Predictive Validity. As the name suggests, in predictive validity one is trying to predict scores on some future criterion measure. Perhaps the most common example in higher education is admissions. Scores from a given test are said to have validity in admissions if they can predict future student success (grades, retention, graduation) for certain groups in certain contexts (for instance, Latino students at college X). In the best form of demonstrating predictive validity, all applicants would be admitted, criterion measures on each student would be obtained, and the most accurate prediction equations possible would be developed. A variety of statistical techniques can be used, including multiple regression, multiple discriminant analysis, logistic regression, and LISREL (Cizek & Fitzgerald, 1999; Tracey & Sedlacek, 1985, 1989).

In practice, however, one rarely if ever has a chance to get criterion scores on an unselected sample, even though this is required for the best estimate of predictive validity. If the range of possible scores is restricted on the predictors or criteria, the size of the statistic representing the extent of the relationship (for example, correlation coefficient) is artificially reduced. One can estimate the amount of this reduction, but it is a problem to do so accurately. Restriction of range is discussed further in Chapter Four.

Predictive validity is a useful method, especially when it matches the logic of what one wishes to accomplish (for example, selecting students). In a way, it is the ultimate method of estimating the validity of scores from a measure. If one can predict future outcomes with a measure, it must be good. The major disadvantage to predictive validity is that it takes time. One has to develop a measure, wait for the criterion results, then go back and revise the measure, and wait again. Establishing predictive validity evidence for scores from a measure of student success could take years, and many are not willing to wait for the results. I recently reviewed a manuscript for a journal where the authors said their new measure of student potential looked good, but they had no predictive validity evidence. My recommendation was that they do the necessary research and then resubmit the manuscript.

Concurrent Validity. In concurrent validity, one identifies those who are successful (or unsuccessful) on a criterion measure, and a measure is developed that reflects the characteristics of the successful group—ideally, contrasted with the unsuccessful group. In creating the Minnesota Multiphasic Personality Inventory (MMPI), the test developers compared people with certain clinical symptoms with a "normal" group on their responses to many items (Hathaway & McKinley, 1943). Items that differentiated between the two groups were retained in the instrument.

This technique has the advantage of yielding more immediate validity evidence for scores on a measure than predictive validity does. A disadvantage may be the difficulty of getting criterion information. For example, in estimating the value of a procedure used in awarding financial aid, it may be more difficult to get the cooperation of students who were academically dismissed, compared to successful students. The resulting scores are empirically derived and may not have face validity. Some critics of testing examine an item or a measure on the basis of its apparent validity rather than its statistical properties. Even if misinformed, this reasoning can cause problems for a test developer, and many move toward face validity rather than try to explain the empirical validity.

Congruent Validity. Congruent validity is a technique that could be employed more often than it is. It is estimated by correlating scores from a new measure with those from an existing measure against a specific criterion (Fuertes et al., 2000; Woods & Sedlacek, 1988). It is an easy way to check the validity of scores on a measure. The most obvious problem with congruent validity is the logic that if we already have validated scores from an existing measure, why develop a new measure? Possible answers are that it is a shorter version, perhaps in another format (online version, for instance) or with updated items and more face validity. It should be incumbent on the developer of any new measure to demonstrate how it is similar to and different from existing measures.

Convergent validity is demonstrated when several measures are shown to achieve the same result using different measures, while *discriminant* validity is achieved when one measure is differentiated from another. For example, if two personality assessments give the same profile, there is evidence for convergent validity, whereas if the two measures show different results, there is evidence for discriminant validity. Depending on the purposes for developing the assessments, one or the other type of validity might be preferred. Suppose one is developing a new measure of the same variables covered by another measure; convergent validity evidence is desirable. If, however, the goal is to develop a measure of something other than what is covered by an existing measure, establishing discriminant validity is preferred. To illustrate, if one is developing a measure of shyness then a negative correlation of the new scale with a measure of aggression is desirable.

Wherever possible, multiple measures of the same phenomenon are recommended to establish convergent and discriminant validity. The logic of the multitrait-multimethod approach (Campbell & Fiske, 1959) is that different measures of the same trait should correlate more highly with one another than similar measures of different traits. For example, a questionnaire and an interview assessing a person's long term-goals should agree more than one questionnaire assessing long-term goals and another questionnaire employing the same measurement format but assessing nontraditional knowledge acquired. The multitrait-multimethod logic allows determination of any variance that is due to the method of measurement itself, as opposed to the true variance of an attribute.

Reliability

The reliability of scores on a measure refers to their consistency of measurement: Will I get the same score if I take the test again? If the score isn't exactly the same, how far off can I expect it to be? Often no estimates of reliability are reported for scores on a measure. As with validity, reliability estimates are specific to a particular group at a particular location. Scores from an assessment technique, for instance, may have reliability for undergraduates at a certain college but not be reliable for faculty at that school.

Test-Retest Reliability

The most basic form of demonstrating reliability is to apply a measure twice to the same people over a relatively short period of time. A limited period is necessary because intervening events or changes in the respondents may occur otherwise. If one is assessing entering new students in the fall of their first year, they may have different responses on the measure in the spring owing to changes in them, or in the campus climate, rather than problems in the measure. If one were studying student attitudes before September 11, 2001, and again after that date, student feelings might have changed, and therefore the lack of consistent results may not be a lack of reliability in the scores employed.

An interval that is long enough so respondents cannot remember exactly how they responded, but not so long that they may have changed, is recommended.

Usually, this is a one-to-two-week period. Responses can be related using Pearson Product Moment correlation, from time one to time two, to estimate reliability. If responses are not continuous (for example, categorical), various other correlational methods can be employed, or a percentage agreement of responses across the two times can be estimated (Bakeman & Gottman, 1986).

Test-retest reliability is generally the best form of reliability if one can get it, although it takes time and the cooperation of a sample of approximately thirty or more. Other estimates of reliability are attempts to approximate test-retest estimates. Generally, test-retest works best with paper and pencil or online measures, rather than focus groups or interviews.

Internal Consistency Reliability

If one can't get test-retest estimates of reliability, there are several ways to estimate reliability with just one application of the measurement. For a technical discussion and comparison of types of internal consistency reliability, see Henson (2001).

In *split-halves reliability*, as the name suggests, the measure is split into two parts and the two halves are correlated as if they were separate measures. This has the advantage of not requiring a second assessment of a group, but a disadvantage is that it assumes the measure is only half as long as it really is. Generally, the longer the test is, the more reliable the scores are from it. The more chances one has to measure something, the more stable is the resulting measurement. There are ways to correct for the true length of the test (Anastasi & Urbina, 1997; Linn & Gronlund, 2000). However, each time one estimates something, some precision is lost, because there is error in any estimate. Split halves may not be practical for a number of assessment methods.

Odd-even reliability involves correlating a score from the odd items on a measure with a score on the even items. It is a form of split–halves reliability and has the same advantages and disadvantages.

One of the best methods for estimating internal consistency reliability is *Cronbach's alpha* (Cortina, 1993; Henson, 2001). This is a widely used method, available in most statistical analysis packages; however, it is limited to continuous data and traditional test items.

In this chapter, some of the problems with commonly employed tests have been discussed. Methods of determining the validity and reliability of scores from measures were also covered. In the next chapter, the implications of reliability and validity for diversity are examined.

CHAPTER THREE

RELIABILITY, VALIDITY, AND DIVERSITY

Chapter Two discussed methods of determining validity and reliability. This chapter describes how those methods apply to diversity-related issues.

Higher education has become a highly diverse enterprise (Hurtado, Milem, Clayton-Pedersen, & Allen, 1998). Colleges and universities in the United States. are much different now than they were when the SAT and other tests were developed in the last century. Women, people of color, gays, lesbians, bisexuals, and people with disabilities among others are participating in the country's society in more extensive and varied ways. For example, even though women have attended U.S. colleges and universities for many years, they are now interested in studying a much wider range of fields than was previously the case (Ancis & Phillips, 1996; Ossana, Helms, & Leonard, 1992). People of color are also applying to institutions of higher education in unprecedented numbers (W. B. Harvey, 2002; Knapp, Kelly, Whitmore, Wu, & Gallego, 2002; McTighe Musil et al., 1999; Wilds & Wilson, 1998). This mix includes international students and those from lower socioeconomic levels. The Internet and distance learning programs have made education possible in many formats that were barely imaginable decades ago. Our tests have not kept up with these changes (Sedlacek, 2003a).

Studies have shown that racism, sexism, homophobia, and other forms of prejudice are among the issues many of these new and diverse students are facing as they enroll in higher education (Mohr & Sedlacek 2000; Schlosser, 2003;

Sedlacek, 1996a). Most of our current measures don't identify these issues or evaluate how important they are to students, let alone suggest any guidance for how to help students deal with them after they enter college. We need assessment methods that consider the impact of these issues on a student's ability to succeed. We also need answers to such varied questions as these:

- Am I teaching my students anything?
- To whom should we give scholarship money?
- How should I evaluate my residence hall program?
- Am I being fair to my students of color?

These questions are not being answered adequately by existing evaluation measures.

Those who develop assessment methods have struggled with providing adequate validity and reliability evidence for their measures for women, people of color, people with disabilities, gays, lesbians and bisexuals, international students, and others who may not have had a "traditional" experience in the United States. It is important to consider how experiences on the basis of race, culture, and other aspects of diversity affect the lives of those being evaluated, because out of those experiences come the new measures discussed in this book.

Possible Goals for Diverse Campus Environments

To offer the best possible education for all students, educators must develop academic and nonacademic programs that consider the needs of students with varying experiences and abilities.

The increase in the variety of students attending colleges is an opportunity for an improved and richer multicultural environment, but research suggests that such improvements are not as naturally occurring as one might think. Students of color attending predominantly White institutions frequently perceive the environment to be hostile, concerning interracial interactions, while White students there have fewer experiences with hostile interracial environments (Ancis, Sedlacek, & Mohr, 2000; Helm, Sedlacek, & Prieto, 1998b; Loo & Rolison, 1986; Pascarella, Edison, Nora, Hagedorn, & Terenzini, 1996). Thus, measures of student attitudes and behaviors on a campus should reflect these group differences in experience.

In addition to having separate perceptions of the institution's environment, students of color and White students hold differing perspectives on the establishment of groups within a campus environment. Whereas White students tend to view groups composed solely of one ethnicity as racial segregation (Loo & Rolison, 1986), students of color may perceive the same groups as a support mechanism related to their retention (Sedlacek, 1998, 2003a, forthcoming). Although it may seem likely that students within a multicultural environment would have frequent interactions, these findings suggest that interaction among racial groups may not be a typical occurrence.

The "contact hypothesis" supports the assumption that close contact among members of different races increases the possibility for positive racial attitudes to develop, and the lack of such contact fosters prejudice and ill will (Allport, 1954). Supporters of the contact hypothesis view racial segregation as a source of ignorance, and ignorance as a building block for derogatory stereotypes and racial hostility. Those who hold this view contend that intergroup contact is a desired outcome and is most successful under certain conditions: equal status among group members, cooperative interdependence among group members, a strong degree of interaction, and egalitarian norms (Allport, 1954; Amir, 1969, 1976; Cook, 1985; Gaertner et al., 1994; Gaertner, Dovidio, & Bachman, 1996). If stronger social bonds could be forged among races, they contend, racial attitudes would improve dramatically (Sherif, 1973; Sigelman & Welch, 1993). Therefore the more frequent contact students have with people of other races, particularly under the conditions described, the more likely positive relationships are to develop. The contact hypothesis and subsequent related work constitutes a theoretical basis for understanding the conditions that might foster positive interaction, but less seems to be known about the conditions that actually exist in the variety of interactions on and off campus. Assessments that are sensitive to these issues are required to achieve validity and reliability for their resulting scores.

Effects of Inequity

Research has shown that handling racism and other inequities well has predicted success in school in prior years. But is racism still an issue in the twenty-first century? There is ample evidence that racism as defined here (to include all of the inequities that various groups of nontraditional students face) is well established in the United States and causes problems for many people (Feagin, 2000; Feagin & Feagin, 1978; Horseman, 1981; Sedlacek, 1988, 1995b; Sedlacek & Brooks, 1976; Sivanandan, 1983; Stanfield, 1994). The effects of racism are not only psychological or sociological; there is also a physiological dimension. For example, Krieger and Sidney (1996) found that young Blacks who perceived discrimination had higher blood pressure than their Black peers who did not perceive discrimination.

Learning to make the systems of society work for them is important for all students, but the overlay of racism and other forms of discrimination upon those systems makes it more difficult to understand and negotiate for nontraditional students. Hence it is critical to their success in school.

M. Bowen (1978) suggested that people learn social coping mechanisms from their parents, grandparents, and great-grandparents, or equivalent older people who have socialized them. When people are under stress, they are particularly likely to fall back on strategies learned from those who came before them. A student of color, struggling with the current environment at a high school, college, or university, could easily reach back to negative messages from his or her family history, some of which were developed at times of more overt racism, when mistrust was prudent and appropriate.

Models for Handling Racism

Two models of dealing with racism have been developed that may help in understanding this complex noncognitive variable.

Sedlacek-Brooks Model. Sedlacek and Brooks (1976) proposed a six-stage model for the elimination of racism in educational settings; the model is based on a series of studies. They felt that individuals or organizations needed to proceed through a linear series of stages before racism can be reduced or ended. The six stages are:

1. Cultural and racial differences
2. Understanding and dealing with racism
3. Understanding racial attitudes
4. Sources of racial attitudes
5. Setting goals
6. Developing strategies

The first is an awareness stage in which information is presented about racial/cultural groups, and how they perceive issues differently and need different programs and services. Many current programs emphasizing diversity stress this stage. Institutional data on the number of people in various groups as well as social science research on the problems, attitudes, and needs of these groups are useful at this developmental level. Research plays an important role in this stage because it can yield information about diversity within the institution and challenge assumptions and stereotypes. Sedlacek (2004) discussed a multicultural research program supporting this model.

The second stage concerns learning to identify manifestations of racism (both individual and institutional) and recognize what might be done to ameliorate them. Research on barriers to achievement by students and faculty of color—

admissions and retention policies, biased curricula, the effects of a negative interracial climate—are all useful in this stage.

Stage three involves an analysis of interracial attitudes. Getting the individual or institution to recognize its role in promoting negative interracial attitudes is a critical component of this stage. The SAS was developed for this purpose (Sedlacek, 1996a,—appendix 3-1).

Stage four focuses on understanding the sources of interracial attitudes and acceptance of one's role in the process of racism; it leads to later stages. In stage four, research on the history of racial issues at the university or college can be presented and discussed. For instance, an analysis of examples of racism from the campus newspaper can be used in this stage (M. D. Hill & Sedlacek, 1994).

Stage five involves a synthesis and study of the research material to generate a set of accomplishable goals; in stage six one develops a series of strategies to match each goal.

The goal of the model overall is to move the person or school through these stages using a variety of research-related activities. One of the problems for any change agent is recognizing how long it may take an organization to move through these stages (Sedlacek & Brooks, 1976). The change agent must also recognize that the parts of an organization may change at different rates, and not necessarily in the same direction. Individual progress in the model can be more monotonic, although individuals can move back and forth through the stages. See Sedlacek (2003) for examples of applications of this model.

Helms Model. Helms (1995) has proposed a model of racial identity development for Black and White individuals that can also be applied to organizations. In Helms's White Racial Identity model, the first status (formerly stage) is called "contact." An individual (or organization) is "color blind" and unaware of racial differences in this stage. The person (organization) assumes that people of other races would want to assimilate into the White culture (the only viable one).

Helms's second status, "disintegration," involves guilt and confusion at being unable to reconcile being White with the treatment of people of other races. Reintegration is the next phase, wherein the White person or organization professes its lack of racism and directs anger and hostility toward people of color. A state of denial exists during this phase.

White culture is still seen by the person at this status as superior, but there is recognition that racism exists and that a few Whites other than themselves are responsible for it in the "pseudo-independence" status. Whites are seen as having advantages over other racial groups, but this gap can be eliminated by helping other racial groups to pull themselves up to the level of White culture.

Though not directly comparable to the Sedlacek-Brooks model at this point, the client (organization) could be seen as processing research or experience on cultural and racial differences (status one), understanding racism (status two), and examining racial attitudes (status three).

The "immersion/emersion" status entails taking responsibility for the process of racism and feeling angry and embarrassed about it. Again, though not directly comparable to the Sedlacek-Brooks model, it is at this point that an individual (or organization) might begin to set goals (status five).

The final status, "autonomy," involves the attempt to interact with other races from a positive, nonracist perspective. Here the person or organization truly values diversity. This has been called universal-diverse orientation (Fuertes, Miville, Mohr, Sedlacek, & Gretchen, 2000; Miville, Molla, & Sedlacek, 1992), and several versions of an instrument have been developed to assess this construct. Helms's last status could be seen as an action phase similar to Sedlacek and Brooks's stage six, where strategies are carried out. Helms believes it is possible to move back and forth from one status to another and to be at some statuses simultaneously.

Measures Reflecting Diversity

Use of inappropriately designed measures is a common problem in multicultural assessment (Sedlacek & Kim, 1995). The Association for Assessment in Counseling and Education (AACE) has developed a compilation of multicultural assessment standards (Prediger, 1994). The resulting document incorporates information from many sources, including publications from the American Counseling Association (ACA), the American Educational Research Association (AERA), the American Psychological Association (APA), the National Council on Measurement in Education (NCME), and two divisions of ACA: AACE and the Association for Multicultural Counseling and Development (AMCD). Additionally, the National Academy of Sciences has developed an extensive report on professional standards in testing (Heubert & Hauser, 1998).

The standards presented in Prediger (1994) are grouped by major assessment tasks: selection of instruments (content), selection of instruments (norming, validity, and reliability), administration and scoring, and use or interpretation of results. Prediger discussed standards, and a reference to the source of the standard is given under each task. For example, the standard on norming involves ensuring that appropriate norms have been developed for the population being tested. A particularly important point related to validity is the necessity of providing evidence of both predictive and clinical criterion-related validity for all populations for which a measure is used. In the area of administration, the effects of examiner-examinee differences in ethnic and cultural background, attitudes, and values are noted. Prediger also recommended that those interpreting the assessments have experience and skill in interpreting information for the populations being assessed.

Many problems with our assessment systems regarding diversity that affect validity and reliability could be addressed, but five are discussed here.

The Quest-for-the-Golden-Label Problem. The idea with the first problem is that if we could just find the right label, everything would be solved. There is often much confusion about how diversity is defined, which groups should be included, and what terms should be applied to those groups.

Even though labels and terminology are important and contain many symbolic and connotative elements, those concerned with assessment can help cut through some of the ambiguity by helping to define terms operationally. Differences or similarities among groups can be demonstrated through measurement. See the section on the terminology of diversity in Chapter One for more information.

The Three-Musketeers Problem. The rallying cry of "all for one and one for all" is used often in developing what is thought of as fair and equitable measures (Sedlacek, 1994a). One interpretation of how to handle diversity is to hone and fine-tune our measures so that they yield equally valid results for everyone (Berk, 1982; Sackett, Schmidt, Ellingson, & Kabin, 2001). However, if different groups have their own experiences and ways of presenting their attributes and abilities, it is unlikely that one can develop a single measure or test item that works equally well for all. If there is a concentration on results rather than intentions, one can conclude that it is important to do an equally good job of assessment for each group, not that there is a need to use exactly the same measures for all to accomplish that goal. Equality of results, not process, is desired.

Recent work in assessing intelligence may help in better understanding the Three Musketeers Problem. Several models of including a wider range of attributes as constituting intelligence have emerged. Gardner (1983) proposed seven relatively independent abilities to be part of intelligence:

1. Linguistic
2. Logical-mathematical
3. Spatial
4. Musical
5. Bodily-kinesthetic
6. Interpersonal
7. Intrapersonal

Some of Gardner's attributes seem to be reflected in typical intelligence or scholastic aptitude measures (linguistic and logical-mathematical) but others do not (musical, intrapersonal, interpersonal).

Gardner's work is a beginning, but there is little research support for it.

The term *emotional intelligence* began to appear in the 1960s (Van Ghent, 1961; Leuner, 1966), but it was not described specifically. Goleman (1998) has popularized the term but not been clear about the components that are included in the concept. Mayer (1999) and Mayer, Salovey, and Caruso (2000) have conducted research to support the contention that emotional intelligence consists of four areas:

1. Emotional perception and expression
2. Emotional facilitation of thought
3. Emotional understanding
4. Emotional management

These four areas have low correlations with general intelligence and personality measures (Mayer, 2001). Additionally, there is some evidence that adolescents and college students with high scores on Mayer's emotional intelligence measures are less likely to be violent or use drugs. However, Mayer (2001) has intentionally tried to study aspects of emotional intelligence that are universal, rather than those that may vary by the dimensions of diversity noted earlier. To date, Mayer's conception of emotional intelligence has not been studied in relation to success in college.

Sternberg (1985, 1986, 1996) has suggested three kinds of intelligence, for which he provides some theoretical and empirical support:

1. Componential
2. Experiential
3. Contextual

Componential intelligence is the ability to interpret information hierarchically and taxonomically in a well-defined and unchanging context. People who do well on standardized tests have this type of intelligence. Experiential intelligence involves the ability to interpret information in changing contexts, or to be creative. Standardized tests do not appear to measure this type of intelligence. Sternberg calls his third type of intelligence contextual; it has to do with the ability to adapt to a changing environment, the ability to handle and negotiate the system. If we apply Sternberg's types of intelligence to what typically is done in assessment in higher education, the emphasis is generally on componential intelligence. If there is a concentration on componential intelligence, less useful assessments may be done for nontraditional persons than for those with more traditional experiences in the system.

Componential intelligence is certainly important to nontraditional people, but experiential and contextual abilities may be more likely prerequisites to componential intelligence for people from nontraditional backgrounds (Westbrook & Sedlacek, 1988). If people are struggling with the system, they may not have the time and energy to show their componential talents.

In one example of the Three Musketeers Problem, Herrnstein and Murray (1994) failed to consider intelligence types other than componential in their analysis of the intelligence of African Americans in their controversial book *The Bell Curve.*

The Horizontal-Research Problem. It is possible to conclude that because there is a growing body of literature on diversity issues in higher education, great progress must have been made in understanding those issues. The answer appears to be that some progress has been made, but much remains to be made.

Unfortunately, the most common paradigm for a study that involves nontraditional persons is probably "we are doing the study anyway, so let's add some (African Americans, women, Latinos, and so on) to it and see how they look." The study wasn't designed with these other populations in mind, but they are included. Motives are probably varied, from being politically correct to having a genuine interest in a given nontraditional group. But as I have already stated, results, not intentions, are what count. If this methodology is employed over and over again in different settings, the same results are achieved over and over again. This shows a reliability of sorts, but the research is generally not developmental or sophisticated. It is not vertical or inductive; it is not going anywhere. It also tends to give a false sense of security or self-righteousness by having us count the number of studies and reach an erroneous conclusion.

This is what appears to have happened in college admissions testing. Samples of available nontraditional students have been drawn on campus after campus, their scores have been correlated with grades, and conclusions have been reached. Much less often have studies been built upon theory and earlier research, and new measures developed or higher-order constructs described.

But this does not apply only to admissions testing. An African American graduate student and I were recently attending a presentation by a colleague who was developing a new instrument in the career area. I introduced the graduate student to my colleague, indicating that she was interested in career issues for African Americans. I asked him if he had any information on how useful the instrument was for African Americans. He said he had not checked that out yet, but that it was a good idea. I then said that some important issues, such as handling racism, might need to be included in developing an instrument that was useful with African Americans. He admitted he had never thought of that.

My colleague is a highly respected, well-trained, humanistic person. He would not intentionally engage in racism, but it is likely that scores from his new instrument will not be as valid for African Americans as for others. He was caught in the horizontal research problem, not engaging in developmental or sophisticated thinking or planning relative to diversity.

The Bias-Is-Bias Problem. Any good methodological reference will caution against a loss of subjects in doing assessment research and in developing norms for instruments (see Mehrens & Lehman, 1991; Upcraft & Schuh, 1996). However, in practical situations there is almost always missing or incomplete data, and the assumption is commonly made that the missing individuals do not cause the sample to be biased. If the missing people are from nontraditional groups, however, that assumption is frequently incorrect.

In my first undergraduate course in statistics, the instructor pointed out the distinction between statistical bias, "a consistent overestimate or underestimate of a parameter," and prejudice or social "bias" of some sort. I now wonder if that was a good idea. Much of the work done in assessment has become so esoteric and molecular that there is a tendency to forget, or perhaps never think of, the larger implications of the bias issue (Berk, 1982).

The institutional research office at a university documented an example of sampling bias. To develop regression equations for use in student selection, data were included for all students whose SAT scores and high school grades were in the university's database. The equations resulting from this process were found to predict equally well for all races. However, upon further probing, it was noted that students with incomplete data were not included in the equation-generating data set, and students in special programs were less likely to be included than others. The rationale was that the number of exclusions was small and the researchers were using all the data available.

Analysis of the data from the missing groups showed that the relationships between predictors and criteria were very different for these students. On closer inspection, it was discovered that students for whom the SAT and high school records did not predict as well were less likely to have data in the student database, because either they didn't turn it in or they didn't take the SAT, or they were in a special program that generated its own data. Such students also were much more likely to be nontraditional.

In this example, the loss of subjects resulted in more sampling bias for nontraditional students than for traditional students. The regression equations produced on the biased data set were used to select students for admission for several years. Consequently, in this case sampling bias resulted in the use of selection procedures whose results were less valid or invalid for many traditional applicants. Sampling bias that invalidates assessments for nontraditional persons is common. The problem of differential quality of samples when studying African Americans in career development studies was noted by Carter and Cook (1992).

Sampling bias can be reduced by checking the characteristics of population members with missing data, asking what the effects might be on people with similar characteristics if the missing data are ignored, and working to get data from all members of the sample or population. If it is not possible to obtain complete data, extraordinary efforts should be made to get data on a well-drawn sample of those missing, so that the extent of the sampling bias can be estimated by comparing the missing sample to the larger sample.

Overall parameter estimates for the population can then be modified, or at the very least cautions can be given so that the biased equations or norms are treated as fallible. This should avoid rigid application of the results of assessment studies to people for whom they may not be appropriate. However, as is discussed next, if assessment specialists lack knowledge of nontraditional populations this often prevents a sophisticated examination of variables on which sampling bias may occur.

The I'm-OK-You're-Not Problem. At the present time, few assessment specialists are adequately trained in developing measures for use with nontraditional populations. Hence many people who develop and evaluate tests tend to feel what works for them is "OK," and those who claim otherwise are misinformed or politically motivated. Many graduate programs produce methodologists with good technical and quantitative skills, but few of these graduates have even a rudimentary appreciation of racial and cultural variables, let alone any sense of how to measure them. Conversely, those most interested in cultural and racial variables tend to have little training or interest in quantification or assessment. As a result of the dearth of well-trained professionals working in the area, few good assessment techniques are available for work with nontraditional groups.

It may be that variation in career interests explains the lack of quantitatively oriented programs working on issues relevant to nontraditional persons. Holland's research on vocational preferences (1985) suggests that "investigative" and "realistic" types tend to be interested in assessment and quantification, while "social" types tend to be interested in issues related to culture, race, and nontraditionality. Helms (1992) felt that the relatively small number of visible racial and ethnic group (VREG) members of the American Psychological Association (3.1 percent, and no psychometricians among them; see Russo, Olmedo, Stapp, & Fulcher, 1981) requires that those trained under the Eurocentric tradition in testing must develop the needed culturally sensitive measures.

Obviously, requiring those interested in assessment to take courses in multicultural issues, and requiring those with multicultural interests to take measurement courses, is one answer. However, this already takes place in many training programs, and it is inadequate to change much behavior in the profession. More opportunities for collaboration in instrument development through grants and workshops, as well as theses, dissertations, and other everyday professional activities, should be made available.

When I introduced my African American graduate student to my colleague who was developing a new career instrument, I was trying to accomplish several things. First, I have since completed a collaboration with the student and the colleague on this topic. The student learned from the experience and the colleague benefited from her input. Had I not suggested they work together, the student might not have been able to identify a problem with the measure, and the issue of using the measure for nontraditional populations might have never come up for my colleague. Nevertheless, simply putting the two together without some further effort on my part would not have reduced the skepticism of the student, changed the reluctance of my colleague, or improved the validity of scores on the measure for African Americans.

There are initiatives in higher education that can help on this issue. More publications, either freestanding or as part of a journal or newsletter, are recommended. Regular and preconvention programs and efforts to obtain grants and contracts can also be supported, including more collaboration between multicultural groups and technical groups.

Conceptualizing Errors in Support of Diversity

Several problems that work against promoting diversity have been discussed here. These problems are in no sense independent. Some are easier to reduce or control than others, but suggestions have been offered as to how each problem can be remedied. What can be done about these problems and many others that are undoubtedly present in our procedures may be conceptualized in terms of the classical statistical error model: Type I versus Type II.

Type I errors occur in concluding that differences are present when they are not. In other words, we are wrong when we attempt to reflect cultural, racial, gender, and other differences in our measures. There would be no problem with the Three Musketeers approach.

Type II errors happen when we conclude there are no differences among people on the basis of the nontraditionality of their experiences, when there really are. The Three Musketeers approach would be wrong if we committed a Type II error. We will always err in one direction or another, but we can choose our direction.

If we proceed to implement some of the approaches discussed here and the hypotheses proposed are false, a Type I error is made and considerable time, effort, and money are wasted. Conversely, if the hypotheses are true, and it is concluded that differences based on nontraditionality are not present, or at least not worth investigating further, a Type II error has been made. With a Type II error, there is the risk of producing an extremely negative series of outcomes for many groups, by perpetuating biased approaches to testing and measurement. The very least that should be done, if we are serious about promoting diversity, is to tolerate the possibility of a Type I error and increase the power of the currently used procedures by working to eliminate the molar problems presented here as well as more molecular problems, such as differential item bias.

Determining Nontraditionality Through Measurement

To help determine which groups we might consider nontraditional, I suggest using two measures: the Situational Attitude Scale (SAS) and the Noncognitive Questionnaire (NCQ).

The SAS assesses prejudicial attitudes toward groups. The SAS procedure uses experimental and control forms to isolate reaction to a particular group. Examples of two forms are shown in Appendix 1. Versions of the SAS have been developed to measure attitudes toward these groups:

- Blacks (Balenger, Hoffman, & Sedlacek, 1992; R. T. Carter, White, & Sedlacek, 1987; Evans, 1997; Leitner & Sedlacek, 1976; Minatoya & Sedlacek, 1984; Mitchell & Sedlacek, 1996; Sedlacek, Brooks, & Mindus, 1973; T. J. White & Sedlacek, 1987)
- Latinos (R. T. Carter et al., 1987; T. J. White & Sedlacek, 1987)
- Arabs (Miville & Sedlacek, 1994; Sergent, Woods, & Sedlacek, 1992)
- Jews (Gerson & Sedlacek, 1992)
- Mormons (Gilman, 1983)
- Japanese minority groups (Forrer, Sedlacek, & Agarie, 1977)
- Australian minority groups (Chaples, Sedlacek, & Miyares, 1978)
- Danish minority groups (Brooks, Sedlacek, & Chaples, 1974; Chaples, Sedlacek, & Brooks, 1972)

Additional forms of the SAS have been developed to assess prejudice toward:

- Women (Herman & Sedlacek, 1973; Minatoya & Sedlacek, 1983)
- Older people (Peabody & Sedlacek, 1982; Schwalb & Sedlacek, 1990)
- Gays and lesbians (Engstrom & Sedlacek, 1997; Fox, 1995; Washington, 1993)
- People with physical disabilities (Linnell, 2001; Marshall, 1983; McQuilkin, Freitag, & Harris, 1990; Stovall & Sedlacek, 1983)
- American Indians (Ancis, Bennett-Choney, & Sedlacek, 1996)
- Asian Americans (Leong & Schneller, 1997; Liang & Sedlacek, 2003a)
- Student protesters (Hopple, 1976)
- Commuter students (Foster, Sedlacek, Hardwick, & Silver, 1977; Lea, Sedlacek, & Stewart, 1980; Wilkshire, 1989)
- Counseling clients (Gill, 1993; Shanbacher, 1980; Stovall, 1989)
- Children (Carney & Sedlacek, 1985; Knight, Seefeldt, & Sedlacek, 1984)
- Athletes (Engstrom & Sedlacek, 1991, 1993; Engstrom, Sedlacek, & McEwen, 1995; Hirt, Hoffman, & Sedlacek, 1983)

If a group is the target of prejudicial attitudes, it meets the first criterion for inclusion as a nontraditional group. Scores on the various forms of the SAS have shown content validity, construct validity, and internal consistency reliability in measuring attitudes for many samples and contexts. The race of the administrator has also varied, and consistent results have been found across samples (Sedlacek & Brooks, 1972a).

The second measure that has been developed is the Noncognitive Questionnaire (NCQ). It is designed to assess attributes that are not typically measured by other instruments and that may be a common way for persons with nontraditional experiences to show their abilities (Sedlacek, 1989, 1998a, 1998b, 2003). The NCQ is discussed in more detail in the next chapter, on noncognitive variables. If the NCQ systematically correlates more with the success of members of a given group (such as African Americans) than it does for traditional White males, then the group meets the second criterion for inclusion as a nontraditional group.

In this chapter, some of the issues that diversity introduces into testing have been discussed. In the next chapter, a system of employing noncognitive variables that can overcome many of those problems is presented.

CHAPTER FOUR

NONCOGNITIVE ASSESSMENT MODEL

This chapter grows out of the analysis in the last chapter and proposes guidelines for assessments that yield useful data for those with traditional and nontraditional experiences. It discusses the development of the noncognitive assessment model and the logic and research behind it. Definitions of noncognitive variables and how they can be measured are at the core of the discussion.

Development of the Assessment Model

The noncognitive assessment model was developed from more than thirty years of research and practice demonstrating that:

- Those from diverse racial and cultural groups have been particularly ill served by measures currently available
- Test results might not suggest any developmental actions
- There was no theory or overall model coordinating separate assessments
- Decision makers frequently could not use assessment results
- Little or no research supported many of the measures available
- Evaluation results were usually not tied to outcomes such as grades or retention

In developing the model, I started with research results of scores from items, scales, or measures that seemed to have some validity for diverse groups. I chose measures that yielded scores on dimensions that suggested developmental actions and had policy implications. I then developed new versions of the measures and tested out the validity and reliability of their resulting scores in a number of research studies. Upon examining the results of one study, I would make revisions in the measures and do another study, always seeking to improve the measurement. After some years of doing this, I sought some overall theories or explanations for the findings. This chapter shows the product of these efforts and documents the literature behind them.

Noncognitive Variables

The term *noncognitive* is used here to refer to variables relating to adjustment, motivation, and perceptions, rather than the traditional verbal and quantitative (often called cognitive) areas typically measured by standardized tests. Noncognitive variables are useful for assessing all students, but they are particularly critical for assessing nontraditional students, since standardized tests and prior grades may afford only a limited view of their potential.

Although *noncognitive* appears to be precise and scientific sounding, it has been used to describe a variety of attributes. As long ago as the 1950s, attempts were made to include personal and social dimensions in assessment (Fredericksen, 1954; E. S. Wilson, 1955). Brown and Marenco (1980) recommended use of the noncognitive variables shown in Table 4.1 to achieve cultural diversity in law school admissions. Willingham (1985) studied high school honors, high school follow-through, personal statements, and references and concluded that they added to the prediction of college success. Other researchers have included student involvement (Astin, 1993); academic and social integration (Milem & Berger, 1997; Tinto, 1993); study skills (Nisbet, Ruble, & Shurr, 1982); and socioeconomic background, institutional, and environmental variables (Ting & Robinson, 1998) in their conception of noncognitive variables related to student success.

The Graduate Record Examination (GRE) Board, which is part of the Educational Testing Service, conducted a symposium in 2001 to determine if noncognitive variables could be included in the GRE program. At the symposium, scholars from several academic disciplines came together to present what they thought were noncognitive variables and how those variables could be measured. Goldberg (2001) asserted that noncognitive variables consisted of personality attributes, noting that the personality literature has yielded a "big five" series of traits identified through factor analysis:

1. Extraversion
2. Agreeableness

TABLE 4.1. DESCRIPTION OF NONCOGNITIVE VARIABLES.

Variable Number	Variable Name	Description
1	Positive self-concept	Demonstrates confidence, strength of character, determination, and independence
2	Realistic self-appraisal	Recognizes and accepts any strengths and deficiencies, especially academic, and works hard at self-development; recognizes need to broaden his or her individuality
3	Successfully handling the system (racism)	Exhibits a realistic view of the system on the basis of personal experience of racism; committed to improving the existing system; takes an assertive approach to dealing with existing wrongs, but is not hostile to society and is not a "cop-out"; able to handle racist system
4	Preference for long-term goals	Able to respond to deferred gratification; plans ahead and sets goals
5	Availability of strong support person	Seeks and takes advantage of a strong support network or has someone to turn to in a crisis or for encouragement
6	Leadership experience	Demonstrates strong leadership in any area of his or her background (church, sports, noneducational groups, gang leader, and so on)
7	Community involvement	Participates and is involved in his or her community
8	Knowledge acquired in a field	Acquires knowledge in a sustained or culturally related way in any field

3. Conscientiousness
4. Emotional stability
5. Intellect and imagination

Extraversion consists of demonstrating independence, decisiveness, and negotiating skills. *Agreeableness* includes relating and cooperating with others. *Conscientiousness* involves organizing, performing administrative tasks, following regulations, integrity, and motivation. *Emotional stability* includes reacting to stress, adapting, and making decisions. *Intellect and imagination* consists of planning strategically, demonstrating knowledge, analyzing, writing, and communicating orally.

Measures yielding scores on the big five have construct validity as relatively distinct characteristics. Scores from self-report measures of these traits have been shown to possess validity in predicting employee and military performance for a number of samples, but they have not been applied to educational settings (Goldberg, 2001). Even though self-report personality measures might appear to be subject to "impression management," this may be more difficult to do than one would think (Ellingson, Smith, & Sackett, 2001). In other words, trying to complete the measures in a way that is not reflective of oneself may not work. It also appears that scores from most of the measures of big-five attributes are similar across ethnic groups, so they may not pick up variance that is due to nontraditional experiences (Goldberg, Sweeney, Merenda, & Hughes, 1998).

Reeve and Hakel (2001) felt that it was important to specify what criteria are being predicted with noncognitive measures and for which groups. They noted seven areas to consider in evaluating undergraduate or graduate student performance:

1. Classroom and examination proficiency
2. Academic effort
3. Personal discipline and self-management
4. Personal administration skills
5. Interpersonal relations
6. Nonacademic effort
7. Career vision and self-directedness

Reeve and Hakel concluded that the noncognitive dimensions of personality, interests, and motivation are potential predictors of these criteria. The validity of scores from the predictors might vary by the criterion predicted. Using research from job settings, Reeve and Hakel gave the example of extraversion having a positive correlation with performance in sales but a negative correlation with performance in management. This finding implies that scores from any predictor may have validity for certain types of students in higher education, such as majors or by race, gender, or other nontraditional grouping.

Noncognitive Variables to Include in Assessment Systems

Research has identified eight noncognitive variables (NCVs) that are valuable in assessment systems for diverse populations, and that may help guide policy.

These NCVs appear to be in Sternberg's experiential and contextual domains (1985, 1986, 1996), although standardized tests tend to reflect the componential domain.

Positive Self-Concept. A positive self-concept is predictive of success in higher education for students of color and other nontraditional students. Having a good self-concept is important for any student, but it becomes even more so for those with nontraditional experiences because of the added complexity of dealing with a system that was not designed for them. A number of studies have shown that a positive self-concept correlates with college grades, retention, and graduation—particularly the latter two—for regularly admitted African American students (McNairy, 1996; Milem & Berger, 1997; Sedlacek,1999; Tracey & Sedlacek, 1984a, 1984b, 1985, 1987, 1988, 1989; Tracey, Sedlacek, & Miars, 1983). O'Callaghan & Bryant (1990) found self-concept important for the success of Black American students at the U.S. Air Force Academy.

Successful students possess confidence, a strong sense of self, strength of character, determination, and independence. The student who feels confident of making it through school is more likely to survive and graduate than those without such confidence. A strong self-concept seems important for students of color and women. Although many students of color have had to overcome incredible obstacles and setbacks even to reach the point of applying to college, they need still greater determination to continue. Determination is needed precisely because many of their unique culture and gender-related experiences have involved dealing with those setbacks developmentally, which helps them after entering college.

An important component of self-concept is seeing oneself as part of the system and feeling good about it, which is generally easier for traditional students since so much of the system is designed for them. Studies demonstrate that how students of color feel about themselves is related to their adjustment and success in college (Kim & Sedlacek, 1996; Neville, Heppner, & Wang, 1997; Patterson, Sedlacek, & Perry, 1984; Trimble, 1988; Trippi & Cheatham, 1989). Patterson, Sedlacek, and Scales (1988) found self-concept to be important for the adjustment of students with disabilities, and Adelstein, Sedlacek, and Martinez (1983) had similar conclusions for older women returning to college. Sedlacek and Sheu (forthcoming, a) found that for Gates Millennium Scholars, who were all students of color with low family incomes, having a positive self-concept correlated positively with their college grades. Bennett (2002) showed that for "underrepresented minorities" who went into teaching a positive ethnic identity was associated with their graduation from college.

In addition to the usual school pressures, nontraditional students typically must handle racial, cultural, and gender biases and learn to bridge between the culture in which they were raised and the prevailing one. DiCesare, Sedlacek, and Brooks (1972) found that African Americans who stayed in college and adjusted to these obstacles were usually absolutely certain they would obtain their degree, in contrast to those who left school.

The successful student of color is likely to be experienced in going against the grain, as well as being atypical. Thus there is good evidence to suggest that important cultural differences exist between African Americans and Whites in the manner in which self-concept is operationalized. On some measures, the opposite use of the same predictor may select the best students from different cultures. For example, Pfeifer and Sedlacek (1974) found that Blacks who got high grades tended to have personality profiles that varied dramatically from Whites who got high grades, according to norms based on White students.

Race and gender identity are important aspects of how one shows ability. Helms (1992) has developed identity models for Blacks, Whites, and people of color. Neville et al. (1997) found racial identity attitudes of African American college students related to perceived stressors and coping styles. Ossana, Helms, and Leonard (1992) have studied "womanist" identity as an important part of self-esteem, and Jones (1997) found that race varied in its importance in the identity development of women in college, depending on their race. Kim and Sedlacek (1996) found that there were differences in self-perceptions among African American men and women as they entered college. Frankenburg (1993) discussed the relevance of exploring the concept of "Whiteness" in the identity development of White women.

Other aspects of self-concept have been explored that might be worth further consideration. There has been work on religious identity (Fowler, 1981; Suthakaran & Sedlacek, 2001) and lesbian, bisexual, and transgender identities (D'Augelli & Patterson, 1995; Mohr, Israel, & Sedlacek, 2001).

Berger and Milem (2000) and Fries-Britt and Turner (2002) found that successful African American students found their self-concept bolstered on historically Black campuses, while Fries-Britt and Turner noted that successful Black students had to learn to cope with self-concept issues on traditionally White campuses.

Fuertes, Sedlacek, and Liu (1994) demonstrated the importance of a strong self-concept for Asian and Pacific Islander university students. Bennett and Okinaka (1990) found that Asian Americans often had feelings of social isolation and dissatisfaction on campus. Chung and Sedlacek (1999) also noted that Asian Americans had lower career and social self-appraisal than students of other races.

For Latinos, a possible self-concept problem is how "Latino" to be. Should I speak Spanish? Should I join a Latino group or a general group? Fuertes and Sedlacek (1995) noted the importance of a Latino self-concept; Longerbeam, Sedlacek, and Alatorre (forthcoming) found that Latinos were more likely to feel they lacked academic ability than other racial groups. Latinos have also been found more likely than other groups to be uncomfortable on a campus stressing diversity issues (Ancis, Sedlacek, & Mohr, 2000; Helm, Sedlacek, & Prieto, 1998b). However, as entering first-year students Latinos were more likely to be looking forward to interacting with other racial groups than were other students (Longerbeam et al., forthcoming). It may be that Latinos enter college with high expectations of diversity, but the reality causes them difficulty.

Sedlacek and Adams-Gaston (1992) found self-concept related to grades for student athletes. They demonstrated that the athletes might be considered nontraditional in that they experience prejudice, and their performance can be predicted with noncognitive variables.

Stericker and Johnson (1977), Betz and Fitzgerald (1987), and Ancis and Sedlacek (1997) have all found women's self-concept related to their academic success. T. J. White and Sedlacek (1986) reported self-concept to be predictive of success for students in special programs, and S. P. Boyer and Sedlacek (1988) determined that self-concept was predictive of grades and retention for international students.

Realistic Self-Appraisal. Realistic self-appraisal is the ability to assess one's strengths and weaknesses, allowing self-development. Realism in self-appraisal by nontraditional persons does not connote cultural, racial, or gender deficiency or inferiority. Students of color and women of all races who are able to make realistic assessment of their abilities, despite obstacles to making such an assessment, do better in school than those less able to make that judgment. Realistic self-appraisal is also a predictor of success for traditional students.

White students do well pursuing their own interests (internal control) in a society designed to meet their needs, but students of color need to be aware of the external control on their lives that negotiating the racism in the system requires (Gurin, Gurin, Lao, & Beatty, 1969; Sedlacek, 1988, 1993, 1995a, 1996b, 1998a, 1998b, 1999, 2003a, forthcoming, a; Sedlacek & Brooks, 1976). Supporting this conclusion, DiCesare et al. (1972) found that African Americans who were better able to assess their strengths and weaknesses were more likely to remain in school than those who were less realistic. Sedlacek and Sheu (forthcoming) showed that realistic self-appraisal was correlated with high college grades for students of color (African Americans, American Indians, Asian Americans, and Latinos) in the Gates Millennium Scholars program.

Perrone, Sedlacek, and Alexander (2001) found that White and Asian American students perceived intrinsic interest in a field as the major barrier to achieving their career goals, suggesting that they were not so interested in the fields they were studying as were other students. African Americans, Latinos, and Native Americans cited personal finances as their major barrier to achieving career goals.

White faculty members may give less consistent reinforcement to African American students than they do to White students (Allen, 1992; Sedlacek & Brooks, 1976). Note that lack of consistency is not the same thing as negativity.

For African Americans who are trying to make a realistic self-appraisal, faculty reinforcement that is too positive causes as many problems as one that is negative. For example, Christensen and Sedlacek (1974) demonstrated that faculty stereotypes of African Americans can be overly positive, and S. L. Carter (1996) discussed an example of a colleague who defended his practice of grading Black students more leniently than White students.

Some researchers have identified poor communication with faculty, particularly White faculty members, as a problem for African American students (Allen, Bobo, & Fleuranges, 1984; Fleming, 1994; Sedlacek, 1993, 1995a, 1995b; Sedlacek & Brooks, 1976). Helm et al. (1998b), and Ancis et al. (2000) found that a communication problem with faculty could make it more difficult to do assessments of African American and Asian American students. Hargrove and Sedlacek (1997) wrote that African American students were more likely to feel they needed career advising and counseling than were students from other racial groups.

Much evidence exists of women experiencing an academic climate that interferes with the ability to do realistic appraisals of their academic abilities (Ancis & Phillips, 1996; Brush, 1991; Fitzgerald et al., 1988; Sandler, 1987). These difficulties bring about a corresponding decrease in academic and career aspirations from their first year to their last year in school (El-Khawas, 1980; Ossana et al., 1992). Women who are able to make realistic self-appraisals have been shown to get higher grades in a university than those who have difficulty with such assessments (Ancis & Sedlacek, 1997).

Tracey and Sedlacek (1984a, 1984b, 1985, 1987, 1988, 1989) and Tracey et al. (1983) showed realistic self-appraisal correlating with college grades, retention, and graduation for students of all races, but the relationships were particularly strong for African Americans. Webb et al. (1997) identified realistic assessment of the degree of difficulty of academic work as a correlate of grades for female African American medical students. S. P. Boyer and Sedlacek (1988) and Moore (1995) reported that international students with more realistic self-appraisal got higher grades in college than those that did not make such appraisals. S. P. Boyer and Sedlacek also found that international students with realistic self-appraisal were more likely to stay in school than those with lower scores on the variable.

Successfully Handling the System. The successful nontraditional student is also:

- A realist with personal experience of discrimination
- Committed to fighting to improve the existing system
- Not submissive to existing wrongs, nor hateful of society; able to handle a racist or otherwise discriminatory system
- Assertive that the school has a role or duty to fight discrimination

As was discussed in Chapter One, racism is used in this book to cover all the -isms that may adversely affect people.

For traditional students, this noncognitive variable takes the form of handling the system without the addition of racism (Sedlacek, 1993, 1996a, 1996b, 1999; Tracey & Sedlacek, 1984a, 1984b) and might better be labeled "negotiating the system." For example, Sedlacek, Bailey, and Stovall (1984) showed that students of all races and genders who followed directions in their applications to a precollege orientation program got higher grades in college (.05 level) than those who made certain mistakes. Interestingly, those who did not make mistakes had significantly lower SAT scores than those who did.

How we learn to handle the circumstances with which we are confronted tells us much about our ability and potential. For example, someone from a wealthy background may have to learn how to develop himself or herself without being tested by circumstances (that is, having to earn a living), something that develops character in most people.

Research has consistently shown that students of color who understand racism and are prepared to deal with it perform better academically and are more likely to adjust to a predominantly White school than those who do not (Bandalos & Sedlacek, 1989; Barbarin, 1981; DiCesare et al., 1972; Tracey & Sedlacek, 1984a, 1984b, 1985, 1987, 1988, 1989; T. J. White & Sedlacek, 1986). How well African American students are able to negotiate the campus system is associated with their success in school (Deslonde, 1971; Feagin, 2000; Feagin & Sikes, 1995; Fries-Britt & Turner, 2002; C. Garcia & Levenson, 1975; Harris & Nettles, 1996; Sedlacek, 1989, 1996a, 1996b, 1999; Tatum, 1992; Webster, Sedlacek, & Miyares, 1979; West, 1993). Even on a relatively unique campus—the U.S. Air Force Academy—successful Black American students scored high on a handling-racism scale (O'Callaghan & Bryant, 1990).

Bennett (2002) wrote that ability to handle racism was predictive of college graduation for "underrepresented minorities" in a teacher training program. Sedlacek and Sheu (forthcoming, a) found that the better Gates Millennium Scholars (who were African American, American Indian, Asian American, and Latino) handled racism the higher were their college grades.

Steele's work on "stereotype threat" (1997) supports the importance of the psychological set with which examinees approach a test. If African Americans are told they do not usually do well on a test, then they do less well than if a more positive set is given. According to both professional and popular literature, African Americans don't do as well as Whites on standardized tests (Sedlacek, 1998a, 1998b, 2003a; Lemann, 2000). Consequently, for African Americans the act of taking a test probably involves dealing with the racism that might have been involved in helping to create a stereotype threat in the first place. Hence the variance that is being measured when African Americans take the SAT is likely to be in part handling racism.

That women face many systemic obstacles—discouraging comments, differential opportunities, sexual harassment—has been well documented (Ancis & Phillips, 1996; Brush, 1991; Fitzgerald et al., 1988, Sandler, 1987). How well they learn to make the system work for them inside and outside of education is predictive of their college grades (Ancis & Sedlacek, 1997). This noncognitive variable has also been shown to relate to the academic success of Asian Americans (Fuertes et al., 1994), Latinos (Fuertes & Sedlacek, 1995), and international students (S. P. Boyer & Sedlacek, 1988).

Fuertes and Sedlacek (1993) identified barriers to leadership development in higher education among Latinos. There is evidence that Latinos enter college with positive feelings about diversity but encounter an atmosphere other than what they expected (Ancis et al., 2000; Helm et al., 1998b; Longerbeam et al., forthcoming). Those students who have demonstrated the ability to use the system to their advantage prior to college have more success once they get there compared to those who have not shown that ability.

Allen concluded that "the institutional barriers that serve to insure the perpetuation of a status quo rooted in an unfair system of racial stratification" were "admissions requirements that rely heavily on culturally and economically biased standardized tests; faculties dominated by middle-class White males; soaring cost accompanied by inadequate financial aid programs; destructive pedagogical style that emphasized 'dog-eat-dog' competition; the embrace of exclusionary entries that undercut attempts to achieve cultural pluralism and diversity; and norms that elevate sorting out procedures over approaches that emphasize student learning" (1992, p. 42).

Fries-Britt and Turner (2002), Garrod and Larimore (1997), and C. J. White and Shelley (1996) presented case studies from students of color exemplifying Allen's points, indicating how widespread the problems are.

A variety of models for handling racism were discussed in Chapter Three. They can be usefully applied to help individuals and groups achieve better results on this noncognitive variable.

Preference for Long-Term Goals. Having long-range goals is a predictor of success in college for students. Developing those goals, however, can be more difficult for nontraditional students. Because suitable role models are often hard to find and the reinforcement system has been relatively random for them, many nontraditional students have difficulty understanding the relationship between current efforts and future outcomes.

In other words, since students of color or other nontraditional students tend to face a greater culture shock than White male students in adjusting to the dominant student-oriented campus culture, students of color tend to be concerned with immediate issues of adjustment. This conclusion is supported by research that indicates students of color are not as predictable in their academic performance in the first year as are traditional students (Farver, Sedlacek, & Brooks, 1975). However, by the second year, when they have had an opportunity to adjust to their environment, students of color are about as predictable as others.

Astin (1975) demonstrated that those African Americans with lower aspirations and vaguer goals than other African Americans were more likely to leave school. Tracey and Sedlacek (1984a, 1984b, 1985, 1987, 1988, 1989) and Tracey et al. (1983) presented evidence that having long-term goals predicted college grades, retention, and graduation for African American students. Bohn (1973) concluded that Black students who were able to make long-term plans performed better on work-study jobs than those who did not have such plans. S. P. Boyer and Sedlacek (1988) found a significant relationship between setting long-range goals and grades and retention for international students. Moore (1995) concluded that having long-range goals correlated with persistence in school for international community college students. Thus students who show evidence of having long-range goals do better in college than those without such goals.

Availability of Strong Support Person. Students who have done well in school tend to have a person of strong influence who confers advice, particularly in times of crisis (Sedlacek, 1998a, 1998b, 1999, 2003a, forthcoming). For traditional students, this individual may be in the educational system or in the immediate family, but for nontraditional students he or she is generally a relative or a community worker. Students of color, women, and others for whom the educational system was not designed do better in college if they have a history of developing supportive relationships than do those who have not had this experience.

Many students of color, however, do not have the support to fall back upon that traditional students typically have (Allen, 1992). For instance, an African American student who is about to enter college may not have members in the immediate family or neighborhood friends who have been to college (or to that particular college or university) or understand the ins and outs of the system, which most educated Whites take for granted. White persons, individually and collectively through institutions, often do not have high expectations of persons of color and therefore are not oriented to help them to seek education (Trippi & Cheatham, 1989).

Because of random reinforcement of the relationship between individual effort and positive outcome, a relatively small obstacle or set of obstacles may make a student of color drop out or fail school (Mallinckrodt, 1988). If a White student drops out, numerous forces in the society might bring him or her back into the educational system. But the student of color is more likely to drop out and never be heard from again (Allen, 1992).

Students of color often find difficulty forming relationships with faculty and staff (Nettles, 1990; I. H. Johnson, 1996). However, research has indicated that these relationships are important (Fries-Britt, 2000). Davidson and Foster-Johnson (2002), in their review of the literature on mentoring graduate researchers of color, concluded that a mentor is a critical part of success for such researchers. Successful mentors are aware of many cultural and racial variables that are relevant to the relationship with their mentee.

Having a strong support person has been shown to be a significant correlate of grades, retention, and graduation for African Americans (Tracey & Sedlacek, 1984a, 1984b, 1985, 1987, 1988, 1989), women (Ancis & Sedlacek, 1997; Betz & Fitzgerald, 1987; Tidball, 1986), athletes of all races (Sedlacek & Adams-Gaston, 1992); international students (S. P. Boyer & Sedlacek, 1988), and students in special support programs (including Asian Americans, African Americans, and Whites; Ting, 1997; T. J. White & Sedlacek, 1986).

Leadership Experience. Students of color and women who show evidence of leadership prior to matriculation in college, often in some form related to race or gender, are more likely to be successful students than those without such leadership experiences. Leadership ability is important for any student, but it may take various forms for students of color; since traditional students have more supports built into the system, it is not so critical an attribute for them to demonstrate for admission to college.

Nontraditional students who are most successful in higher education have shown the ability to organize and influence others. What seems to be important is obtaining nontraditional evidence of the student's ability to lead. Application forms and interviews typically yield less useful information about the backgrounds of nontraditional students. Many White applicants know how to play the game and have joined (and then are sure to list) a variety of offices held in traditional school organizations. Many students of color have not had the time or inclination for such activities (Allen, 1992).

The most promising nontraditional students may have shown their leadership in some less typical way, such as working in their community, through a religious organization, or even as a street gang leader (Allen, 1992). It is important to pursue the cultural and gender-relevant activities of the individual applicants rather than treat them as if they all come from similar environments. For example, Liu and Sedlacek (1999) reported that Asian American students had unique and culturally related ways of expressing their leadership, as through family and cultural organizations. If an applicant succeeds in his or her culture and is ready to take on college, there is evidence that the student has the potential to succeed.

An important component in leadership as a predictor of success is assertiveness (Sedlacek, 1989, 1993, 1996b, 1998a, 1998b, 1999, 2003a, forthcoming). A passive style of relating to others for students of color denies many opportunities in a system that is not optimally designed for them. Seeking out resources, human and environmental, is correlated with success for students of color. Such activities are positive for any student but particularly important for nontraditional students. Gates Millennium Scholars, who as a group had high GPAs (3.25 on a 4-point scale), were more involved in leadership activities than a comparison group with similar backgrounds. All Gates Scholars are students of color (Sedlacek & Sheu, forthcoming, a, b).

Tracey and Sedlacek (1984a, 1984b, 1985, 1987, 1988, 1989) and C. J. White and Shelley (1996) showed evidence of the value of leadership in retention of Latinos and Native Americans. They also found leadership predictive of success in school for African American undergraduate students, as did Webb et al. (1997) for female African American medical students. Ancis and Sedlacek (1997), Astin (1977), and Betz and Fitzgerald (1987) all identified leadership as a correlate of success for women in college, and S. P. Boyer and Sedlacek (1988) noted a similar relationship for female and male international students. Ting (1997) and T. J. White and Sedlacek (1986) concluded that leadership correlated with academic success for students in special support programs.

Community Involvement. Having a community with which students of color and women can identify and from which they can receive support is critical to their academic success. Those who have been involved in such a community are more successful than those not so involved.

The community is often based on racial, cultural, or gender issues for nontraditional students. Students of color, women, and other persons with nontraditional experiences who are active in a community learn how to handle the system, exhibit leadership, and develop their self-concept in such groups. Mallinckrodt and Sedlacek (1987) reported that African American students who used campus athletic facilities and certain student union programs were more likely to stay in school than those who did not; the relationship was not present for White students. Thus African Americans need to develop communities within the larger society to find support. Webster and Sedlacek (1982) offered further evidence for the importance of student unions for African American and international student retention.

Allen (1992); Tracey and Sedlacek (1984a, 1984b, 1985, 1987, 1988, 1989); Tracey et al. (1983); and C. J. White and Shelley (1996) supported the value of community involvement as a predictor of academic success for African Americans. Fuertes et al. (1994) reported that identification with a community was important for Asian American success in school, as did Sedlacek and Adams-Gaston (1992) for male and female athletes of all races. C. J. White and Shelley (1996) indicated the importance of community in retaining Latino and Native American students. Bennett (2002) concluded that having a race-based community correlated with college graduation for "underrepresented minorities" in a teacher training program. Scoring high on a community involvement scale was related to high college grades for Gates Millennium Scholars of color (African American, American Indians, Asian Americans, and Latinos).

Ancis and Sedlacek (1997) found community to be a correlate of success for undergraduate women, as did Ting (1997) for White students in special programs. S. P. Boyer and Sedlacek (1988) and Moore (1995) also reported community involvement to be important for the academic success of international students.

An interesting technique called perceptual mapping can help in identifying communities that may be of relevance to students or others on campus (Mitchell, Sergent, & Sedlacek, 1997; Sergent & Sedlacek, 1989). The perceptual mapping approach allows respondents to indicate locations of interest to them and their perceptions of those areas. The unique aspect of perceptual mapping is that respondents use actual maps of interior or exterior spaces, and they project feelings and perceptions on the maps. Research has shown that African American and White students choose different areas of a campus as positive or negative, depending on their experience with communities in those areas (Mitchell et al., 1997).

Using perceptual mapping helped identify areas that might cause difficulties for some student racial and cultural groups. For example, at one university the plans to renovate a part of a campus student union were changed because African American students tended to congregate in an area that would have been affected.

Knowledge Acquired in a Field. Persons of color are more apt to learn and develop by way of methods that are less traditional and outside the education system. The methods may be related to culture or gender, and the field itself may be nontraditional.

A number of researchers have shown the predictive value of nontraditional learning for the academic success of certain groups: Tracey & Sedlacek (1984a, 1984b, 1985, 1987, 1988, 1989) and Tracey et al. (1983) for African Americans; Fuertes and Sedlacek (1994) for Latinos; S. P. Boyer and Sedlacek (1988) for international students; Ting (1997) for special program students; and Ancis and Sedlacek (1997) for women.

Women and students of color who have shown evidence of nontraditional learning prior to college tend to be more successful in college than those who show no such evidence. For example, a person who has learned some principles of accounting by working in a food cooperative in their neighborhood, or another who learned about chemistry by volunteering in a hospital, demonstrate this type of learning. Volunteering can be an important source of potential learning experiences (Altman & Sedlacek, 1991; Balenger & Sedlacek,1993; O'Brien, Sedlacek, & Kandell, 1994; Sergent & Sedlacek, 1990). However, the important point is whether the person learns from the opportunities presented.

Table 4.2 describes how a high or low score on each of the eight noncognitive variables might be reflected in a person's behavior.

Measuring Noncognitive Variables

The noncognitive variables can be assessed in a number of ways. Several are described here.

The Noncognitive Questionnaire (NCQ). The Noncognitive Questionnaire (NCQ) was designed expressly to assess the eight noncognitive variables. Tracey and Sedlacek (1984a, 1984b), Woods and Sedlacek (1988), and Ting and Sedlacek (2000) presented construct validity evidence for scores on the eight dimensions measured by the NCQ for African American and White samples (see Appendix 2). Woods and Sedlacek (1988) also showed some congruent validity evidence that the NCQ correlates with a measure of stress. Faubert (1992) found concurrent validity evidence that the NCQ was related to the success of ninth and tenth grade rural African American students.

There is a great deal of evidence that NCQ scores can predict grades, retention, and graduation for nontraditional and traditional students (see Ancis & Sedlacek, 1997; Bandalos & Sedlacek, 1989; S. P. Boyer & Sedlacek, 1988; Carstens, 1993; Fuertes & Sedlacek, 1995; Fuertes et al., 1994; W. Hill, 1995; McNeill, 1992; Moore, 1995; O'Callaghan & Bryant, 1990; Sedlacek, 1989, 1991, 1993, 1996a, 1996b, 1998a, 1998b, 1999, 2003a, forthcoming; Sedlacek & Adams-Gaston,1992; Ting, 1997; Tipling, 1993; Tracey & Sedlacek, 1984a, 1984b, 1985, 1987, 1988, 1989; Tracey et al., 1983; T. J. White and Sedlacek, 1986).

Several forms of the NCQ have been developed and employed in a number of admissions contexts. The questionnaire can also be administered online; Appendix 2 shows a basic form that can be employed including scoring instructions. Tracey and Sedlacek (1984a) reported two-week test-retest reliability estimates on NCQ scores ranging from .74 to .94, with a median of .85 for the NCQ items with differing samples. Interrater reliability on scores from the three open-ended NCQ items ranged from .73 to 1.00.

TABLE 4.2. POSITIVE AND NEGATIVE EVIDENCE OF EACH NONCOGNITIVE VARIABLE.

Noncognitive Variable Items 1 Through 8

In this table, you will find definitions of the eight noncognitive variables and a list of questions to guide you in assessing each variable.

Variable Item 1: Positive Self-Concept

This variable assesses the applicant's confidence, self-esteem, independence, and determination, all vital components of future achievement and success.

Positive Evidence	*Negative Evidence*
Does the applicant feel confident of making it through graduation?	Does the applicant express any reason he or she might not complete school or succeed in attaining his or her goals?
Does the applicant make positive statements about himself or herself?	Does the applicant express concerns that other students are better than he or she is?
Does the applicant expect to achieve his or her goals and perform well in academic and nonacademic areas?	Does the applicant expect to have marginal grades?
Does the applicant show evidence of how he or she will attain his or her goals?	Does the applicant have trouble balancing his or her personal and academic life?
Does the applicant link his or her interests and experiences with his or her goals?	Does the applicant appear to be avoiding new challenges or situations?
Does the applicant assume he or she can handle new situations or challenges?	

Variable Item 2: Realistic Self-Appraisal

This variable assesses the applicant's ability to recognize and accept his or her strengths and deficiencies, especially in academics, and works hard at self-development to broaden his or her individuality.

Positive Evidence	*Negative Evidence*
Is the applicant aware of his or her strengths and weaknesses?	Is the applicant unaware of how evaluations are done in school?
Does the applicant know what it takes to pursue a given career?	Is the applicant not sure about his or her own abilities?

Positive Evidence	*Negative Evidence*
Is the applicant realistic about his or her abilities?	Is the applicant uncertain about how his or her peers or superiors rate his or her performances?
Does the applicant show an awareness of how his or her service, leadership, extracurricular activities, or schoolwork has caused him or her to change over time?	Does the applicant overreact to positive or negative reinforcement rather than seeing it in a larger context?
Has the applicant learned something from these structured or unstructured activities?	Is the applicant unaware of how he or she is doing in classes until grades are out?
Does the applicant appreciate and understand both positive and negative feedback?	Is the applicant unaware of positive and negative consequences of his or her grades, actions, or skills?
Does the applicant show evidence of overcoming anger, shyness, or lack of discipline?	Does the applicant face a problem, such as a bad grade, with determination to do better?

Variable Item 3: Successfully Handling the System (Racism)

This variable assesses the applicant's ability to understand the role of "the system" in life and to develop a method of assessing the cultural or racial demands of the system and respond accordingly/assertively.

Positive Evidence	*Negative Evidence*
Is the applicant able to overcome challenges or obstacles he or she is confronted with as a result of racism in a positive and effective way?	Is the applicant unaware of how the system works?
Does the applicant understand the role of the system in his or her life and how it treats nontraditional persons?	Is the applicant preoccupied with racism or does the applicant not feel racism exists?
Does the applicant reveal how he or she has learned to deal with the system accordingly?	Does the applicant blame others for his or her problems?
Does the applicant react with the same intensity to large and small issues concerned with race?	Is the applicant's method for successfully handling racism that does not interfere with personal and academic development nonexistent?

Variable Item 4: Preference for Long-Term Goals

This variable assesses the applicant's persistence, patience, long-term planning, and willingness to defer gratification and success in college.

Positive Evidence	*Negative Evidence*
Does the applicant reveal experience in setting both academic and personal long-term goals?	Does the applicant lack evidence of setting and accomplishing goals?
Does the applicant provide evidence that he or she is planning for the future?	Is the applicant likely to proceed without clear direction?
Has the applicant determined a course of study and anticipated the type of career or path he or she might (or could) pursue?	Does the applicant rely on others to determine outcomes?
Is the applicant aware of realistic and intermediate steps necessary to achieve goals?	Does the applicant focus too much attention to the present?
Has the applicant participated in activities (volunteer work, employment, extra courses, community work) related to his or her anticipated career goal?	Is the applicant's plan for approaching a course, school in general, an activity, and so on, nonexistent?
	If the applicant states his or her goals, are the goals vague or unrealistic?

Variable Item 5: Availability of Strong Support Person

This variable assesses the applicant's having a strong support network, help, and encouragement, and the degree to which the applicant relies solely on her or his own resources.

Positive Evidence	*Negative Evidence*
Does the applicant have a strong support system? (This can be personal, professional, or academic support, so long as it is someone the applicant can turn to for advice, consultation, assistance, encouragement, and so on)	Does the applicant avoid turning to a support person, mentor, or close advisor for help?
Is the applicant willing to admit that he or she needs help and able to call on other resources, other than himself or herself, to solve problems?	Does the applicant keep his or her problems to himself or herself?

Positive Evidence	*Negative Evidence*
Does the applicant state that he or she can handle things on his or her own?	Does the applicant state that access to a previous support person may have been reduced or eliminated?
	Is the applicant unaware of the importance of a support person?

Variable Item 6: Leadership Experience

This variable assesses the applicant's skills developed (or influence exercised) from his or her formal and informal leadership roles.

Positive Evidence	*Negative Evidence*
Has the applicant taken leadership initiative—for example, by founding a club or organization? What evidence is there?	Is the applicant unable to turn to others for advice or direction?
Does the applicant describe the skills he or she has developed as a leader, such as assertiveness, effectiveness, organizing, and time management?	Does the applicant lack confidence or leadership skills?
Has the applicant shown evidence of influencing others and being a good role model?	Is the applicant passive, or does he or she lack initiative?
Is the applicant comfortable offering advice and direction to others?	Is the applicant overly cautious?
Does the applicant describe a commitment to being a role model for siblings, community members, or schoolmates?	Does the applicant avoid controversy?
Does the applicant show sustained commitment to one or two types of organization with increasing involvement, skill development, and responsibility?	Does the applicant take action and initiative?

Variable Item 7: Community Involvement

This variable assesses the applicant's identification with a cultural, geographic, or racial group and his or her demonstrated activity within that community grouping.

Positive Evidence	*Negative Evidence*
Does the applicant show sustained commitment to a service site or issue area?	Does the applicant lack involvement in cultural, racial, or geographical group or community?

Variable Item 7: Community Involvement, *continued*

Positive Evidence	*Negative Evidence*
Does the applicant demonstrate a specific or long-term commitment or relationships with a community?	Is the applicant involved in his or her community in name only?
Has the applicant accomplished specific goals in a community setting?	Does the applicant engage in solitary rather than group activities (academic or nonacademic)?
Does the applicant's community service relate to career or personal goals?	

Variable Item 8: Knowledge Acquired in a Field

This variable assesses the applicant's experiences gained in a field through study and beyond the classroom. It pays particular attention to how the applicant gains nontraditional, perhaps culturally or racially based, views of the field.

Positive Evidence	*Negative Evidence*
Does the applicant use his or her knowledge to teach others about the topic?	Does the applicant lack evidence of learning from the community or nonacademic activities?
Is the applicant working independently in his or her field? (Be sensitive to variations among academic fields and the experiences that can be gained—for example, if in the sciences then by doing independent research, or if in the arts or crafts then by participating in competitions or compositions.)	Is the applicant traditional in his or her approach to learning?
	Is the applicant unaware of his or her possibilities in a field of interest?

Appendix 3 shows norms, means, and standard deviations for a number of colleges and universities that have used the basic NCQ. Appendix 4 shows two alternate forms of the NCQ. Both alternate forms have shown test-retest reliability estimates in the .80s and congruent validity (median $r = .79$) for resulting scores for a variety of samples from the basic NCQ shown in Appendix 2.

Tracey and Sedlacek (1989) reported some reliability and validity evidence, with different samples, for scores on a revised version of the NCQ containing more items but no open-ended items, with a somewhat revised factor structure. Lockett (1980) reported validity and reliability data for scores from a modified version of the NCQ for Black students at a large Midwestern university. Ting and Sedlacek (2000) published information on the validity and reliability of scores from a revised NCQ in predicting retention for White students at a large Southeastern university.

Another version of the NCQ was shown to correlate with college grades of traditional and nontraditional students in health programs at a western state community college (Noonan, Sedlacek, & Suthakaran, 2001). Also, Webb and colleagues (1997) wrote that a version of the NCQ predicted success on National Board Examinations for students of color at two medical schools. Students are evaluated in project ACCESS at Prairie View A&M University using the NCQ, and the school reported greater predictability of college success for scores from the measure than for prior grades or test scores.

Short-Answer Questions. The Gates Millennium Scholars program (which is discussed in detail in the following chapter) assesses the eight noncognitive variables using short-answer questions in awarding higher education scholarships to students of color. Raters were trained to score the applications and interjudge agreement was established for a sample of raters (Pearson $r = .83$).The Cronbach alpha reliability estimate for the total noncognitive score from all raters in 2001 was .92 (Sedlacek & Sheu, forthcoming, a). Restriction of range problems appear to have been avoided in the Gates program since a normal distribution of scores for more than sixteen thousand applications was achieved. In the first three years of the Gates program, more than six thousand students of color received awards, and they attended more than nine hundred colleges and universities.

In another example, a short-answer version of a noncognitive questionnaire, based on the dimensions shown in Table 4.1, has been presented by the plaintiffs in *Castañeda et al.* v. *The University of California Board of Regents.* It was indicated as the preferred method of increasing minority student enrollment at the University of California-Berkeley. Appendix 5 shows a short-answer questionnaire designed to assess the noncognitive variables in Table 4.1.

Interviews. Noncognitive variables can be used to interview prospective students, although interviewers must be trained to identify how applicants may demonstrate high or low scores. Table 4.2 contains descriptions of how an individual might present information on the noncognitive variables in an interview, and Appendix 6 shows a series of interviewing principles. Appendix 7 contains the interview protocol used in the Lilly Endowment evaluation program.

The admissions program of the Louisiana State University Medical School has used interviews to assess noncognitive variables. In the ten years since introduction of noncognitive variables, the school's enrollment of students of color doubled to 21 percent, with an 87 percent retention rate.

The university's admissions committee members were trained by using simulated cases to conduct interviews in assessing the eight noncognitive variables (Sedlacek & Prieto, 1982). More than 80 percent of the committee members felt the noncognitive variables were useful in admissions, while 92 percent thought the training helped them identify the noncognitive variables in applicant interviews (Helm, Prieto, & Sedlacek, 1997). The admissions committee reported that self-concept (97 percent), realistic self-appraisal (95 percent), leadership (84 percent), support person (83 percent), and handling racism (81 percent) were the most useful indicators of "minority" student success. Sixty-one percent indicated grade point average and 57 percent identified Medical College Admission Test scores as being useful for minority admissions.

The University of Maryland Medical School has also employed interviews to assess applicants on the noncognitive variables shown in Table 4.1. It has defended their use in an ongoing lawsuit challenging their fairness (*Farmer* v. *Ramsay et al.*). As discussed in Chapter One, the court in *Farmer* has ruled that it will permit the university to employ noncognitive variables in admitting students; the ruling is currently under appeal.

Portfolios. Portfolios are yet another way to assess noncognitive variables (LaMahieu, Gitomer, & Eresch, 1995). Portfolios have been commonly used in the arts to demonstrate the work of applicants for admission. Chen and Mazow (2002) have discussed the value of electronic learning portfolios for students to present their accomplishments.

The school of design at one university has required an additional admissions procedure beyond the general one employed for all undergraduates. Traditionally, it has required a portfolio containing design-related materials produced by the applicant. Administrators and faculty at the school wished to broaden the content of the portfolio to contain information on noncognitive variables, such as how the applicants had overcome obstacles, how they saw themselves, and what their goals were. The school officials felt this would give them better information with which to judge their applicants, particularly those of color. To avoid one potential problem in portfolio assessment—that middle-class students may benefit most —faculty evaluators were trained in identifying examples of high and low scores on noncognitive variables (Koretz, 1993). Tables 4.1 and 4.2 can be employed in training for portfolio assessment.

The University of California, Irvine, has employed a Personal Achievement Profile along with SAT or ACT scores, grades, and specific courses completed, as part of its admission profile (Wilbur & Bonous-Hammarth, 1998). The university included, among other things, the noncognitive variables of leadership, community service, and creative achievement. After applicants were screened on their academic credentials, about 60 percent of the entering class was determined. The additional 40 percent of the class was selected on the basis of the Personal Achievement Profile. Using a double-blind procedure, admissions staff who were trained in reviewing the profiles made the judgments. No interviews or letters of recommendation were employed, and the entering class varied across a number of dimensions.

Essays. With appropriate training, it is possible to have raters score essay material on noncognitive variables. For example, in the Gates Millennium Scholars program, readers were able to score essays on the applications with high interjudge agreement (Pearson $r = .81$) on the noncognitive variables shown in Table 4.1. Validity studies are under way to relate those scores to academic and nonacademic outcomes (Sedlacek & Sheu, forthcoming, a).

Table 4.2 can be employed to help identify how people may evince noncognitive variables in an essay. Appendix 8 contains some sample cases that could be used in training for evaluation of essays.

Application Review. Application review can be seen as similar to essays or portfolios in that an application containing many facets (among them essays and presentations of information on a person) can be evaluated for noncognitive variables. Applications can be reviewed even if there was no *a priori* intention to evaluate noncognitive variables. For example, in the first year of the Gates Millennium Scholars program, the applications were designed and completed by applicants before a determination was made as to how evaluation of the applications would be done. Despite this, the applications contained information that could be evaluated for noncognitive variables.

Appendix 8 shows examples that can be employed in the scoring and training of raters and a suggested scoring system. Interjudge Pearson correlations of between .81 and .85 were achieved using this process in several situations involving admissions and financial aid.

Application review is a good way to start the process of using noncognitive variables in that one can review application materials of current matriculants to do a retrospective study of which noncognitive variables appeared to relate to successes or failures among students. This technique was employed as one of the evaluation methods in the *Farmer* v. *Ramsay et al.* medical school case.

In summary, noncognitive variables present a method of improving assessments for all students and are particularly useful for nontraditional students. Noncognitive variables can be assessed in a number of ways: questionnaires, interviews, essays, portfolios, and reviewing materials not specifically designed to elicit information on noncognitive variables. In the next chapter, the use of noncognitive variables in admissions and scholarship selection is discussed. The chapter includes many examples of how noncognitive variables have been used by schools and programs in higher education.

CHAPTER FIVE

ADMISSIONS AND FINANCIAL AID

Traditional and Nontraditional Measures

This chapter discusses the logic and rationale for selecting students for admission or financial aid awards, including the fairness of standardized tests for different racial, cultural, and gender groups; evaluates some of the alternatives to traditional tests; and presents examples of using an assessment model that is based on noncognitive variables.

The Problems with Using Standardized Tests in Admissions

Despite extremely widespread use of standardized testing for admissions, criticism of it for this purpose is common. Questions about current tests range from their legality (Connor & Vargyas, 1992; C. Harvey & Hurtado, 1994) to the validity of their scores (Hughey, 1995; W. M. Williams, 1997) and their fairness for all groups (Crouse & Trusheim, 1988; *FairTest Examiner,* 1997; Sedlacek, 1974, 1996a). Additionally, many have called for new approaches to be developed (Cole, 1997; Gardner, 1995; Kornhaber, 1997; Latino Eligibility Task Force, 1997; Tapia, 1998). Here is a summary of conclusions on the validity of scores on standardized admissions tests (SAT, ACT, and so on):

- They predict first-year grades fairly well for traditional students (that is, White middle-class and upper-class males).

- They predict first-year grades less well for nontraditional students (cultural, racial, gender groups).
- They do not predict grades well beyond the first year for any students.
- They do not predict retention or graduation well for any students in any year.

Fairness

Even though it may seem logical to *hope* that a single standardized test could fairly equate applicants, *expecting* such an outcome is unreasonable. As discussed in Chapter Three, this has been called the Three Musketeers problem in assessment (Sedlacek, 1994a). The premise of "all for one and one for all" is often employed in developing fair and equitable measures. As Cole (1997) noted, the myth of test scores is that any test will provide a single unequivocal yardstick by which we can measure all comers.

Ease of Use

The fact that standardized tests are easy to use should not be a compelling rationale for using them, especially as the only assessment instruments. A simple overall solution to a complex assessment issue is likely to work better for some groups than others and result in a form of institutional racism (Sedlacek, 1995b). The challenge of any professional in education is to do the *best* job, not necessarily the easiest.

Predicting Success

Another problem with standardized tests is how well they are able to predict college grades, retention, and graduation for various groups of students. Both overprediction and underprediction indicate that scores on a measure are invalid. In other words, if a group performs differently on a criterion measure than it was expected to do, the predictor is not measuring what it should.

The SAT and ACT are doing the job they were designed to do: predict first-year grades for White upper-middle-class and upper-class males. Thus decision makers who are primarily concerned with the first-year performance of White men can use the ACT or SAT by itself to select a class that will perform better on first-year grades than a group selected by chance.

W. M. Williams (1997) concluded that "the bottom line is basically the same for the GRE (Graduate Record Examination), the SAT, and other related tests: those tests weakly predict course grades during the first-year of a multiyear program but they predict little or nothing else" (p. A60). The higher the ability of the group being selected, the greater is the problem of restriction of range in the test scores. This occurs because the scores of higher-ability people tend to bunch up as they near the top of the distribution. Sternberg and Williams (1997) published empirical data on the GRE supporting this conclusion. Darlington (1998) also noted restriction-of-range problems for the GRE, and Sedlacek and Hutchins (1966) discussed the problem for the Medical College Admission Test. Restricting the range of scores on tests artificially lowers their correlation with criteria.

But standardized tests fall short when predicting (1) grades beyond the first year for any student, (2) retention or graduation for any student, and (3) grades or retention for students of color or women. Grade predictions beyond the first year present statistical problems because of a loss of students who receive grades, since students leave school for a variety of reasons. The loss is nonrandom and could cause statistical artifacts (Sedlacek, 1986). However, W. G. Bowen and Bok (1998); Bridgeman, McCamley-Jenkins, and Ervin (2000); Burton and Ramist (2001); Tracey and Sedlacek (1984a, 1984b, 1985, 1987); Vars and Bowen (1998); and Wilson (1980, 1983) have demonstrated that it is possible to do such studies. Some of these studies have shown correlations of the SAT with grades beyond the first year, but the bulk of the evidence demonstrates that the SAT works best in predicting first-year grades.

One reason that longer-term predictions are important in the context of nontraditional students is that many students of color and other marginalized groups may take longer to adjust to their college or university environment because of racism, and so they do not show their true abilities until later in their curriculum (Neville, Heppner, & Wang, 1997; van Rossum, 2002). The less familiar the curriculum for the student, the more time it may take. For example, women in an engineering program may take relatively more time to "do their best" than men do because of the adjustments to the system that they must make (Trippi & Cheatham, 1989). Ossana, Helms, and Leonard (1992) reported that women increasingly were pursuing degrees in areas that were less common for them than men. Therefore predictions of first-year grades would favor men, whose performance is more stable at that point.

Standardized tests typically *overpredict* college grades for racial and cultural groups (Noble, Crouse, & Schulz, 1996; Sedlacek, 1996a, 2003a, forthcoming; Vars & Bowen,1998) and for students with learning disabilities (Ziomek & Andrews, 1996). Sedlacek (1994a) argued that a sampling bias problem may be the cause. Researchers often do not study a representative sample of a given racial or cultural group because applicants might not have taken the test or supplied the score, or they are in a special program where the scores are either not required or pooled with the rest of the applicants. Vars and Bowen (1998) studied students with a limited range of high SAT scores at selective institutions and found that Blacks got lower grades than expected. In fact, they determined that the greatest discrepancies in using the SAT to predict grades for Blacks occurred for those with the highest SAT scores. Thus, restricting the range of scores or subsamples studied can reduce or eliminate the least traditional in a group, and statistical relationships derived from data on such samples may result in overprediction (Darlington, 1998). Ziomek and Andrews (1996) discussed the problem of sample bias in studying students with learning disabilities.

It is also not clear who is included when SAT results are reported by race or ethnicity. Wainer (1988) noted that the percentage of applicants who do not answer the race/ethnicity question on the College Board Student Descriptive Questionnaire that accompanies the SAT ranged from 12 to 14 percent. More recent information ("Students . . .," 1996/1997) suggested additional problems. For example, SAT-takers often decide whether or not to disclose their race or ethnicity according to their perceptions of how the information will be viewed by the colleges to which they are applying. Such sampling problems may contribute to overprediction for some groups.

On the other hand, some researchers have found that standardized tests commonly *underpredict* college grades for women (Betz & Fitzgerald, 1987; Gamache & Novick, 1985; E. S. Johnson, 1993; Rosser, 1989). However, Willingham and Cole (1997) felt that if other variables are considered along with test scores the underprediction is lessened. Stricker, Rock, and Burton (1993) found that underprediction for women was reduced when studiousness was added to prediction equations.

The reasons standardized tests underpredict or overpredict college grades for nontraditional groups are not completely clear, and further research on the topic is indicated. However, as discussed above, sampling bias and self-concept issues relating to taking tests can contribute to less-than-accurate predictions. These issues and others are discussed later in this chapter.

The results are mixed when standardized tests are used to predict retention or graduation as a criterion. Some studies have found little or no validity for test scores against such criteria (Sedlacek, 1989, 1991, 1996a, 1996b, 2003a, forthcoming; Sternberg & Williams, 1997; Tracey & Sedlacek, 1987; Willingham, 1985). Other researchers have shown some evidence for such validity (Adelman, 1999; Astin, Tsui, & Avalos, 1996; W. G. Bowen & Bok, 1998). However, standardized tests were not designed to relate to retention and graduation and cannot be expected to do so. But now many colleges and universities are more concerned with keeping and eventually graduating their students than concentrating on the grades student receive (McNairy, 1996; C. J. White & Shelley, 1996; Wyckoff, 1998). This interest in retaining students is another example of a change in policy direction where standardized tests have not kept up with the needs of higher education.

Legality

Connor and Vargyas (1992), in their discussion of standardized testing for women, concluded that such tests do discriminate against women and may be considered illegal under Title IX of the Educational Amendments of 1972 and the Equal Protection Clause of the Fourteenth Amendment to the U.S. Constitution, which prohibits sex discrimination in any educational program or activity receiving federal assistance. Yalof-Garfield (1997) argued that a model—and legal—admissions policy for law schools would, among other things, be flexible and would not favor one gender or racial group over another.

It is clear that standardized tests do not predict either grades or retention for students of color or women as well as they do for White men (Sedlacek, 1989, 1991, 1996a, 1996b, 2003a, forthcoming; Vars & Bowen, 1998). Exhibit 5.1 presents some common questions and answers that could be applied to standardized tests.

Alternative Admissions Measures

As suggested here, there are a number of alternatives to employing standardized tests in admissions, among them considering students' prior grades, socioeconomic status, and recommendations. Some alternatives have been studied extensively, while others have received less attention, and some show more promise than others. Let us turn to discussion of some of these alternatives.

Prior Grades

High-school grades have always been a staple in college admission formulas. The logic is that the best predictor of future performance is past performance. Researchers have suggested that past grades combined with test scores may be a better predictor of future grades than a test alone (Camara, 1997; Carnevale, Haghighat, & Kimmel, 1998; Cole, 1997; Willingham, Lewis, Morgan, & Ramist,

EXHIBIT 5.1. COMMON QUESTIONS AND ANSWERS ABOUT STANDARDIZED TESTS.

Question: Do admissions tests such as the SAT and ACT measure everything important to know in an applicant?

Answer: Admissions tests measure only one of the three areas important for academic success, problem solving. The two areas not measured by admissions tests are creativity and ability to negotiate a system.

Question: Are admissions tests equally fair for all candidates?

Answer: Nontraditional applicants (some racial groups, women, older applicants) often show their abilities in ways not measured by admissions tests. Some have questioned the legality of traditional admissions tests.

Question: Is it possible to assess abilities not covered in the admissions tests?

Answer: It is difficult but not impossible. Additional variables can be systematically and inexpensively measured.

Question: Is achievement more important than potential aptitude in college admissions?

Answer: Both are important, but some assessment of a candidate's potential or aptitude is critical in teaching and learning.

Question: Should we abandon admissions tests because of all the problems with them?

Answer: No. We should recognize the purpose and limitations of admissions tests and add additional measures to our admissions procedures.

Question: Why have admission tests become so widely used by colleges and universities?

Answer: They allow candidates to be compared on a common yardstick, they are easy to obtain, and they tell us some useful things about candidates.

Question: Aren't critics of admissions testing just being extreme?

Answer: Some may be regarded as such, but there are serious scholars who have criticized our current testing procedures and produced research to back their criticism.

1990; K. K. Wilson, 1983). Tests and grades both probably measure one of Sternberg's types of intelligence (componential ability), which were discussed in Chapter Three (Sternberg, 1985, 1986). Camara (1997) concluded that high school grades or ranks were worse predictors of first-year college grades for African Americans than was the SAT.

Adelman (1997) found that grades predicted college degree completion for students of color when the quality of high school curriculum was considered. However, evaluating students of color on their past performance may limit their potential for change and development; it may take students of color more time to learn how to handle racism and begin to demonstrate their abilities than other students. Trippi and Cheatham (1989) noted the significance of special counseling programs for African American students, particularly in their first year of college. Such programs are necessary, they argued, because of the unique problems and adjustments African Americans face at a predominantly White university. Neville et al. (1997) presented further evidence of the stressors faced by African American students on White campuses that interfere with their problem-solving ability.

Using prior grades as a predictor works against students in the process of change. Prior grades generally have not correlated well with academic success for students in special programs, as with those who have relatively more developing to do than other students (Houston, 1980; Stanley, 1971). However, Ting (1997) found that high school rank correlated with first-year college grades for White students in a special program.

One additional problem with using prior grades as a predictor is "grade inflation." Ziomek and Svec (1995) concluded there is considerable evidence that students are receiving higher grades in high school, particularly at the higher end of the grade distribution, than ever before. A report by *Career World* indicated that the use of test preparation programs for the SAT and ACT as well as grade inflation make it difficult for colleges to identify the high academic achiever ("Top Colleges . . .," 1999). The percentage of students who had an A average (A+, A, A-) has increased nationally from 28 percent to 37 percent, with no corresponding increase in postsecondary achievement (Rigol & Kimmel, 1997). This results in a restriction of range in high school grades, which lessens their utility as a predictor of college performance. Rojstraczer (2003) reported that average (mean) grade point average (GPA) in higher education nationally had risen from 2.94 in 1991–92 to 3.09 in 2001–02, on a four-point system. Thus the grade inflation problem seems to exist at all levels of education.

Some institutions use "altered grades" as an admissions predictor. Altered grades can include awarding extra credit to the GPA for honors courses the student has taken, or because the student participated in a particular program or attended a particular school. This practice tends to work against the interests of applicants who have not had access to such courses, programs, or schools. It also adds some potential invalidity to GPAs since it is not a good practice to add unknown variance to preexisting measures.

The logic of institutions employing what is sometimes called an "uncapped GPA" is that because of grade inflation there is a need to spread out the GPA distribution. The University of California, Berkeley, has developed such measures for use in its admissions program (Thomson, 1995), and it has been challenged in the *Castañeda et al.* v. *The Regents of the University of California* (1999) case as being unfair to applicants of color.

Socioeconomic Status

Socioeconomic status (SES) has been studied as an alternative to using race or ethnicity as a direct consideration in the college admission process. Researchers at the University of California, Berkeley, concluded that the use of SES in admissions would not result in the same level of ethnic diversity that currently existed at UC campuses (Galligani, Caloss, & Ferri, 1995). African American, American Indian, and Chicano/Latino enrollments would decrease while Asian American, lower-SES, and White enrollments would increase.

Kornhaber (1997) noted that although SES had some correlation with first-year success, it did not seem "fair" as a predictor. Aside from being unfair, it also oversimplifies the complexities of race, culture, and gender. The assumption here is that if the lower SES classes are somehow to be uplifted, there will be no implications to being a woman, a Chicano, an African American, and so on. Adelman (1997) concluded that inadequate educational resources, which are correlated with SES, are a major reason for lesser performance in college by students of color. However, a great deal of evidence exists to suggest that beyond SES, racial, cultural, and gender-related issues affect many aspects of the lives of individuals, including how they demonstrate their abilities (Chernin, Miner-Holden, & Chandler, 1997; Ponterotto & Pedersen, 1993; Sedlacek, 1994a, 1996a, 1996b; Sedlacek & Brooks, 1976).

Recommendations

Recommendations suffer from a number of measurement problems (Sedlacek & Prieto, 1990). They tend to yield unreliable and invalid results, and they commonly include a positive "halo effect." Letters of recommendation, especially if the candidate chooses the recommender, are frequently overly positive and are not a useful way to distinguish among candidates.

The results of recommendations tend to be more reliable and valid if the recommender is known to the evaluator or the evaluator solicits the recommendation from a particular person. Another element that can improve validity of recommendation evaluations is to request that specific topics be covered in the letter, such as examples of behavior or answers to specific questions. If a recommendation is carefully evaluated as one piece of application evidence, then reliability, in the form of corroborative information, might be established.

In a case mentioned in previous chapters (*Farmer* v. *Ramsay et al.,* 1998), recommendation letters were an important part of the evaluation of the plaintiff's application to a medical school. Because the letters were written by people known to the medical school and they could be related to other application materials, the recommendations could be used effectively.

Scores from recommendations were also shown to have some validity in Gates Millennium Scholar applications by presenting evidence of noncognitive variables in a corroborative manner.

The Use of Noncognitive Variables in Admissions

Noncognitive variables have been found effective in predicting student success in higher education and employed by many institutions in their admissions and retention programs. Here are case studies of colleges and universities that have studied or included noncognitive variables in such programs. Some are brief snapshots; others include more detail. These examples are intended to illustrate some of the possibilities in employing noncognitive variables, rather than to cover all situations.

A Southeastern State University: General Admissions

Based on several studies, the noncognitive variable questionnaire (NCQ) was found to be predictive of success for undergraduate students at North Carolina State University (W. Hill, 1995; Hoey, 1997; Ting, 1997; Ting & Sedlacek, 2000). The studies showed predictive and construct validity for NCQ scores of White applicants and applicants of color. For White applicants, self-concept and long-term goals were the best predictors of college GPA, while self-concept and negotiating multicultural experiences were the best predictors of retention. For applicants of color, self-concept, strong support person, and handling racism were the best predictors of college grades and retention.

Hoey (1997) found that a combination of first-year fall GPA and NCQ scores could correctly predict 92 percent of the retention of African American students from first to second year at NC State. For other students of color (Asian American, Latino, American Indian, and other), a combination of fall first-year credit hours enrolled and NCQ scores also correctly predicted 92 percent of the retention from first to second year at that institution. Multiple regression and multiple discriminant analyses were employed in these studies.

Construct validity evidence through a factor analysis showed that seven of the eight noncognitive variables described students at NC State. The community dimension took the form of extracurricular activities, but all of the other NCQ dimensions emerged in the factor analysis. The NCQ was administered in paper and pencil format to all undergraduate applicants to NC State; the eight scores were considered along with high school grades and SAT scores for admission. The institution sent out more than seventy thousand copies of the NCQ to prospective applicants for the class entering in fall 1998, of which about 9 percent were African American.

An Eastern Private Liberal Arts College: Competing Successfully

A moderately selective liberal arts college in the East felt it was losing out to its competitors in getting students with the highest SAT scores and grades. It wished to continue to enroll good students. The school began to use the NCQ, both as a recruiting device to attract a broader range of students and as a selection tool. The school had never done a comprehensive study of its admissions predictors, and what was found surprised officials at the college. The SAT scores it had been employing showed poor correlations with grades at the school (.23), and precollege grades showed even less of a relationship with college grades (.15). With the NCQ, higher correlations (.55) were obtained with first and second year grades, and the college was able to increase its applicant pool by 18 percent over three years. Self-concept and long-term goals correlated highest with success at the college. Thus the college was able to increase its number of applicants and improve its ability to select students in a three-year period by stressing noncognitive variables in its admissions process.

A Large Southern State University: Clarifying the Gray Area

A large state university had about six thousand applications for three thousand places in the first-year class. The primary goal in the admission process was to select fairly but at the same time to maximize the number of nontraditional students, particularly African Americans. The mean for all the applicants was 22 on the ACT composite, and the mean ACT for the 520 African American general applicants was just about five points lower. If it chose strictly by ACTs, the university would accept only about 150 African American applicants and might get only half of those to actually enroll. These numbers were unacceptably low, but it did not want to lower the ACT scores required for admission. It also did not want to require the students to go into special programs.

The institution decided to consider both traditional measures (ACT and high school grades) and noncognitive measures. It required all general applicants to complete the NCQ. The school developed two multiple regression equations based on some pilot studies and the NCQ norms (see Appendix). One regression equation was for traditional applicants, and the other was for nontraditional applicants. The approximate weights given were about two-thirds to traditional measures and one-third to noncognitive variables for traditional applicants. For nontraditional applicants, the NCQ was weighted about 60 percent, compared to 40 percent for the ACT and grades.

Admissions office personnel were trained to make a determination of how traditional the experiences of each applicant were. These judgments were used to determine which of the two equations would be used for each applicant. Any difficult decisions were assigned to a committee consisting of admission staff, faculty, students, and campus administrators. The assumption was that if the institution wanted nontraditional students, it would have to consider traditionality of experience in its admission process and ensure that judgments from the assessments were as valid for nontraditional applicants as possible.

The institution did not change any other aspects of its admission, retention, or recruiting programs, or any of its special programs or curricular offerings. By employing the new procedures it admitted 64 percent of the African American applicants, and 208 actually enrolled. The usual graduation rate after six years, before implementing the new procedure, was about 60 percent for traditional students and about 30 percent for African American students. After employing the new admission procedures, the six-year graduation rate for traditional students was 65 percent, while it was 56 percent for African Americans. A control group was not employed for comparison, but officials at the institution were pleased with the new system; they have begun to think of ways to provide recruiters and advisors with more admission information to perform those functions better.

A Medium-Sized Private Western College: Special Programs

A medium-sized private college had several special programs into which students who could not meet the fairly high admission standards were admitted. The means for the entering first-year students outside of these special programs on the SAT were 618 verbal and 580 math, with B+ high school grades.

Most of the funds for the special programs were from public and private grants, but college administrators were not pleased with the high attrition rate (80 percent never graduated from the school) and the isolation of the students in the special programs from the rest of the student body. The general student body, faculty, administrators, and the students in the programs themselves felt the programs were for inferior students. Sixty percent of the students in the programs were Latino, 28 percent were African American, and the rest were from a variety of other racial and cultural groups.

The admissions office, and the administrators and counselors in the special programs, tried to work together smoothly, but with little success. Admissions staff generally favored admitting students with the highest SATs and grades. Staff in the special programs tried to assess recommendations from teachers and an on-site interview, but they were not able to quantify or articulate their impressions of the applicants to the satisfaction of the admissions staff.

The president of the college decided to implement a system based on noncognitive variables. Any applicant who did not meet the usual admission requirements could apply via a second procedure. The applicants were sent the NCQ with a letter explaining that there were many ways to do assessment, and they would be given every chance to demonstrate their qualifications for admission. Applicants were also requested to supply any further evidence of their accomplishments (artwork, writing, community work, and so on) that was not furnished with their initial application.

Admissions and program staff were trained in making assessments of noncognitive variables and a procedure was implemented that gave scores on each of the eight noncognitive variables shown in Table 4.1, as modified by their judgments of the additional materials supplied. (See Appendix 8, which contains training materials on the noncognitive variables.) Evaluators began to develop a consistent language focused on noncognitive concepts (for example, long-term goals), and more consensus on decisions was reached. Additionally, a program to educate the campus about the positive abilities suggested by noncognitive variables was begun. The program has involved seminars, workshops, classes, speakers, and articles in campus publications. Although evaluations are incomplete, results of surveys have shown a change to a more positive perception of multiple ways of showing ability through the noncognitive variables.

An Eastern State University: Athletes as Nontraditional Students

It might be useful to conceptualize student athletes as nontraditional students. Athletes appear to have a unique culture and set of experiences in life that differentiate them from others (Sowa & Gressard, 1983). They tend to spend a great deal of time together and often have common goals and values generated by their experiences. They also may experience prejudice and discrimination, much as students from nontraditional cultures or groups do. For instance, Engstrom and Sedlacek (1991) and Engstrom, Sedlacek, and McEwen (1995) reported that students and faculty tended to have negative stereotypes of student athletes. As discussed in Chapter Three, two conditions define a group as nontraditional: prejudice against them and prediction of their ability with noncognitive variables (Sedlacek, 1996a).

The admission of student athletes to U.S. colleges and universities has been the subject of increased attention and heated debate in recent years (Sedlacek & Adams-Gaston, 1992). The controversy has moved from admissions offices and campus units to the public press. Much of the attention has been focused on the three National Collegiate Athletic Association (NCAA) propositions that limit participation of male student athletes in their first year (Propositions 16 and 48) and their ability to receive financial aid (Proposition 42) on the basis of their SAT or ACT scores. Many have expressed additional concern because of the potentially negative consequences for African American student athletes (Roper & McKenzie, 1989). Unfortunately, there has been more talk than research on predicting the success of student athletes.

The University of Maryland compared the ability of the SAT and the NCQ to predict the academic success of student athletes (Sedlacek & Adams-Gaston, 1992). The study included male and female revenue (such as basketball and football) and nonrevenue (such as tennis and swimming) athletes in an NCAA Division 1-A athletic program.

SAT math and SAT verbal scores showed essentially zero correlation with first-semester grades. As individual predictors, the NCQ scales of strong support person, self-concept, realistic self-appraisal, and community all had significant (.05 level) correlations with first-semester grades. Strong support person, community, and self-concept combined in the regression equations as significantly predicting first-semester grades (.05 level). Cronbach alpha reliability estimates for NCQ scale scores from this sample ranged from .73 to .90.

A Midwestern Medical School: Recruiting Pays Off

A Midwestern institution had a small percentage (3 percent) of students of color and wanted to do something about it. It decided to employ noncognitive variables in recruiting students of color. In the past, representatives from the school had gone to college fairs and visited some historically Black colleges. However, they had no particular unique message to give to students of color about the school or why a student of color might want to come there. The school developed materials highlighting how it was prepared to work with students on each of the noncognitive variables shown in Table 4.1.

The school also communicated with its feeder schools and other institutions at which it had not been successful in recruiting, indicating that it was looking for students with certain noncognitive abilities rather than only those with high grades and test scores. The school increased its enrollment of students of color by 50 percent over a three-year period and improved the retention rate of those students by 22 percent over the same period. University officials are still evaluating their efforts, but their behavioral goals are being exceeded.

An Historically Black Southern University: We Were Never Traditional

Prairie View A&M University, an historically Black school in Texas, was under pressure from the state legislature to defend its admissions policies—and the very existence of the institution. Officials at the university needed a way to assess the talents and abilities of their students that were not shown in prior grades and test scores. They knew traditional measures were never useful in measuring the potential of their applicants. They decided to employ the NCQ in admissions to a program that extended educational assistance and opportunity to students considered at risk to persist to graduation.

An institutional study showed that students in the pre-first-year summer program (called ACCESS) selected with the NCQ got higher grades and completed more credit hours in the year after completing the program than a control cohort. Ninety percent of the ACCESS students completed the program. Applicants to the program also submitted three letters of recommendation and participated in a telephone interview. Use of prior grades and standardized test scores as criteria for admission were minimized owing to their lack of validity for students at the school. About seventy-five students entered the program each year.

A Midwestern State College: Open Admissions

A Midwestern state college had open admissions and was required to admit all students who applied who had received a high school diploma from the state. The enrollment of students of color was about 2 percent, although about 10 percent of the students were over twenty-five years of age and about 50 percent of the students did not complete a degree.

Applicants were not required to take the SAT or ACT. This left the institution in the position of knowing very little about its incoming students. The academic advisors and student service staff felt particularly lacking in information.

Therefore, during orientation at the beginning of each semester, new students were administered a version of the NCQ that was modified to fit the needs of the school (see Appendices 4.1 to 4.4 for examples).

Results were supplied to advisors and student services staff, including the career center, counseling center, and student activities, and the academic advisor of each student. Students signed a consent form indicating that they understood that the results would be used in their behalf in advising and student services, and anonymously for research purposes. Nearly all students consented. Advisors and student personnel workers consistently reported using the information in planning programs and advising students. The college held training sessions for faculty and staff in understanding and using the NCQ results in a helpful and ethical manner.

Research indicated the NCQ, as revised, had statistically significant (.05 level) correlations with GPA in the first year for all students, but the correlations were particularly high for older students and students of color. At the time of this writing, the school has begun a series of retention programs based on the noncognitive variables.

An Eastern Catholic College: Two Functions for Noncognitive Variables

St. John Fisher College implemented use of the NCQ for several purposes. First, it served as a general admissions measure to predict success at the college. Additionally, the NCQ was employed as a way to determine entry into a special educational development program at the school. Students who had a low GPA and low scores on the SAT, but who had high scores on the NCQ, were considered the most likely to benefit from the special program. The program covered tutoring, study skills, adjustments to the campus, and financial and general support. Counselors in the program used individual NCQ scores to work with students in improving on dimensions relevant for them. Results of studies at St. John Fisher showed that the number of students of color increased, and that students in the special program did particularly well in school. There is evidence that such a coordinated program between admissions and special student programs can have good benefits for the institution and its students (T. J. White & Sedlacek, 1986).

A Western School of Veterinary Medicine: Our Own Noncognitive Measure

For a ten-year period, a Western school of veterinary medicine used noncognitive variables in its admissions procedures. It was trying to identify worthy applicants to the Health Careers Opportunity Program (HCOP), which was designed for "disadvantaged" applicants. The school was highly selective in its admissions program and wanted disadvantaged students who could compete favorably with its other students once they were admitted. The HCOP students received financial aid, tutoring, and other support services.

The school developed its own supplementary interview procedure based on the NCQ dimensions. Applicants were administered a semistructured questionnaire (see Appendix 5 for example) on the noncognitive dimensions and then interviewed by trained faculty and administrators on their responses. The interviewers had been trained over a ten-year period using the Simulated Minority Admissions Exercise (SMAE; Prieto et al., 1978). Applicants accepted into the HCOP were highly successful, with 95 percent graduating. Interviewers reported learning some valuable information about noncognitive variables that they could use in teaching and advising students, and the HCOP administrators got information they could use in program planning for their students.

A Large Midwestern State University: Summer Residential Program

The University of Nebraska, Lincoln, offered a six-week summer residential learning community as a bridge to the first year at the university for students of color (van Rossum, 2002). Participants had to show a strong commitment to their own racial or ethnic community, leadership potential, and a desire to complete a degree at the university. The NCQ was administered to participants, and the NCQ scales of strong support person and knowledge acquired in a field correlated significantly with summer and second semester grades for the students. Although the ACT correlated higher than the NCQ scales for summer grades, by the second semester NCQ scores correlated higher with student GPA than did the ACT. This is an example of the potential value of the NCQ in predicting later, rather than earlier, performance for some students of color since they may take time to adjust to the institution.

Scholarships and Financial Aid

In addition to helping assess a student's ability to succeed in college, noncognitive variables can be employed in evaluating candidates for scholarships and financial aid. Here is a discussion of some issues in financial aid, to set a context for description of some programs where noncognitive variables have been used in making financial awards to students.

In the 1970s, adequately funded federal student aid programs attempted to promote equal opportunity (Gladieux & Wolanin, 1976). At that time, traditional college-aged African Americans attended colleges and universities at about the same rate as Whites (U.S. Department of Education, 1998).

By the 1990s, federal policy on higher education desegregation shifted from attempting to desegregate predominantly White institutions of higher education to attempting to desegregate historically Black colleges and universities (St. John & Hossler, 1998; St. John & Musoba, 2001; J. B. Williams, 1997). During the 1990s, the federal government's need-based money available to low-income students had declined to the point where student net costs were beyond affordability (Advisory Committee on Student Financial Assistance, 2001; College Board, 2000; St. John, 1994).

Private financial aid through scholarship programs has emerged as an important part of assisting students in need. Cofer and Somers (2000) published evidence that there is a negative correlation between family income and continuous enrollment in higher education. Lower-income students may start school, but they are more likely to drop out for financial reasons than other students. Scholarships are often awarded to students of color using the same criteria that have been used in admissions: grades and test scores. Here is a description of several programs that have provided scholarships to students of color on the basis of noncognitive variables.

Gates Millennium Scholars

The Gates Millennium Scholars (GMS) program sets out an ambitious and socially important series of goals for itself. Scholarships are provided to financially needy African Americans, Native Americans, Hispanic Americans, or Asian Americans who are, or will be, studying mathematics, science, engineering, education, or library science. Applicants are required to be eligible for Pell Grants as a way of determining that they are in financial need, and awards cover all educational expenses at whatever institution the student is attending.

Students are selected for awards on the basis of their leadership ability, as expressed through their participation in community service, extracurricular activities, or other activities. Such qualities are desired of any applicant by college admissions offices, but they tend to be difficult qualities to judge and may be particularly so among applicants of color. Historically, intentional or unintentional discrimination has taken place against applicants other than those from traditional White upper-middle-class backgrounds. The assessments made in the GMS program are done using great care and sensitivity to the unique and valuable experiences and accomplishments presented by applicants.

To accomplish the task of selecting the scholars, a series of dimensions that reflect the goals of the program and give the applicants the best chance to show their potential in a variety of ways are employed. The noncognitive variables shown in Table 4.1 are used to select the scholars, along with assessments of the academic rigor of the applicant's high school curriculum and their ability to write a good essay explaining their interests in becoming a Gates Millennium Scholar. The goals of the selection process are to judge the academic potential of students of color who show their abilities in ways other than the more traditional standardized tests and prior grades. As with White scholarship recipients, most financial aid awards tend to go to students of color who show attributes in terms of Sternberg's componential intelligence.

Two methods of determining applicant potential on the noncognitive variables have been used in the GMS program. In the first year, applications were scored on the noncognitive variables according to materials furnished in personal statements, letters of recommendation, and other parts of the application that provided information. Raters were trained to identify and consider this information in scoring each of the eight noncognitive variables. Reliability was established among the raters, who were educators of color familiar with multicultural issues in education and working with the kind of student who was applying. In the first year of the program, awards were given to new entering first-year students, returning students, and graduate students.

In the second and third years of the program, the GMS application was redesigned to include short-answer questions focused on each of the noncognitive variables shown in Table 4.1. Again, raters of color were trained to interpret the new items, along with the other information on the application, to develop scores for each noncognitive variable. Reliability of judgments was also established employing the new system. In the second and third years of the program, awards were given to new first-year students only. In the first three years of the program, more than six thousand students of color were attending more than nine hundred institutions in the United States and receiving full scholarships for as long as they matriculated successfully in an institution of higher education. As of this writing, Gates Scholars had college GPAs of 3.4 on a 4-point system, so their early success in school has been established, and the method of selecting them appears to be working well.

The GMS Program is a $1 billion program, planned to last over a twenty-year period. At present, a longitudinal study is under way, tracking scholars (as well as those not selected) to determine the correlates of the noncognitive variables with a range of academic and nonacademic dimensions over the twenty-year period (Sedlacek & Sheu, forthcoming, a, b). This study should yield data that are unprecedented and rich in their potential to afford insight as to how to better understand, and better educate, people of color who have shown great potential in ways that typically are not considered, let alone assessed.

Other Applications of Noncognitive Variables in Financial Aid Programs

The Washington Education Foundation administers the Washington State Achievers program, which is designed to serve students from lower-income backgrounds from the state of Washington who are admitted to a college or university in the state. Raters are trained to identify noncognitive variables and score them along with other information in making awards. Many of the applicants are White students from rural and urban settings who are seen as showing ability on noncognitive dimensions. The program began in 2001 and will be studied for thirteen years after inception. Here is another important sample of students being monitored where correlates of noncognitive variables may yield much that educators and social service providers can use (Sedlacek & Sheu, 2003).

The National Action Council for Minorities in Engineering (NACME) makes available scholarships for African American, American Indian, and Latino male and female engineering students through its Engineering Vanguard program. The program employs the NCQ and other application materials in evaluating candidates. Those awarded scholarships are placed in partnership universities. The program maintains contact with scholarship recipients and makes use of noncognitive variables such as leadership and community to help with student needs after matriculation.

The financial aid staff of a large Midwestern state university has developed a creative way to use the Gates Millennium Scholar application. They are interested in attracting scholar applicants to their institution. Their plan is to allow the GMS application to be used as the financial aid application to their school. This streamlines the process for applicants and avoids the problem of discouraging many applicants of color from applying to the school because of excessive "red tape" and procedures. The school recognizes the racism in the typical financial aid application procedures and wishes to reduce the barriers many applicants of color might face in applying for financial aid.

Financial aid professionals from a large Western state university took a somewhat different approach by including a measure of noncognitive variables they have developed themselves with their financial aid application. The noncognitive variables are then used along with other application materials to make decisions on awards. Problems in using standardized tests, GPA, and other possible measures such as SES and interviews in determining admissions and financial aid are particularly critical for those students with nontraditional experiences. Noncognitive variables offer a way to avoid those problems by yielding some new information that is related to student success.

How a number of colleges, universities, and scholarship programs have employed noncognitive variables with some success has been covered in this chapter. The next chapter shows how noncognitive variables can be used in teaching.

CHAPTER SIX

TEACHING A DIVERSE STUDENT BODY SUCCESSFULLY

Noncognitive variables (NCVs) can be useful in assessment after a student matriculates. The noncognitive variables shown in Table 4.1 can be employed in a variety of settings involving teaching. Most teachers are constantly searching for a way to communicate more effectively with their students, and today's teachers are also trying to reach a diverse group of students in their classes. Noncognitive variables are a unique and valuable way to approach this diversity in class and to evaluate the outcomes of teaching.

Teachers have successfully incorporated NCVs into their classes by taking field trips to various off-campus communities, discussing research on NCVs, and giving students experience in problem solving across diverse groups. Some faculty members have trained their teaching assistants to handle diversity topics as they come up in class.

This chapter begins with some specific examples of courses or seminars that incorporate NCVs to improve the performance of various nontraditional groups as well as the understanding of diversity issues for all students; it ends with a discussion of results of a large-scale evaluation of curricular change in forty schools.

A Course on Racism

Since the ability to handle racism and inequity has been shown to be important to the success of nontraditional students, courses in handling racism can be useful to improve the success rate. What follows is an example of one way to conduct such a course. Parts of it could be included in any course where racism might be raised as a relevant issue. A brief history of the course illustrates some of the racism in existence at the University of Maryland that made the course valuable to many students.

History of the Course

The idea for the course was developed in the late 1960s, during a time of political and social turmoil in the United States. At that time, the University of Maryland offered a few specialized courses touching on racism, taken mainly by graduate students. The content was largely academic and theoretical, rather than practical or focused on what people could do about racism. In response to what was happening in the country and in the education system, a colleague and I developed a course that could be taken by undergraduate and graduate students, and we wrote a book to be used in the course (Sedlacek & Brooks, 1976).

The dean of the College of Education was opposed to what he viewed as "pop sociology," so he had to be convinced with research evidence that the course was needed (Sedlacek & Brooks, 1973). The evidence supported three key conclusions:

1. White students at all levels at the university had generally negative attitudes toward Blacks.
2. Those attitudes were associated with dogmatism and authoritarianism (Sedlacek & Brooks, 1972b).
3. The climate created by those attitudes had an adverse effect on Black students (Sedlacek & Brooks, 1973).

By 1985 the university had moved to about 15 percent undergraduate students of color, up from 1 percent in the late 1960s. As more students of color entered the university and expectations for diversity programs grew, the course was allowed to meet a "diversity" requirement for undergraduate students added in 1988 (Roper, 1988). Currently, the course is typically offered every semester and is consistently oversubscribed. New faculty were hired, including some of color, in part to teach the course. The university continued to increase its diversity through adding students of color (36 percent of all undergraduates in 2003) and implementing campus diversity programs (Helm, Sedlacek, & Prieto, 1998b; Ancis, Sedlacek, & Mohr, 2000).

Thus the course moved from being a special topics oddity, of little apparent interest on a nearly all-White campus, to becoming a visible part of many multicultural offerings on a highly diverse campus. What would be next for the course? Heretofore it had been taught with a blend of required texts and readings, along with class projects and presentations to facilitate learning (see Roper, 1988, for a syllabus and class activities from 1987).

Roper also demonstrated that not only were students learning some new information about racism, their attitudes and behaviors toward other groups were changed as a result of the course. The course directly addresses NCVs, among them positive self-concept, realistic self-appraisal, and handling the system (racism). For example, students tended to show less dogmatism and prejudice toward other groups and engaged in more interracial behavior than they had before the course. Whites, in particular, felt less distance from Blacks than they had previously. Roper (1988) also found that over a relatively short period of time (several weeks), interracial attitudes and behaviors may become more negative. Positive change takes time. The course could have continued along what seemed to be a successful path; the students demonstrated that they were learning and changing and course ratings by students were good. However, the Internet is with us in the early twenty-first century, and its possibilities suggested some course revisions.

The Redesigned Course

In redesigning the course, I made an attempt to explore possible uses of the Internet, including doing the entire course online or as a distance learning experience. By doing some reading and talking to distance learning colleagues, I reached a number of conclusions:

- The Internet provided the potential for vast amounts of information, but most of it was not evaluated as to quality.
- Most of the journals and other professional literature were not completely available on the Internet. In some cases, abstracts rather than complete documents were available.
- Online courses promoted isolation among students by limiting or eliminating interpersonal interaction.
- Limited interpersonal interaction might make it difficult to achieve some course goals (for instance, learning to work with other racial groups in a noncomputer situation).
- The Internet is a tool. Like the printing press, radio, or television, technology will not do the teaching for you.

The students were also issued the challenge to learn with the instructor, rather than to have everything come from the instructor. This approach, when it works, can have a significant effect on student self-concept. The university was enrolling talented students, and it seemed that placing students in a compelling situation where they are required to be active participants would be the best way to learn online (*Joint Task Force on Student Learning,* 1998). As opposed to being directed to specific references only, students were told in the first class meeting that they were to use the many resources the university was providing so they could *teach themselves* along with their instructor. Several students asked to have that point repeated so they understood it.

In organizing the latest incarnation of the course, I attempted to build on the history and experience with the course while addressing each of the points noted here.

Course Evaluation

The course was evaluated in the areas of information, attitudes, and behavior. Each goal is discussed in more detail in this section. These three areas are considered relatively independent in research and evaluation studies (Sedlacek, 1998c). That is, one may achieve certain outcomes in one area but not in another.

Course Format. The three-credit course typically meets once a week for three hours during the semester. A limit of fifty students was enrolled, with many more expressing interest. Four graduate student teaching assistants played a crucial role in implementing the course. Each student in the class was randomly assigned to one assistant, and a separate classroom was made available for each group aside from the primary classroom.

Course Assignments. *Paper* (20 percent of grade). A five-to-eight-page double-spaced paper on a definition of racism with ten to twenty references, at least five of which must be Website URLs, was required. The paper was graded on the student's ability to organize the references and use logic to reach his or her own definition. The first two meetings of the class included a discussion of racism by the instructor and three assigned readings, one of which was available only on the class Website (Hill & Sedlacek, 1994; Sedlacek, 1995b; Westbrook & Sedlacek, 1991). In addition to the general class Website, students had individual and group sites. Students were required to post their papers on their individual sites. They received training from staff at the campus technology center in developing and using their Websites and online resources (see Appendix 9). This paper was designed to cover the information goal of the course.

Racism log (20 percent of grade). Students were required to record examples of racism they encountered throughout the semester from personal experience, media, class, the Internet, and so on. Each example was to include a description of the incident (with a copy of an article or other reproducible material where appropriate) and answers as to why it was racism, as well as their reaction to the incident. The best logs would include examples of a number of kinds of racism from a variety of sources. Logs were kept confidential. Students could use the Internet, but they were encouraged to express themselves in any way they wished. This assignment met both information and attitude course goals and has the advantage of calling for types of intelligence beyond the componential (Sternberg, 1996).

Debates (20 percent of grade). Each student was assigned randomly to the pro or con position on a controversial topic on racism in education (for example, admissions in higher education, diversity programs, affirmative action, bilingual education). Working in groups with the teaching assistants, students developed their own references, materials, and arguments. The format was pro twenty minutes, con twenty minutes, con fifteen-minute rebuttal, pro fifteen-minute rebuttal over opening argument not on con rebuttal, pro fifteen-minute summary, and con fifteen-minute summary.

Debates were to include all group members making use of a variety of resources, including at least six Internet sites, in addition to those covered by teaching assistants in a lecture to the whole class on each topic. Students were given study guides on each topic. The use of witnesses, audiovisual or creative materials, computer presentations, and so forth was encouraged. Class members not involved in the debate posted their reactions to the debate on their individual Websites. They were to discuss the strengths and weaknesses of each presentation and conclude which side presented its case best, independent of the students' position, and which side had the toughest case to present.

This requirement covered information, attitudes, and behavior. By working in groups, many students would confront their feelings while dealing with information and behavior. Teaching assistants were trained to process such feelings. Students were also given guidelines on handling group feelings and behaviors (for example, some members not doing their share). Again, this course requirement calls for more types of intelligence than simply the componential, and it encourages realistic self-appraisal and skills in handling racism.

Debate written report (20 percent of grade). Each side of each debate was to prepare a group written report to be posted on the subgroup Website (one for each debate position). The report was to include arguments and counterarguments covered and develop the logic taken by the pro or con group. References were to be evaluated using an online reference guide made available on the class Website. This guide covered such topics as the authority or site author, accuracy, objectivity, currency, and coverage. This assignment covered the information and behavior goals of the course.

Final exam (20 percent of grade). A short answer and discussion format exam was given covering all material presented, including debate content and what students had learned and done about dealing with racism. This assignment would cover the information and behavior goals of the course.

Information Course Goal. The examinations and evaluations of content just noted indicated that the students had learned some things about racism, including how to define and identify examples of it. They had the most trouble knowing that the exact same situation may be racism for one group and not for another. For example, a common final exam question used in the course describes an incident where a person approaches a White magazine seller at a newsstand and is treated in a rude manner. The first customer is an African American female, who feels insulted and charges the man with racism. The next customer is a White man who is treated exactly the same way by the salesman. The White man does not take it personally and thinks the salesman is a "jerk" or having a bad day. The question for the students to answer is, "Can you have racism in the one situation and not the other?"

The students who give the best answers discuss the possibility that the African American was hurt by the remarks, likely because of a history of discrimination in similar situations involving friends, family, ancestors, and her; as a result, there is a negative outcome for her. The White man has no such history of discrimination and assumes the remarks have nothing to do with him. He is not harmed by the remarks, and there is no racism. The key is that an apparently identical stimulus can have different effects depending on the experience of the group a person represents. A focus on results, not intentions, is a concept that I hoped students would understand.

Attitudes Course Goal. Several versions of the Situational Attitude Scale (SAS) (Sedlacek, 1996a; see Chapter Three) were administered to students at the beginning, middle, and end of the course (see Appendix 1 for SAS forms). Roper (1988) also administered dogmatism and social distance scales in a pre-post design to students in the course. Students were also asked weekly about their optimism or pessimism that racism could be eliminated in education (see Appendix 10).

Most students tended to start the class with a negative attitude toward nontraditional groups (other than their own). At the end of the class, they had somewhat more negative attitudes. Students were also more dogmatic and pessimistic about racism at the end of the class. On the average, students felt some social distance from other groups at the start of the class; this did not change during the course.

Several groups of students showed differing patterns of change in their attitudes toward nontraditional groups. Students in each group showed individual differences, but on average the patterns discussed in this section were demonstrated. Many African American students struggled with their feelings about other groups—such as gay, lesbian, bisexual, or transgender students; people with disabilities; and Asian Americans—as they considered whether racism could be relevant to those groups. Some African Americans had strong emotional reactions to racism before taking the class, but this is not the same as learning how to handle racism.

Latinos tended to have problems with where they fit in the racism picture. Are they perpetrators? Are they victims? Are they both? These are self-concept issues, and their feelings were supported by findings in studies exploring Latino reactions to diversity programs (Ancis et al., 2000; Helm, Sedlacek, & Prieto, 1998b; Longerbeam, Sedlacek, & Alatorre, forthcoming).

Asian American students had reactions similar to those of Latino students, and often they were dealing with some denial that racism had anything to do with them. Asian American students also tended to feel that the campus "rules" were changing, and they were uncomfortable with that. These are self-concept and handling-racism issues (Liang & Sedlacek, 2003a,b). White students often had a difficult time with their reactions to being in the position of power and the implications of that awareness (Sedlacek, 1996a).

If these changes are interpreted in terms of the Sedlacek-Brooks (1976) model of eliminating racism, students become more aware of their prejudices by taking the class. Even though the outcomes appear to be negative in the short run, this is a stage that they must work through in learning to handle racism in the long run.

Behavior Course Goal. Students completed a log of their behavior in working against racism each week. Generally, all students reported engaging in more behaviors relating to dealing with racism each week as the course progressed. Increases were seen in discussions of racism with friends and family as well as reading, watching television, and using the Internet (other than for classwork) concerning racism topics.

Conclusions

This course is a direct attempt to teach students how to understand and handle racism. For those experiencing some kind of -ism, the course provides a long-term model for dealing with it. For those students who are not experiencing an -ism, the course gives them a way to think about racism and to help eliminate it.

The course is in a constant state of development, but several observations based on class evaluation seem relevant and are discussed in the context of the a priori conclusions reached about the course noted earlier. The important point here is that students were exhibiting more behavior in discussing and confronting racism, even though their attitudes were becoming more negative. It was also known that students had more information about racism. Here one can see how attitudes, information, and behavior may not be moving in the same direction, but all must be confronted and processed if racism is to be handled and ultimately eliminated.

After some stops and starts, the students seemed to be accepting the responsibility for their learning. The teaching assistants and I stated and consistently reinforced the idea that the students were being given many human and technical resources and they could use them to learn. One can evaluate the resources—be they URLs, computer facilities, or quality of instruction—and improve the course the next time.

I had to learn to be comfortable with less control. The students were not necessarily going to cover the assigned material, but they were coming up with new resources that would benefit them.

The students were expected to learn about the Internet and how to use its resources, but there was an attempt to keep the focus on learning about racism and the course goals. By permitting a great deal of human interaction in processing those resources, I hoped to avoid the pitfalls of online courses.

It is clear that there are large individual differences among the students according to their technical ability, race, gender, and life experience. The class is typically 50 percent female, 60 percent students of color, and 80 percent juniors and seniors, with majors from art to zoology. Some students have never thought much if at all about racism, while others have had multiple courses on the topic.

The teaching assistants were from a variety of races and genders, and their work with the class added to a great mix and multilevel quality of interaction in the class. An important secondary outcome for the course was the effect it had on the teaching assistants. They were being trained to teach such a course and deal with racism themselves. They were also learning how to do assessments and research with the noncognitive variables. The lack of such people was noted as a problem in Chapter Three. One of the teaching assistants who was Asian American reported to me that after he completed his graduate work he encountered some racism on his job. He indicated that he used ideas and materials from the class to handle it. All of the teaching assistants have continued to engage in research and teaching in areas of diversity.

Using Noncognitive Variables in a First-Year Student Seminar

The importance of developing a sense of community on campus cannot be overstated. Socially integrating students during their first eight weeks on campus may be the most important thing an institution can do in setting the foundation for a student's successful transition to college (Wawrzynski, 1999). The first years of undergraduate study are critical to student success (Education Commission of the States, 1995). Tinto and Goodsell (1993) posited that the likelihood of dropping out of college is greatest for most students in the first-year because of a period of transition and adjustment. This conclusion is supported by a number of other researchers (Astin, 1993; Pascarella & Terenzini, 1991; Tinto, 1993; Upcraft, Gardner, & Associates, 1989).

To address retention concerns, administrators have implemented support measures to assist students in their transition to the academic and social systems of college. According to the American Council on Education, in 1995 82 percent of colleges and universities had "taken steps to improve the first-year," compared to only 37 percent in 1987 (El-Khawas, 1995, p. 7).

E. Boyer suggested that "in order to give first-year students a sense of the community whose structure, privileges, and responsibilities have been evolving for almost a millennium" (1987, p. 43) institutions should offer a credit-bearing first-year student seminar. Gordon and Grites (1984) reported that the first-year student seminar has emerged as a vehicle for easing the transition of students from high school or the work environment into the college community. Tinto (1993) stated that institutions have recently turned to a range of first-year student programs explicitly designed to assist new students. El-Khawas (1995) noted that the first-year student seminar is the most common step implemented to improve the student's first year.

Even though first-year student seminars have grown in popularity, little is known about how first-year student seminars assist in the student persistence process. Wawrzynski (1999) evaluated a first-year seminar at a large Eastern university, including its effects on noncognitive variables.

The Seminar

A one-credit, letter-graded, eight-week seminar was offered to assist all incoming first-year students in their integration of the academic and social aspects of college life. Students generally self-selected into the seminar, but academic advisors sometimes encouraged them to enroll. Participants were 62 percent White,

15 percent African American, 13 percent Asian American, 5 percent Hispanic, and 0.3 percent American Indian. Fifty-one percent were men; seminar composition generally reflected campus enrollment.

These were the core elements emphasized in the seminars:

- Goal setting (related to realistic self-appraisal and long-term goals)
- Time management (related to realistic self-appraisal and long-term goals)
- Academic study skills (related to self-concept)
- Career exploration and development, including major exploration (related to long-term goals)
- Finding and using resources on campus, or in the community (related to handling the system, strong support person, and community)
- Diversity (related to the entire NCV spectrum)
- Alcohol and sexuality (related to self-concept)

During the eighth week of classes, seminar participants were administered a ninety-five-item survey questionnaire concerning experiences, academic skills and behaviors, future goals, attitudes about the university, and background information. Content validity of questionnaire scores was determined from a review of relevant literature (Spector, 1992), and construct validity was estimated through factor analysis. The test-retest reliability of responses to the questionnaire items was estimated at .79 for the participants.

Wawrzynski (1999) found that students who were able to develop what he called "social integration" were more likely to persist than those who did not. It can be defined as finding a community on campus that provides needed support. His results also showed that peer interactions were the key elements in these communities. Successful students developed communities around peer interactions. Wawrzynski also indicated that the first-year seminars were a way for faculty to help students identify and use campus resources. Thus the seminars helped students "work the system" and were an important link to analyzing campus life and successfully negotiating its demands.

An interesting relationship was found between academic self-concept and negotiating the system. Seminar participants had lower academic self-concepts than those who did not enroll in the seminar. This made it all the more important for seminar participants to learn about campus resources from faculty. Without that opportunity, many of the students would not have persisted in school. Students with better academic self-concepts did not need the extra efforts to find campus resources to be successful.

Curriculum Revision

In the mid-1990s, the Lilly Endowment funded an evaluation of forty schools that were engaged in attempting to add diversity perspectives to their curriculum (Sedlacek, 1995a). The various programs can be grouped into one of four approaches: comprehensive, focused, diffused, or external. Positive and negative experiences with each approach are evaluated here in terms of noncognitive variables.

Comprehensive Curricular Change

A comprehensive plan is defined as a course on diversity that all students would take. The courses, which varied from one to three credits, were offered by different departments or programs at different schools. Some courses were taught by full-time faculty with expertise in the area (often with some additional training), others by part-time or visiting faculty hired to teach that course, and still others by a large number of faculty across disciplines trained to teach the course.

The most successful comprehensive programs tended to stress community in bringing students together to learn and also covered issues on working the system. Successful programs were realistic in their appraisal of where students and the school were in the developmental stages of awareness of racism and its effects.

Successful Comprehensive Programs. Success was variously defined in the schools, and evidence in the attitude, information, and behavior areas was presented by the schools (Sedlacek, 1998c). The most successful program was a one-credit course at one school taught by faculty from all departments. All first-year students were required to take the course, which was designed to expose them to issues of stereotyping and prejudice, and to the relationship of these issues to the exercise of power in the United States. Class size was limited to twenty; formats included retreats, class meetings, field work, and weekly one-hour classes. Faculty received training, including visits to other campuses, and chose one of several collections of readings as a text. Aside from teaching the students, the course was seen as a way to involve faculty across disciplines and encourage them to take an interest in, and assume some responsibility for, diversity initiatives.

Another school reported some success with offering sections of the course according to students' majors. For example, social science majors might have more interest or background in that area or go on to take other courses, so they took their own section of the course, focused on social science content. In turn, the topic could be presented to physical science majors by their faculty in a way that was meaningful to them. The disadvantages were a lack of diversity of students and teachers in the sections and the difficulties that faculty in some areas (such as engineering) had in dealing with the content.

In the most successful comprehensive example, there were extensive evaluations of faculty and student (traditional and nontraditional) reactions to the diversity course content in general and to the several formats. Questionnaires and focus groups were employed at regular intervals, and the feedback was incorporated into retraining faculty or training new faculty. Generally, faculty were enthusiastic about this approach, although it should be recognized that all faculty who taught these courses were volunteers. Faculty particularly liked the retreat format, where the course could be completed in a single session or several extended, often weekend, ones. They felt they could get the material across better in a situation that permitted some warm-up. A disadvantage of the retreat format was that students were unable to do homework, readings, or projects between sessions.

One issue that varied across the academic departments and colleges of the university was how the course would be considered in faculty course load or for tenure and promotion decisions. In some departments, the course was considered part of the regular teaching load, while in others it was considered an overload or extra course. Some departments counted the course as any other in tenure and promotion evaluation; others considered it as service. This lack of consistency caused some confusion and feelings of unfairness among faculty. The course appeared to work best (according to both faculty and students) where it was accorded the status of a "regular course."

Traditional students were varied in their attitudes. Most felt the course was useful, and many said that it was the first time they had been exposed to diversity as a topic or to diversity of students in a classroom. However, a quarter of the traditional students reported being uncomfortable with exposure to these topics, and still other students thought the course was too superficial to do any good.

Most nontraditional students and some traditional ones felt that if the course were only one credit and faculty could be trained to teach it in a short time, the content was being demeaned. Administrators answered this criticism by pointing out the value of involving a range of faculty and students in the topic and the practicality of using current faculty and spreading the workload, rather than hiring new faculty or designating a smaller number of departments to be responsible for the course. As will be seen, how faculty were involved in teaching the diversity course was a key point that distinguished the successful and unsuccessful comprehensive curriculum reform examples.

Nontraditional students were generally in favor of the course, but they wanted it to be three credits, so it would be considered just as important as other courses. Many traditional students felt the course did not affect them, but paradoxically they also reported noticing discussions among fellow students on diversity or becoming aware of interracial dynamics in other areas of their lives.

Unsuccessful Comprehensive Programs. One school's unsuccessful comprehensive program was an attempt to add a three-credit required course on diversity to its first-year curriculum. The president appointed a large committee of faculty and administrators to work out the details. The result was that the course served as a catalyst for raising long-standing animosities. Power issues as to who would be responsible for the course, faculty load, and academic rigor were debated intensively. The department that would be logically responsible for the course felt it was already overburdened and mistreated by the administration. The department insisted that as many as six new faculty had to be hired to staff such a course, and it was not willing to have other departments involved in its area of expertise. The department was also unwilling to add any diversity components to the existing first-year seminar course.

In this case, long-standing organizational issues and the president's failure to anticipate these issues set up a structure that had little likelihood of success. Convening a large campuswide committee without vigorous leadership from the administration did not work. The committee was unable to come up with a workable course plan, and the faculty were polarized by the issue.

At the same time, students were expecting a diversity course to result from the Lilly Endowment initiative and were disappointed when no new course came about. Nontraditional students complained of the inadequacy of the current required first-year seminar course in covering diversity as they saw it. They tended to feel the school had let them down by promising curricular and other reforms but failing to deliver. At this school there is currently little activity related to development of a diversity curriculum or hope of such activity in the near future. Interviews and discussion groups indicated that most faculty members and administrators thought things were worse than before the attempt at curricular change.

Noncognitive Variables and Comprehensive Curricular Change Programs. There are some noncognitive variables, applied in this case to the institution rather than the individual, that appear to differentiate the successful and unsuccessful examples. One issue is realistic self-appraisal, a school's ability to evaluate how ready it is for change. In one successful example, a number of departments were ready to work together on a course; this was not the case in the unsuccessful example. In the Sedlacek and Brooks (1976) model discussed in Chapter One, the successful school was probably at least to the understanding-racism stage (stage two), if not already willing to explore attitudes (stage three). The unsuccessful school was probably still in stage one (examining racial and cultural differences). The school probably had not decided that it wanted to explore these differences, at least in any cooperative way.

According to Helms's model (1995), the unsuccessful school may have been in a preencounter status (that is, contact), and its experience might trigger a reassessment as to whether to move ahead with another strategy or avoid the topic of diversity, at least for the time being.

Any school facing a similar problem might start with more limited goals, such as revising course content only in departments ready to deal with diversity issues, and holding decentralized workshops on racism and diversity for various elements of the campus. Once these smaller projects have been established, it may be easier to launch a campuswide cooperative effort. The unsuccessful school may have tried to do too much too fast, hoping that the grant money would bring people along before they were actually ready.

The most successful school did a great deal of planning and training of faculty in preparation for the course. The extensive evaluations of the course it initiated also established a more adventurous "let's experiment and learn together" atmosphere. This community-oriented approach was necessary to avoid the insecurities and power confrontations so likely to come about without such efforts. The successful school appeared to be handling racism better than the unsuccessful school by working through the difficulties of starting a new course, and by recognizing how it handled a course on diversity. It was aware that students of color would be watching closely, and that their self-concept could be affected by the actions of faculty and administrators. Interestingly, many students felt they were unaffected by the course in terms of attitude or information acquired but were able to note some changes in their behavior and that of others. This observation is a good reminder of the complex relationship among the three areas.

Focused Curricular Change

A focused curricular change is one that occurs in a specific department or area in the institution. There is no attempt to make changes across the curriculum. Examples of successful and unsuccessful focused programs are discussed next. The successful focused programs were able to develop a sense of community within the programs, and to handle racism by working to avoid negative stereotypes of program participants.

Successful Focused Programs. One example of a focused curricular revision took place in an institution's science program. Science was broadly conceived as including physical, biological, and behavioral sciences. The school had determined that it was attracting nontraditional students who were initially interested in science but frequently changed majors and graduated in some other area. The problem was retaining nontraditional students as science majors, not in retaining them in the school as a whole.

Working with a consultant from the education faculty, the administration decided to revise the introductory physics course so that it would be based on cooperative learning rather than on a traditional lecture format. The program was designed to keep nontraditional students in science by giving them positive experiences early in their science coursework. Under the new format, students worked together on projects in small groups (from three to six attendees). Each group had its own work area and computer. The instructors consulted with the groups as needed.

The cooperative learning consultant helped the physics teachers use the new system to its best advantage and helped the students learn to work cooperatively to complete their projects. The students in the program interacted with one another outside the class, and they attended gatherings at the physics course coordinator's house. Students in the program did not seem to be stigmatized as less than competent by science faculty, and faculty outside the sciences seemed to view the program neutrally as the province of the science department. Students outside the program expressed some envy of the students in the program, but their feelings seemed to be primarily positive. The administration supported the program, and the department was able to retain an increased number of nontraditional students.

The science faculty and administration had the view that all their students were capable and could master the content if it were presented optimally to them. Thus problems of institutional racism were less likely to arise. Students in the program were enthusiastic about it, and many planned to go on to graduate or medical school. Further evidence of the success of the program was that program students were taking visible leadership roles on campus in student organizations and student government.

In a separate example—a study of faculty successful in incorporating multicultural content in their individual courses—it was found that faculty with some ingenuity got it done regardless of the field of study (K. K. Johnson & Sedlacek, 1997). For instance, one faculty member in fire protection engineering said he included some material on the differential impact of fire prevention programs on people of various racial groups.

All faculty in the Johnson-Sedlacek study included racial groups in their focus on diverse communities, while a majority included issues affecting women. Other nontraditional groups such as lesbians, gays, and bisexuals, or people with disabilities, were included by only a few faculty in their course content. In other words, even among faculty who were active in diversity efforts, few included many of the groups that would be considered nontraditional as defined in this book.

Unsuccessful Focused Programs. An example of an unsuccessful focused curricular revision was again in a science curriculum. In this case, a special section of a newly developed introduction to a science course was offered for nontraditional students who had shown some interest in science but had not necessarily committed to science as a major. Both the institution and the science department hoped the new program would increase the number of nontraditional students majoring in science.

The instructor was motivated to have the course be successful and prepared a number of new approaches to the material, such as including contributions to science of people of color. There was interest in the course in the first year, but enrollment declined in the next year. The students felt the material was "watered down" and uninteresting. They also felt that other students, and even the instructor, had a negative stereotype of students who took the class. The instructor, who was a tenured, full-time, White male faculty member, admitted he was disappointed in the students' abilities and motivation. He had expected them to be better prepared in science and felt he had to make the course remedial, which was not his original intention. Enrollment was expected to drop further, and it was considered likely that the course would not be offered in the future. Other faculty in the department were not interested in teaching the course after their colleague's bad experience.

Summary and Reactions to Focused Curricular Change Programs. The self-concept of students outside the course was an important difference in these programs. In the successful program, care was taken to present the program as an innovative, positive alternative. As a result, participants were seen positively and treated as such by teachers and fellow students. Use of the consultant on cooperative learning and continuous monitoring of the process and adjustment helped keep the new course moving and developing.

In the unsuccessful example, the instructor was acting substantially on his own. He had no consultant to help him evaluate his classroom techniques, which may or may not have been optimal for his audience. The institution did not appear to be promoting the program, or evaluating its progress in such a way as to provide feedback that would help avoid negative stereotyping. The instructor also had no particular training in what to expect when teaching a group of nontraditional students. The stereotype that nontraditional students lack ability in science could have interfered with the optimal performance of students and could be an example of institutional racism, because it is a common pattern that some nontraditional students face.

As noted earlier, M. Bowen's work (1978) suggests that past perceptions, learned from parents and grandparents, may influence present behavior, particularly when individuals are under stress. It is possible that the inability of the unsuccessful instructor to handle his own bias affected the self-concept of the nontraditional students in his class.

There are long-term reasons some nontraditional students do not major in areas such as science. Historically speaking, African Americans and Latinos were encouraged to study certain fields (education, social science, religion). On the other hand, women were encouraged to study the arts and humanities but not science. Other academic disciplines often seem foreign and hostile to nontraditional students, thereby confirming the negative stereotypes the students may have about those careers. Better planning on the part of the administration might have prevented the negative outcome in the unsuccessful course discussed here. Without considerable training in multicultural issues and support from peers, it would be difficult for any single instructor in one course to turn around the negative preconceptions about the "special" class.

A potential problem, in both the successful and unsuccessful focused programs, was the lack of adequate career counseling built into either program. The assumption was made that it was good for the nontraditional students to major in science. In the overall sense of reducing institutional racism, encouraging nontraditional students to major in a variety of areas is desirable, but at the individual level it may be racist to assume that others know what is best for each student. Nontraditional students are usually encouraged to undertake alternative courses of action to suit institutional goals, rather than for their own purposes.

Another way in which the programs differed was on the noncognitive variable of community. In the successful example, the program served as a basis for developing a positive smaller community on the campus, even though the campus itself was small. The students met outside the science class and socialized together. This did not occur in the unsuccessful example. Students did not want to be identified with a group labeled as inferior. Thus groupings of nontraditional students are necessary and constructive, but they must be kept positive. If there is a perception that nontraditional students have been assigned or de facto placed in a stigmatized group, the consequences for the students are likely to be negative. It takes planning and foresight to help nontraditional students develop a supportive community.

If one examines the models for eliminating racism, the institution in the successful example appears to have had some understanding of the process of racism (stage two), whether they called it that or not, and to have taken action on that basis (Sedlacek & Brooks, 1976). The unsuccessful school did not appear to appreciate the cultural and racial differences it would be facing (stage one), let alone the implications for racism in stage two.

In the Helms (1995) model, the successful school was likely to be at least in the pseudo-independence or possibly the immersion/emersion status and was taking positive steps to work on diversity issues. The unsuccessful school appeared to be in an earlier status (possibly disintegration or contact) and was not able to anticipate what would be needed to make the course a success.

Diffused Curricular Change

In a diffused model of curricular change, an attempt is made to add diversity and related content in many or all courses in the curriculum rather than to have a separate diversity course or to focus on only one area of the curriculum. Hence diversity content is spread across the curriculum. This model can be implemented with any course in a curriculum using noncognitive variables (Sedlacek, 1983).

The most successful schools using this approach were able to develop a sense of community across levels of the institution. Successful schools were also able to make realistic appraisals of where the institution and faculty were in the developmental models of handling racism.

Successful Diffused Programs. The school with a successful diffused program had faculty across departments spend time together in formal sessions where they exchanged ideas for the courses they taught. Many courses were cotaught as a way to infuse new ideas and content into the courses. Faculty also spent informal time together at a weekly dinner meeting where the discussions were not exclusively professional, but where issues related to improving instruction inevitably arose. In these sessions, faculty got to know each other well enough to discuss problems, doubts, and fears. Even though not all faculty members were involved, there were representatives from nearly all departments, and those who participated frequently took ideas back to their department for discussion.

The administration supported the activity through released time or extra pay for the formal sessions and by furnishing food for the informal meetings. Most of the participants in these sessions were regular full-time faculty, although part-time and visiting faculty also participated. One faculty member, hired under the Lilly Endowment program, had expertise in diversity issues and served as a consultant to other faculty members both individually and during the sessions. She was a graduate of the institution, and a number of faculty had taught her some years earlier, thus making it easier for her to discuss some issues with them. The faculty felt they were committed to innovation and regular updating and revising of courses, and diversity was viewed as one more aspect of this process.

Students at this institution reported that diversity content seemed to be appearing in many of their courses, and they reported feeling more positive toward this approach than they thought they would toward having isolated coursework on diversity issues. Nontraditional students were particularly glad to see changes across the curriculum. There did not appear to be any particular backlash among traditional faculty or students.

In a study of the faculty who had been actively involved in changing their curriculum campuswide (Johnson & Sedlacek, 1997), it was found that they had all attended sessions sponsored by the university to help departments make such changes. Activities included meeting with colleagues about possible changes that could be made in their courses, proposing new courses, including special topics offerings, and revising introductory or general courses that were taught by a number of people in the department. Generally, faculty reported success with their courses, although some faculty resisted any change or resented interference. The most success was had by faculty who showed leadership by example and offered themselves as consultants to anyone interested.

Unsuccessful Diffused Programs. One institution that found it difficult to achieve its goal of broad curricular reform regarding diversity solicited proposals from faculty interested in changing their courses. Those selected by a committee of faculty and administrators were given a summer stipend to revise the course, along with funds for materials. The committee tried to encourage interest from all departments, and its selection of faculty proposals was guided in part by the goal of promoting course revisions in many departments.

Unfortunately, few or no proposals were received from some departments, and several faculty members openly challenged the selection process when their proposals were not funded. Articles and letters to the editor in the campus paper criticized the concept of diversity and accused some on campus of trying to be politically correct. The process stalled, and some members of the selection committee resigned from it. Few courses actually got started using this process. The faculty members who did get funded met occasionally but had fundamental disagreements on the definition of diversity, which some felt should be resolved before the course revision process went forward.

Summary and Reactions to Diffused Curricular Change Programs. The successful program seemed to work because of recognition of the necessity for building a sense of community across several levels of the institution. The tradition of innovation and curricular change at this institution expanded smoothly to include diversity issues. The administration supported formal and informal networking of faculty and was realistic in its appraisal of the faculty's needs. The consultant was facilitative, but she was also part of the team rather than an outsider. The style of the administration at the successful institution was also facilitative. The administration did not foster competition among the faculty, as the unsuccessful institution did. A community of faculty working together for change was formed at the successful institution, while the unsuccessful institution stressed individual faculty efforts and did not encourage joint or group activity.

Using the models for eliminating racism, the successful school was more sophisticated in its interpretation of the problems of racism that might be faced in curricular change and used multiple techniques to solve those problems. The unsuccessful school was not prepared for the backlash and negative reactions it received. In the Sedlacek-Brooks (1976) model, the successful school was at least at stage three (understanding racism) and in the Helms (1995) model was likely in the immersion/emersion status. The unsuccessful school had not reached either of those stages in its institutional development.

External Curricular Change Programs

Some schools attempted to change their curriculum by hiring part-time or temporary scholars to teach courses, or to create academic experiences for students. These programs included single lectures, scholars or artists in residence, and faculty exchange and mentor programs. The most successful programs set clear long-term goals and did realistic appraisals of what was needed to accomplish those goals.

Successful External Programs. One institution employed a program of several scholars or artists in residence. The scholars and artists gave lectures, taught classes, put on programs or exhibitions for the larger community, and consulted with faculty. The individuals were in residence for at least several months, so that they were able to get to know faculty and students. Because the guests were all acknowledged experts in their area and were not going to stay at the school, faculty were able to consult them without feeling threatened. Generally, students enjoyed being exposed to another kind of teaching model, and nontraditional students were able to focus on some areas of particular interest to them. The administration generated some positive publicity for the school by bringing in outside experts who also worked with the off-campus community.

In one case, when a visiting artist from a nontraditional cultural group solicited comments on his work, an anonymous person used a racial epithet and said he hoped the artist would die of AIDS. The artist displayed the comment along with his art, and some positive antiracism discussions took place on the campus as a result.

Another school tried a mentor program for its faculty with some success. Mentors from other institutions who were familiar with multicultural content in their field were matched with faculty who wished to revise their courses. Mentors met with mentees on the latter's campus, at the mentor's location, or at professional meetings. Mentors spent some time with the mentee's students and occasionally with others during campus visits. Courses were revised, and ongoing professional relationships developed.

Unsuccessful External Programs. Another school began an exchange program with an historically Black college by inviting a faculty member to spend a semester on its campus. But the goals of the exchange program were not made clear to the visiting faculty member; as a result, expectations on both sides of the exchange were unfulfilled. The visiting faculty member, who was African American, had hoped to learn new material in his field (which was not directly related to diversity), but the other faculty regarded him as a race-relations expert rather than as a colleague. Faculty and students alike consulted him on diversity issues, and the visitor felt overwhelmed by all the attention and requests for information in areas outside his interests and expertise. The administration had hoped to promote some of its diversity initiatives through the exchange program. All involved in the program were frustrated, and both schools were reconsidering the value of the exchange program.

Summary and Reactions to External Curricular Change Programs. Having clear goals and a realistic appraisal of what is needed to accomplish goals will increase any program's chance of success. In the successful program, the visitor was allowed to do his work, and positive outcomes resulted from his successful handling of a racist incident. According to the Sedlacek-Brooks (1976) model, there was a failure to understand racial and culture differences (stage one) and their implications for racism (stage two) at the unsuccessful school by assuming certain interests on the part of the visitors. In the Helms (1995) model the unsuccessful school was still externalizing the issue, seeing it as the responsibility of the visitor rather than its own. The school was probably at the pseudo-independence status. The school that was successful in its mentoring program carefully matched mentors and mentees. Mentors were experts in multicultural content and tried to avoid dependency on them by encouraging mentees to try things on their own. The mentors knew what to expect from the situation and were able to handle it.

Helping to foster a sense of community, even the larger off-campus community, for the visitor was another important part of success at the one school. At the unsuccessful school, the visitor felt isolated and not part of any group. Employing outside experts can be a relatively inexpensive way to add diversity quickly to a curriculum. However, for the change in curriculum to take root and grow, the influence of the outside expert on faculty and students over the long run is important.

This chapter has dealt with the role of noncognitive variables in teaching; the next chapter discusses their role in advising and counseling.

CHAPTER SEVEN

ADVISING AND COUNSELING WITH NONCOGNITIVE VARIABLES

Advising is an important but complicated function in higher education. It is important because the quality of the advising directly affects a student's progress, or lack thereof, through the system. It is complicated because a good advisor must not only understand the rules, regulations, and academic requirements of the institution but also understand the context of the student. That is, an advisor must understand the variables that are affecting a student's life, which include traditional ones such as academic ability and financial need, but also less traditional ones dealing with cultural, racial, and gender background. This chapter discusses how advisors can use noncognitive variables (NCVs) with their students.

Advising Versus Counseling

It can be difficult to determine where advising ends and counseling begins. A major difference may lie in the training of the person performing the function. Nearly all colleges and universities have trained and licensed professional counselors, with a background in psychology, education, psychiatry, or social work. People with such training tend to process some issues differently those without such training. On the other hand, academic advisors are often faculty with unique knowledge of subject matter in an area. It is important that a referral relationship be established between academic advisors and counseling professionals. They must understand their respective roles and work for the benefit of students. In a number of the examples that follow, advisors and counselors have cooperated in their efforts to assist students.

In a study of faculty who successfully incorporated multicultural concepts into their sessions with advisees, most said it was difficult to do so, and they needed advice or training on how to do it better (Johnson & Sedlacek, 1997). Many were uncomfortable in raising diversity issues, but those who were successful often used classroom work as a point of departure to get into other aspects of diversity. For example, a history faculty member used class discussion on a gender topic to help a student seek some personal resources that proved helpful to the student in finding a community on campus and reducing her isolation.

There are many discussions of strategies or issues concerning retention or orientation (see Garnett, 1990; Wawrzynski, 1999; Whitaker & Roberts, 1990), but few comprehensive models to approach advising, particularly for nontraditional students (Peabody, Metz, & Sedlacek, 1983; Sedlacek, 1991, 1994b).

Sternberg's three types of intelligence (componential, experiential, and contextual) can be a starting point in understanding the advising process (1985, 1986, 1996). Many people would agree that experiential and contextual intelligence come into play more in the later years of most programs, because upper-level courses tend to require students to write more, discuss more, and hopefully think more. Componential skills, as defined by Sternberg, appear less useful by themselves beyond the first year in that they require more reasoning in an unchanging context and might be more associated with didactic and introductory coursework. Advisors who understand this intelligence model can help students identify shortcomings, advantages, and strategies to get through the areas where they may be less equipped. In particular, nontraditional students may need more support in the first year, because they are more likely to rely on experiential and contextual attributes than traditional students.

Westbrook and Sedlacek (1988) concluded that students can be advised or counseled by identifying behaviors associated with good or poor performance on each of the eight noncognitive variables discussed in this book (see Table 4.2):

1. Positive self-concept
2. Realistic self-appraisal
3. Successfully handling the system (racism)
4. Preference for long-term goals
5. Availability of strong support person
6. Leadership experience

7. Community involvement
8. Knowledge acquired in a field

Used along with other variables, models, or techniques, NCVs can greatly enhance the ability of advisors and counselors to assist students, particularly nontraditional students. For example, the NCVs can be useful in helping to advise students of color about graduate school opportunities (Sedlacek, 2003b), and good advising for graduate students of color has been shown to be critical for their success (Davidson & Foster-Johnson, 2002).

Advisors and counselors can work with students to improve their development on any of the dimensions (Westbrook & Sedlacek, 1988). Advisors and counselors can help obtain better student outcomes in terms of grades and retention satisfaction by using the noncognitive variables.

Here I present several examples of schools that have employed an advising or counseling system using noncognitive variables. Such examples may be useful in seeing how NCVs have been valuable in successfully advising students.

The Advising/Counseling Session

Whether or not one employs the NCVs, it is common for an advisor or counselor to interview students to make an original diagnosis of abilities, or to probe certain areas more deeply. A variety of interviewing methods can be employed, though principles modified from some originally developed by Bingham and Moore (1959; see Appendix 6) are recommended.

To assess noncognitive variables, an advisor/counselor should listen carefully in a kind of scanning posture using the list of behaviors associated with the NCVs. As a student touches on something that appears relevant, it should be probed using principle six in Appendix 6). Questions can be phrased more directly if this scanning procedure does not yield enough information, so long as rapport is sufficiently established (principle four of Appendix 6). For instance, asking a student how he or she finds the interracial environment at the school might be asked directly if the issue has not come up otherwise.

Another key principle in Appendix 6 is number eighteen, making referrals. It is particularly important that advisors and counselors have extensive and current information on where students can go for further information or assistance. In many instances, it may be best to make an initial diagnosis of shortcomings on one of the NCVs and refer the student to someone else to resolve the problem. It is often difficult for the same person to uncover an issue and then try to resolve it.

A Western Community College: Selection and Advising

Admissions is commonly separated in policy and practice from advising, particularly postmatriculation academic advising. If the two areas can be coordinated, the effect on students and the campus climate can be profound.

As more students from diverse backgrounds seek admission, especially to community colleges that have open admissions, more institutions have to reexamine their admissions policies in the context of how they provide advising (Grimes & David, 1999). For example, a community college in the West chose to investigate the possibility of employing NCVs in selecting students for its health sciences programs. Previously, the college had employed prior grades (GPA) as a predictor of student success. The college was also interested in seeing if noncognitive variables could improve its academic advising system.

The school had a serious problem in using GPA as a predictor because of "grade inflation" (Rigol & Kimmel, 1997; Ziomek & Svec, 1995; Rojstraczer, 2003). As some programs have gotten more selective, the GPAs of applicants have increased to a point where their potential to discriminate among applicants is quite limited. At this college, the mean GPA of applicants to their health programs was 3.76 on a 4-point system. Additionally, 10 percent of all high schools nationally no longer calculate GPAs. Of those that do, 57 percent include nonacademic courses in the figure (College Board, 1998). With the increase in the variety of students attending community colleges, there is also an increase in the number of individuals who are coming to college underprepared, even with high GPAs (Smittle, 1995).

At the same time, the college was receiving pressure from the community, faculty, administrators, and applicants to develop a better admissions and advising system. This community college had a large number of older applicants, as well as about 20 percent applicants of color, primarily Latinos. Thus the college enrolled many nontraditional students. The NCQ scales were designed to yield information for use by advisors in working with students developmentally. Therefore the college conducted a predictive validity study of NCVs that would coordinate admissions and advising (Sedlacek, 1991).

Students in the health sciences programs at the community college ($N = 320$) were administered the NCQ. The NCQ was scored with coefficient alpha reliability of scores estimated at .86. The NCQ scale scores were correlated with cumulative grades, and grades for several semesters.

Multiple regression analyses were conducted using NCQ scores as predictors and GPA as a criterion for each semester and cumulative GPAs separately. Significant (.05 level) multiple correlations were found with spring, fall, and cumulative GPAs for two years.

Community tended to be the most important scale in all equations, while strong support person contributed most to the earlier GPA predictions and leadership to later GPA predictions. Moore (1995) also found the NCQ community scale to correlate positively with grades for international students at a community college.

Overall, even though the relationships between GPAs and NCQ scores were not high, the correlations that were significant indicated some potentially useful relationships to consider in determining policy. The NCQ scales tended to correlate best with early and late GPAs and with cumulative GPAs. Studies have shown that early and late grades in a curriculum are probably the most meaningful (Sedlacek, 1989). Getting off to a good start and finishing well are critical to student adjustment and are points of transition. Students are often exploring or focused on other issues in the middle of their curricula. Cumulative GPAs are the most stable estimate and hence may be more likely to show a relationship if one is present.

Students in the study generally had NCQ scores similar to normative samples, but they tended to be lowest on community, which was the scale most predictive of their performance. Thus community could be used as both a predictor of success and a postmatriculation concept in advising and student services. Students at this community college had the highest NCQ scores on self-concept, long-term goals, and leadership.

As a result of its findings, the college has invested more resources in training advisors to help students find a community, on or off campus. The college is now using the NCQ in admissions and providing scores to academic advisors.

A University Counseling Center Reaches out to Advisors

One counseling center has developed relationships with advisors by assigning each professional counselor to work with the advisors in a specific college of the university. Counselors and advisors share information and learn when and how to make referrals to one another. Joint training sessions were held for counselors and advisors on the noncognitive variables and how they might be employed in their respective roles. The sessions were jointly sponsored by both units, all advisors and counselors were encouraged to attend, and all but one did.

Results of a survey of the advisors and counselors indicated that 91 percent felt the program helped their work with students, and 88 percent indicated that the noncognitive variables were useful. The most common comment was that they felt they had an organized and coordinated way to approach the work by using the noncognitive model. Referrals between the two units increased by 40 percent during the next school year. Focus groups with students showed they were more positive about the information they were receiving in their advising sessions after the noncognitive variable training than before.

A Small Selective Midwest Private College: High Scoring Nontraditional Students

Is this really a problem? Any of us would feel fortunate to have that Native American student with high grades and test scores. Why ask for trouble? The answer to the question is that too often we lose those students because of problems with one or more noncognitive variables. Statistically, the reason we get lower correlations with standardized tests and college grades for nontraditional students is that not only do some students with low scores do better than expected but some students with high scores do worse than expected.

A small, selective institution with mean SATs in the high 600s on each scale for its general student body was successful in attracting and enrolling Native American, Chicano, and African American students with good grades and test scores, but they were not staying. About 85 percent of the traditional students who matriculated eventually graduated, but only 50 percent of the nontraditional students finished. Most students who left did so in good standing somewhere in their first two years.

The school decided to implement a new advising system for all students, traditional and nontraditional, which relied heavily on noncognitive variables. All students were administered the NCQ at orientation, after admission but prior to enrollment. A noncognitive profile was developed for each student, and a specific prescriptive program was developed for each. Faculty and staff were trained to be resource people, specializing in one or more of the NCVs. Thus one individual or a student service might concentrate on self-concept development, another on understanding racism, and another group served as mentors (strong support persons). This proactive approach was embraced and seemed to be enjoyed by most on the campus. As one staff member put it, "This kind of individualized attention is part of our tradition. We just needed to organize and focus it better."

Aside from the positive feelings generated, two years later retention was 90 percent for traditional students and up to 74 percent for nontraditional students. The increased energy and attention may have caused the increases rather than working with NCVs. However, NCVs can set a context for the activity and help foster a new look at what might be old issues.

Who Comes for Counseling? Predicting Counseling Center Use

Aside from teaching and academic advising, the NCQ has also been shown to predict help-seeking behavior, particularly counseling center use (Arbona, Sedlacek, & Carstens, 1987). The rationale for studying the NCQ in this context is that a single set of variables relating to both academic success and help-seeking behavior may assist in designing counseling services that are more likely to be used. Arbona et al. found that for Black students high scores on handling the system (racism) and community, along with low self-concept and a lack of long-term goals, were associated with counseling center use. For White students, the variables associated with coming to the counseling center were the existence of a strong support person, long-term goals, and a more negative self-concept. S. P. Boyer and Sedlacek (1988) found that NCVs also predicted counseling center use for international students. The variables that were particularly important were high scores on handling the system, knowledge in a field, and long-term goals.

In each of these situations, differing patterns of noncognitive variables were associated with counseling center use. Interestingly, in the Arbona, Sedlacek, and Carstens study, having long-term goals predicted counseling center use by Whites, but *not* having long-term goals predicted counseling center use by Blacks. Again, the needs of students vary by race.

A Summer Enrichment Program for Health Careers

An intensive eight-week program for talented "minority" high school and college students interested in health professions was held at the University of Tennessee Center for the Health Sciences (Fogelman & Saeger, 1985). The noncognitive variables shown in Table 4.1 were incorporated into the program along with math and basic science content.

Examples of how the variables were employed included a self-awareness program designed by a Black clinical psychologist to foster a positive self-concept. Topics such as assertiveness, pride in racial origin, historical contributions of Blacks to the health care system, and methods to enhance personal and academic motivation were addressed in a workshop format. The experience also involved students in a variety of self-awareness exercises. Association with other talented minority students also helped build self-confidence in the students. Peer counseling sessions encouraged students to share feelings and evaluations of one another. Comments from the students included these: "In high school you don't get to do much in the labs, but here we were treated as competent students who handle themselves well." "I learned I could compete with all types of students under any circumstances. This program has given me a positive outlook on my future career" (Fogelman & Saeger, 1985, p. 546).

Individual assessment and feedback in regularly scheduled counseling sessions were designed to produce information for realistic self-appraisal of the academic capabilities of students. In other sessions, students were advised on methods for using their time more efficiently and effectively, ways of strengthening their study habits and reading skills, and insights into thinking positively about their own unique capabilities. Focusing on a student's individual capabilities and helping a student maximize those talents had the dual goals of realistic self-appraisal and building self-confidence (Fogelman & Saeger, 1985). Among comments from students on realistic self-appraisal: "The frankness of the program was its most positive feature. There was no beating around the bush, or fooling anyone into believing they were doing good when they weren't." "The knowledge I gained about study habits and reading skills will last much longer than any other information" (p. 547)

Individual sessions on racism and how to deal with it were held. Professionals of color shared their experiences at negotiating the system. As one student put it, "Once a student has been accepted into medical school, his or her hardships are not over; they are just beginning, especially being Black" (p. 548).

Discussion in counseling sessions concentrated on the intentional design of the program to help students develop longer-term goals and to see the longer pathway through school, eventual practice of a health profession, and appreciation of deferred gratification. The comments of a student embodied the program goals: "The program basically gets one ready for that long road ahead, and puts him on the right track" (p. 548).

Each student was assigned to a host family (which ideally included a health professional). Students were encouraged to spend time with the family and to discuss issues of concern to students. This accomplished the support-person goal and to a lesser extent the community goal of the program. Student comments included these: "I have met quite a few people that will help me through my future goals. They have given me that even greater incentive to further my education in a health career field." "I've gotten to know the doctors on a personal basis and will miss them. They taught me a lot and I could never forget them" (p. 549).

Fogelman and Saeger (1985) reported that they felt leadership, community, and what they called demonstrated medical interests were best covered in advising and counseling programs after students had completed the summer program and returned to school.

Advising Transfer Students

A recent report on college enrollment trends indicated that higher education has experienced a rapid growth of students in the last decade (Knapp, Kelly, Whitmore, Wu, & Gallego, 2002; U.S. Department of Education, 2002). Paralleling this rapid growth is the number of students who will transfer from one institution to another (Beckenstein, 1992). The number of transfer students has increased from institution to institution over the past decade, but research on transfer students has not kept pace with this growing trend.

The research on transfer students has been devoted to comparing them to their first-year-student counterparts (Miville & Sedlacek, 1995). Additionally, in their meta-analysis, Pascarella and Terenzini (1991) discussed the problems of two-year colleges in preparing students to transfer to four-year institutions.

Transfer students are a diverse group on many characteristics, among them gender, race and ethnicity, socioeconomic status, and age; they have also grown more diverse in recent years (Laanan, 1996). Smith et al. (2000) have called for more research on transfer students and diversity. Researchers have focused primarily on the differences in grade point average attained (Laanan, 1996) and have failed to study NCVs.

Transfer Students at a Large Eastern University: Race and Gender Differences

In a study of nearly twenty-five hundred transfer students at the University of Maryland, it was found that the academic self-concept of Asian American transfer students was an issue (Wawrzynski & Sedlacek, 2003) as they felt pressure on them to be model students (Liang & Sedlacek, 2003a).

Also, African American and Asian American transfer students expressed a greater interest in working with faculty on a research project or interacting outside of class, than did White students. This suggests a good place for advisors to develop a support-person role with students of color. Additionally, African American and Asian American students were more interested in meeting people from other cultures than were White students, indicating an interest in negotiating the diverse campus environment.

African Americans and Asian Americans were more interested in joining campus organizations than were other transfer students. This supports the research suggesting that both those groups develop support systems through community involvement (Fuertes, Sedlacek, & Liu, 1994; Sedlacek, 1998a, 1998b). This result challenges the myth that transfer students are interested only in the academic offerings of an institution, and it supports the evidence that campus climate can have an important effect on the success or failure of transfer students.

African American transfer students, more than any other group, felt their college education was for acquiring skills for work and life: technology skills, learning to communicate effectively in writing, learning to communicate effectively orally, and learning to think and reason. Latino transfer students were also more likely than White students to desire learning to communicate effectively orally as an important outcome of college. Both these results suggest the importance of considering long-term goals in advising transfer students.

African American and Asian American transfer students felt that gaining an appreciation for attitudes and cultures different from theirs was more important for them than did White students. Thus transfer students of color understood the importance of learning to navigate a new environment and can be helped to do so in advising.

As noted earlier, the idea of developing a sense of community for students of color is critical. African American and Asian American transfer students were more interested in participating in community service as part of their college education than were other students.

Asian American students indicated they had trouble deciding what to study, suggesting another area in which to focus advising. However, speaking up in class is likely to occur more for African American, Latino, and White students than for Asian American students. These students may view this as a leadership opportunity by offering advice or taking action where called for. Additionally, African Americans were more interested than any other racial group in developing leadership skills.

African American and Asian American transfer students were more likely to study with other students than were White students. Helping students develop peer study groups as a community is something advisors can facilitate.

Transfer Student "Hassles"

As part of an ongoing program evaluation, the academic dean of the University of Maryland's social science college wished to learn more about the academic service experiences of students within that unit. Junior students were selected for study because they could be surveyed during one academic year and appropriate service changes could be made before the all-important senior year. The responses of native and transfer students were compared throughout the investigation. The hassles of junior native and transfer students enrolled in two majors, government and criminal justice, were examined (Mitchell, Beardsley, & Sedlacek, 1997) This was an attempt to help transfer students negotiate a system that was not optimally designed for them (handling an -ism).

Transfer and native students showed significant differences on college advising questions. The three highest hassles for transfer students were (1) determining which advisor is appropriate for particular questions, (2) receiving adequate information about scholarship sources, and (3) learning which courses will count toward requirements. The three lowest hassles reported by transfer students were (1) getting information about appropriate procedures for applying for graduation,

(2) finding out the procedure to change one's major, and (3) getting unofficial copies of one's transcript.

Several changes in the advising system were introduced as a result of the survey:

- A centralized unit evaluating transfer student course credit evaluations was established.
- All college advisors received some specific training on the hassles faced by transfer students.
- A transfer student open house was held where college advisors and counselors from the counseling center and career center were available, and students had their individual questions answered.
- A one-credit course for transfer students dealing with their concerns was developed.

Individual Case Studies

Case studies are presented here to allow the reader to examine NCVs that have been a problem for a given student. These are real cases with names changed to protect their identity. Some are from a workshop developed by Westbrook and Sedlacek (1988), and others have been discussed in Sedlacek (1991). Before reading the discussion on each case, take the list of behaviors associated with each NCV in Table 4.2 (p. 50) and see if the major noncognitive variable problems for each student can be determined.

Sara Davis

Sara Davis is an African American junior. She started her courses well but has now begun to slip in everything. Sara has SAT scores of 420 math and 600 verbal.

Sara went to an inner-city high school, and she always read the material assigned and performed well on the tests. When she was not doing her course assignments, she was always busy working, taking care of her brothers and sisters or studying ballet—a field she almost pursued seriously. She decided that ballet was an impractical career given her financial needs and the difficulties of succeeding in that field.

She had always performed well in her science courses in high school. Consequently her advisor suggested that she consider a career in medicine, so she switched to premed. Medicine offered her a real opportunity for a career beyond anything she had thought of previously.

As Sara began her first-year in premed, she did fairly well on the early material but gradually seemed to be falling further and further behind. As she discussed the courses with her peers, she found that many knew much more about the course content than she did. They were working in labs or on science-related projects currently or had done so before they came to college.

What really surprised Sara was that one of the other African American premed students was working in a walk-in medical check-up and first aid program several blocks away from where she lived. Another student had learned some information and procedures that went beyond what was covered in the book.

Advising Sara. Sara illustrates the dilemma of many nontraditional students who come to an academic area via a nontraditional route. She had not been thinking about medicine for many years, like some of her colleagues. She had not really shown interest in medicine, but she moved in that direction because it seemed financially rewarding and she was recruited. However, she had not learned any medicine-specific background knowledge from community or nonacademic activities and thus was a "mismatch." Unless she was given information or help in understanding that she might not have had the same experiences as traditional students, or encouraged to pursue her interests, she was done a disservice. She needed some good career counseling, and her major noncognitive variable problem was in the area of *knowledge acquired in a field.*

The Outcome. Sara's advisor diagnosed her dilemma and referred her to the counseling center for career counseling. She decided to stick with ballet and eventually went on to graduate school and is currently teaching and performing.

Joe Martin

Joe Martin is a Latino sophomore who got through his first year in fine shape and is doing passable work in his second year; but he is considering leaving school because he is lonely and unhappy.

Joe's parents were born in Mexico and originally came to this country illegally as migrant workers. Joe was born in the United States and was bilingual in his early years. He was called José until his parents moved to the Midwest, just as he started high school. Joe was bright and a good student, but he was not comfortable being singled out as a Chicano. So he worked hard at disguising his accent and started calling himself Joe and pronouncing the family name in English rather than Spanish. He loved his parents, but he avoided having his friends meet them because their English was poor and they were clearly Chicanos.

Joe was smart enough to get a scholarship to a school away from home and took the opportunity to move away from any identification as a Chicano. However, he has been somewhat lonely and feels removed from the other students. His father died during his first year in college, and he chose not to return for the funeral.

As the first-year students got to know one another better, Joe sensed that he was not like any of the other students. The Chicano student group was active and provided many academic and nonacademic services for the students, but he was not comfortable declaring himself a Chicano and joining them.

At the same time, Joe was uncomfortable with the Anglo students whose families, backgrounds, and interests were much different from his. He stayed to himself and did reasonably well. However, when he started his second year somehow it came out that he was a Chicano and he felt really embarrassed and isolated. He felt that people were laughing at him and did not respect him. He felt so bad about things that he was about to leave school under the pretext that he was more interested in attending another school in another field.

Advising Joe. Because José decided to deny his Chicano background, he lost a needed community resource. *Community support* is vital to nontraditional students; loners have great difficulty. Mallinckrodt and Sedlacek (1987) showed that one group of nontraditional students (African Americans) who used campus gyms and student unions were more likely to stay in school than those who did not. Such was not the case for traditional students. White students had a larger community that accepted them on campus; the African American students did not and had to develop one for themselves.

The Outcome. José's advisor put him in touch with someone in the campus activities office who gradually got him involved in Chicano student activities. José earned a master's degree and works for an electronics company.

John Freeman

John Freeman is a smart, first-year White student who has planned for as long as he can remember to go to medical school. His father is an anesthesiologist, his mother a bank executive, and his older brother and sister are medical students at the University of Chicago. Additionally, most of his friends are from professional families. Given this background, his entering college was assumed without much discussion.

John did not have the grades and SAT scores to gain admission to a highly selective undergraduate college, as his brother and sister had done, and he was surprised when he was accepted at a Midwestern state school. He was pleased but thought maybe he should have taken some extra work in chemistry before starting college. Chemistry was John's most difficult subject, and he wanted to feel sure he knew it before tackling the college and medical school curriculum.

John had long talks with his girlfriend about the problems he would have in spending time with her since he would have to study so much. He was about to suggest they break up, and this was worrying him. John also hoped to continue a part-time job he had held in a laboratory for several years, which would give him something to count on financially and be something to fall back on if he decided to leave or was not successful in college. John felt lonely and isolated during the early part of his first year in school. He also could not bring himself to ask questions in class—particularly in chemistry, where he was not as certain of his knowledge as were his fellow students.

When John received low grades at the end of the first semester, he was too embarrassed to discuss them with his brother, sister, or parents. He felt his fellow students already knew he was having trouble, so he was less reluctant to talk about grades with them. John started seriously thinking of leaving school so he could get into some kind of job that suited him.

Advising John. John had *self-concept* problems because he was comparing himself to his family members. Although his family was close and apparently supportive, they could not provide him the support group he needed to process his concerns. His advisor worked with him on the strengths and weaknesses within himself, not in comparison to other people. The advisor helped John find an interest group off campus so he could more easily relate to some new friends. Eventually John was able to make more *realistic self-appraisals.*

The Outcome. John and his advisors chose some medical schools to which he could apply that matched his interests but were not those associated with his family members. John successfully completed medical school and is a pediatrician in a Midwestern city other than (but close to) where most of his family of origin lives.

Eric Loo

Eric Loo is an Asian American graduate student in political science. He is unhappy and struggling in his studies. Part of his struggle is that he does not seem to have enough time to study. He wanted to fit in with the other students in his department, and when they asked him for help with their computer problems he was glad to oblige. He was adequate but not highly proficient in data analysis and spent a great deal of his time trying to keep ahead of his peers so he could fulfill their expectations of him. Generally, he was helpful but found that all his relationships were based on his supposed technical abilities. He was not forming social or academic relationships on the basis of other dimensions. He was unhappy and overworked and felt he was stuck. He was considering leaving school.

Advising Eric. Eric seemed to be stuck in a "model minority myth" stereotype (Liang & Sedlacek, 2003a): that all Asian Americans are supposed to be good in technical areas. Not only was this not particularly true for Eric, it was affecting him in many negative ways. He wasn't *handling racism* well. Even though it was an apparently positive stereotype to be considered proficient at something, it made him seem unidimensional. He needed a *community* where he could process issues and enjoy the benefits of contact with others.

The Outcome. Eric and his advisor worked out a plan where Eric would be friendly but unavailable for help sometimes. He was also encouraged to assert his needs and show some leadership by demonstrating his other interests, which included movies and hiking.

Eric initiated some group events with his fellow students, and in turn they saw him differently. He continued to discuss and evaluate how he was handling things with his advisor as he worked on his plan.

Tyrone Smith

Tyrone Smith is an African American sophomore who is on academic probation as a result of failing one class and making D's in two others. He lives alone in an apartment near the university, which is located in his home state. His father has been deceased for a year, but Tyrone stated that his father had not lived with him since he was five years old, that he adjusted well to having no father, that he was self-taught, and that some children need a father but he did not.

Tyrone apparently chose his major (child psychology) using his mother's best friend, Anna, as a role model. Anna is a school psychologist who works with children in several schools, including the one where Tyrone's mother teaches special education. He was able to name several schools where his mother's friend works. Tyrone's course sequence has been difficult because he failed to register for a required course. The reason given was that he misread the departmental requirements.

Tyrone studied a great deal and did not spend much time with friends of either sex, feeling he did not have the time for socializing. Tyrone had always earned A's and B's in high school, and his SAT scores were 560 verbal and 580 math. Tyrone showed no strong reaction to his low grades in school and said he felt he could work things out by working harder on his studying.

Advising Tyrone. Tyrone seems to have vague *long-term goals* in that he chose his major on the basis of what his mother's friend was doing; she was someone he did not know well or seek out for advice. He is also a loner and does not have an individual *support person* or a *community* to give him what he needs. Tyrone's advisor tried calling him in for appointments and encouraging the young man to come in to see him.

The Outcome. Tyrone started to miss more classes and eventually flunked out of school. His advisor does not know what happened to him.

The advisor probably needed to take more assertive action with Tyrone, even though he had many other students to deal with. Catching him after class, discussing academic and nonacademic topics with him, and making some good referrals to resources on campus such as the counseling center or career center were likely worth trying. The advisor never established sufficient rapport with Tyrone to be in a position to take the next steps that he needed.

Glen Haskins

Glen Haskins is a White senior in college who is barely passing his courses. He is the older son of a second marriage for both his mother and father. He has a younger brother by both parents and four half-brothers and a sister from first marriages. He has a good child-adult relationship with one of his half-brothers. Glen's parents are high-level career employees with the state government.

His parents, and most of their children, are college educated, and they have always encouraged Glen to do well in school. Because his school performance and finances were never a problem for him, he cannot pinpoint a time when planning began for his graduation from college. He thinks it was always assumed that he would complete college. The major question in Glen's mind was where, not whether, he would attend college.

He had a stable and successful elementary and high school background. He was accepted at several undergraduate schools, including a quite prestigious one. He chose a less prestigious school primarily because it was close to home. His biggest current problem is in locating three teachers who have known him well enough to write a letter of recommendation for him.

Glen's parents were very proper and progressive. They were educated and believed in, and worked toward, the education of their children. They were productively employed and expected their children to be productively occupied (in school, school activities, part-time jobs). He was told to speak softly when spoken to by adults, and in public to be seen and not heard.

Glen is an avid basketball fan and a good athlete. He was noticed playing pick-up games and asked by his high school coach to try out for the team. He tried out in the tenth and eleventh grades but did not make the team. He is also good at other sports, so long as there is not organized competition. When the performance stakes go up, his skills diminish.

Advising Glen. Glen has a problem with being very passive and letting things happen, rather than showing *leadership* skills. Assertiveness is a key part of leadership. Glen has received some ineffective advice from his parents on how to conduct himself.

His advisor has taken a gradual approach in being a *strong support person* to Glen. First, he went with Glen to watch some basketball games, particularly intramural games. Eventually he encouraged him to get on an intramural team.

The Outcome. Glen was successful on the team, and with the help of his advisor he has gradually become more assertive about his coursework and what he wants to do with his life. His advisor did not want to just tell Glen what to do, which is a common problem in advising (see Appendix 6).

Myra Wilson

Myra Wilson, an African American, is a second semester sophomore who is on academic probation as a result of unsatisfactory performance in math and physics. She is a lesbian and the only child of a private-duty nurse who has never been married.

Myra appears to have been raised with a relatively high level of independence. She has not mentioned the academic probation to her mother and indicates that she would not show her mother her semester grade report. She feels certain she will perform better in her second semester. She will then be able to discuss grades with her mother and spare her the disappointment of hearing about the first semester.

Other evidence of Myra's independence is found in her expressed reason for not dropping one or both classes she failed. She said that dropping either one would have reduced her credits below the number required for her to remain on financial aid. Despite her borderline academic position, Myra has found it necessary to take a part-time position several miles from the campus. Her mother has not taken issue with this decision.

Myra came to college in a relatively advantaged position. She attended a summer orientation program and obtained significant exposure to what the school might be like for her. She declared her intention to pursue a double major in anthropology and biology. Her study habits were quite immature. Regardless of the complexity of the course, she reported "trying to devote an hour of study daily to each course." She often did not meet her study time goals for the reasons that beset most students. But she had an additional, more unusual problem: she enjoyed certain courses so much that she would not stop studying for them when the planned hour was up. She would often continue with it until she was too tired to study anything else.

Myra accepted responsibility for taking too many difficult courses at one time, but she was not willing to do so for her failure in math. She thought a great many graduate students enrolled in the class "hoping for an easy A," and she was too angry to talk to her professor about it. The professor knew about it and stated in class that he intended to raise the standards to prevent that. He planned his work for students who knew what they were doing and destroyed students like her.

When her mother asked how she was doing compared to the other students, she replied she did not know any more about them than they knew about her, nor did she know how other students figured out what would be on the tests. She said she always seemed to do worse on the exams than she thought she would. Furthermore, Myra was not "out" as a lesbian to her peers. This prevented her from developing a supportive community on campus.

Despite Myra's disappointing third semester, she says college is a perfect place for her. She says she has had plans for going to graduate school since she entered junior high school.

Advising Myra. Myra had poor *realistic self-appraisal.* She is getting feedback from a variety of sources that she cannot handle a double major, and that she needs help with study habits. Her advisor pointed out her difficulties, but Myra wouldn't listen. She felt her advisor was prejudiced toward her and he did not think she could do well. In fact the advisor was uncomfortable with her aggressive style and did not go beyond giving her information.

Eventually Myra got another advisor (also a male) who had a "safe space" sign on his door, suggesting he was open to discussing issues that might concern a lesbian in a nonthreatening environment. Myra tested him, but the advisor spent considerable time establishing rapport and trust. She had a *self-concept* problem and admitted to her advisor that she was aggressive because she was not sure how people would react to her sexual orientation. The advisor realized he could not provide all the help she needed, so he made a referral to the gay-lesbian center on campus.

The Outcome. Myra is seeing a counselor in the gay-lesbian center but is also getting solid advice from her advisor on how to deal with her academic difficulties.

She is more comfortable letting people know of her sexual orientation, and she now has a single major and a reduced course load. She has retained her financial aid, thanks to the advisor's intervention.

Carl Johnson

Carl Johnson, an African American junior, is not doing well, in his opinion, for the first time in his academic career. He was an honor student in high school, and everyone expressed expectations that he would establish an outstanding college record. However, despite his parents' pride in and praise of his performance, Carl was displeased with it and disturbed by the fact that he worked constantly for inconsistent results.

He is majoring in computer science and is interested in graduate school. He enjoyed the content of his courses and the accolades he got from friends and relatives when he described them. However, when people asked him about his grades, he always said he had a B average because he was ashamed, displeased, and puzzled by the fact that his grades were always an array of A's, B's, and C's. No matter how hard he studied, his A's would be equaled by the C's.

Carl was so distressed by the C's that he began to believe there was something wrong with him. From his perception, he was a diligent student in all of his courses. Certainly he studied some of them more than he did others, but that was because of his judgment about what the course demanded. Every one of Carl's courses was going to get just a bit more than they demanded. That is the kind of student he is.

When he was unable to plan his problem away, he went for counseling, thinking that he was out of touch with reality, and not really putting in all of the time he thought he was. He quit the counseling sessions after three visits because he thought the counselor was not taking him seriously, but he was more convinced than ever by the encounter that there was something wrong with him. He did not even have the ability, he thought, to speak convincingly enough to let someone know how he was feeling.

Carl always was, and still is, popular with male and female peers, but he has no one outside his family who would call him a close friend. Although he is interested in women and often daydreams about them, he never thought he could afford the time and commitment that dating requires. He feels very strongly that it would be fun to date. There are even several males in his class that he thinks are a lot of fun, and he would like to double-date with them. Carl does not, however, know how to get a date. When confronted with women in a one-to-one situation, Carl becomes anxious, unless he is involved in a conversation about science or computers and in a public place.

Advising Carl. Carl appeared to have a *poor self-concept* largely stemming from his problems in his social life. Those social life problems were beginning to interfere with his academic self-concept. His advisor realized he could help Carl in some ways, but that Carl needed some professional help as well. The advisor referred Carl to the counseling center and also suggested that he and Carl attend some sporting and social events together.

The Outcome. The combination of activities worked well for Carl. He has been getting out more and has made some male and female friends. His counseling has helped him deal with some of his doubts and anxieties. Carl's grades improved and he has gone on to graduate school.

Gloria Torres

Gloria Torres is a twenty-one-year-old Puerto Rican in her first year as a law student; she is on academic probation with a GPA of less than 1.0 (on a scale of 4.0). She was a sociology major as an undergraduate. Her mother is a security officer for the New York City public school system, and her father is a retired U.S. marine and transit authority employee living in Miami. She and a brother live with her mother; one brother lives with her father. She visits her father regularly.

Gloria is frustrated and angry about her fortunes in law school. Her undergraduate college teachers did not take her legal interests seriously and steered her toward graduate school in social work. She had many problems in undergraduate school: teachers who covered too little material, who refused to answer her questions, who graded too easily, and so on. She came close to enrolling in a school of social work. Her dream, however, was to become a lawyer, and so she decided to apply.

Gloria's LSAT scores were relatively low and raised some questions in her mind about her ability. She was advised to attend a prematriculation summer session, which she did. She is ambivalent about having taken the summer program. On the one hand, she recognized some material studied in college and attended to the courses carelessly because she thought it was going to be easy. She should have worked harder, but she ran into the same kind of difficulty she had in college—problems she could not solve alone, teachers who would either refuse to answer her questions or give answers that were too complex for her to grasp at the speed with which they were given, and so on.

Gloria is having problems in law school similar to those she had as an undergraduate. She thought she was a good student and was understandably upset when, after challenging an initial B grade on a case write-up that was thoroughly marked up, her grades dropped to the borderline failing level and remained there for the semester. She wrote several papers in the course during the semester and always thought she had done better than she was graded.

She became thoroughly frustrated in her efforts to meet her professor's expectations. Through talking to friends about her situation, she was referred to a third-year African American student who critiqued one of her papers. She turned in the paper that the other student critiqued and received an F. Gloria then made her regular appointment to see the professor. When she arrived, she was presented a copy of the student disciplinary code on academic dishonesty. Because it was a polished paper and did not contain many of the errors that were typical of her work, the professor assumed that she had copied the material. By bringing all of the sources she had used to the professor's office and pointing out the sections cited, she was able to convince the professor that she did not cheat. Her grade on the paper was changed to a C.

Gloria reported her problems with the professor to the dean, who read her papers and in each case said he would have either assigned a higher grade or been more explicit about what Gloria could have done better, but he could not say that anything the professor had done was actually wrong. She was told by the professor at her next appointment that he knew about her visit to the dean's office. Gloria interpreted the fact that the dean communicated with the professor after her visit as proof that she had convinced him she had been abused by the professor. She assumed she would have failed the class had she not gone to see the dean, despite the fact that she earned a C.

Gloria is feeling discouraged in her program, and disappointed and angry about having chosen to come to law school instead of a program in social work. She hears from her friends who are progressing in that program and doing fieldwork under supervision.

Advising Gloria. Gloria needs help *working the system* and *handling racism.* Her style of going over the head of the person she feels has wronged her does not always work. Her advisor used a technique of getting Gloria to specify a number of alternatives that she could employ each time she had a problem, including some she could do on her own and some she may have made worse or even caused by her actions. They then listed pros and cons of each alternative. In this way the advisor was able to teach Gloria that there are usually multiple ways to solve a problem, and that the academic system is more complex than she realized.

The Outcome. After some success in discussing options, the advisor discussed whether Gloria was in the right field. With help from the career center advisors,

Gloria concluded that she really belonged in social work, and that in her eagerness to defy stereotypes she had put herself in the wrong place. Gloria left law school and is currently doing well in a social work curriculum.

Fred Hunter

Fred Hunter is a Native American senior, a history major who is on academic probation as a result of having failed two of four courses last semester: Spanish and literature. He is an only child who lives with his mother, although he communicates regularly with his father.

Fred had done passable work in his courses previously. His SAT scores were 480 verbal and 440 math. His explanation for the low test scores is that most of the questions were in areas he had not covered, and the verbal part was mostly words that require definition, many of which he did not recognize. He majored in journalism, biology, sociology, and general studies before settling on history.

Fred reported attending almost all of his classes (he missed only two during the last semester) and spending most of his time in his room, other than going out for class or meals. His study habits were variable. He might study heavily for days and then not at all for some time, depending on his feelings. He describes himself as being at his best when he is spontaneous; this gives him his truest motivation. He is not sure what effect the course failures will have on his progress toward graduation. It appears to be a waste of time to worry about it because, whether he chooses or not, he typically goes to sleep when he attempts to study. He is also easily distracted; in particular, whenever the television is turned on, he usually stops studying and watches it.

He has few friends. He is on good terms with his roommate, but they do few things together. His typical pattern is to go home on weekends to hang out with his long-time friends. He views college as a large, complex place that he would not especially like to try to get to know. Although he says he has been interested in history since he entered high school, he has little information about what he might do with the degree.

Advising Fred. Fred is a loner who does not have an individual *support person* or a *community* group to lend him support. He seems to have no tribal connections (which often serve as an important support mechanism for Native Americans). His advisor had a difficult time seeing him. She e-mailed him, called and left phone messages for him, and even tried to catch him at his residence once. Fred eventually was forgotten by the advisor and everyone else at the school; he sort of disappeared.

The Outcome. No one much noticed when Fred left school, and we do not know what happened to him. He needed a great deal of help, perhaps more than it is reasonable to expect of an advisor. Other methods of contact could have been attempted by getting assistance from campus agencies, since he also appeared to need some career counseling and some help with long-term goals.

Mari Toya

Mari is an international student from Japan majoring in engineering. She is quiet and does her work on time and competently for each class. She speaks and writes English well and had good SAT scores. She got straight A's in her engineering courses until she took a course that required her to work with teams solving practical engineering problems. She did not seem to be doing her part on the teams and had little to contribute to the discussion or to construction of the equipment they were required to build. Her advisor saw Mari for several years and did not detect any problems. She was always polite and said she was doing well, and the advisor simply placed her in the next courses without much thought. When he recently asked her how she was doing that semester, she said "fine," even though her advisor had heard from the professor teaching her course that she was not doing well. When the advisor confronted her, she broke down and began crying. She felt that she was letting her family, her advisor, and her school down by her performance.

Advising Mari. The advisor was surprised by Mari's reaction, and after calming her down he began to probe what was different about the course in which she was struggling. First, there seemed to be several cultural issues that were barriers for her. She was used to being very deferential to her teachers, which was the norm in Japan. The instructor would tell the students what to do, what was correct, what was incorrect, and so on. In this class, the teacher was letting the students come up with the answers and discover for themselves whether the answers were correct. She was uncomfortable doing this, and her classmates learned not to expect anything from her. This reflects her weakness in *negotiating the system.*

Mari also seems to lack much experiential, or systemic, ability (Sternberg, 1996). Her strengths seem to be in the componential ability area. She is good at memorizing material and playing it back to the instructor; she is not good at creative tasks or learning a new system of how to operate. Her advisor went over these issues for her and stressed that it was only one course and she may be better at other aspects of engineering. He also helped Mari deal with her *concept of herself.* For a variety of reasons, cultural and otherwise, she was more proficient at some things than others.

The Outcome. Her advisor helped Mari find a *community* of Asian students who were in technical fields on campus, where she could discuss these issues with peers. Mari got a B in the course, has gone back to Japan, and is working for an engineering firm there.

Alvin Nesser

Alvin is White, a junior prelaw student with a learning disability, attending a college with little in the way of programs to help such students. He did well enough in the introductory, mostly didactic courses in his first two years. Now that he is in his junior year, more writing is required, and he has not been able to keep up with the time demands. A paper that may take most students a week to write typically takes him more than a month to complete. He is smart and verbal, and few would suspect that he has a learning disability. He did not know what to do, so he went to see his advisor.

Advising Alvin. Alvin's advisor was surprised when she was told of his disability. Her first reaction was that there wasn't much she could do. He would have to do the work and try to get some help from a specialist in learning disabilities, although there was none on campus. She also knew that the Americans with Disabilities Act required the school to make a "reasonable accommodation." He needed a *support person* and help in *working the system.*

After the session with Alvin, the advisor thought about the issues further and came up with an idea. He was not trying to avoid work; he worked harder than perhaps any other student on campus. She contacted the professors teaching his classes and proposed something to them. If they would accept the same paper from him for each class, they could each grade it from the vantage point of their respective discipline. Alvin would have the task of choosing a topic that fit all the class requirements and could overcome the systemic barrier presented by his disability.

The Outcome. All but one of his professors agreed, and he has done well in all his classes.

Here we may have equality of outcome rather than process. Clearly, Alvin is not writing as many papers as the other students. However, he is working as hard as the other students, if not harder, and producing a specimen of his work for professors to judge. Without some consideration of the barriers presented to Alvin, he is not likely to complete college, owing to financial and timeline problems that might present themselves. His advisor has been creative in proposing a viable solution.

Carlos Ortega

Carlos is a Latino senior premed student who is on academic probation as a result of failing two courses. He is angry with the dean's office and threatening to transfer to another institution. The dean's office has strongly recommended that he repeat the courses failed during the semester. Carlos has been interested in medicine for a long time, actually since junior high school, but he did not get really serious about it until he started college. He comes from a musical family. His mother, father, and three uncles were a singing cabaret team prior to the birth of Carlos, his two brothers, and his sister. He and his siblings grew up singing and performing. He developed a solo voice, and his parents found him a voice teacher who began encouraging his aspirations for a show business career.

By the time Carlos got to college, he was quite confused about his career. He was interested in medicine and had done all of the right things in high school, but his age and the strength of his voice meant he could do a lot more interesting things in the music area than he had been able to do before. Medicine looked attractive, but it was far into the future. His music was in the present; his fans loved him; and he was earning an excellent income. Because of the early acclaim, he needed to select a major at the university that would allow him the time needed to rehearse and travel. He chose a major in music, but he took at least one course from the premed curriculum each semester. At the end of his second year, he thought he had made the wrong choice.

Carlos loved performing, and he thrived on people's reactions to him, but for him this was not enough. He felt as if he were on vacation, and it was OK to be on vacation for a while but eventually he had to go back to work. He wanted to achieve something he had dreamed medicine would permit. He wanted to change his major to premed.

Carlos's undergraduate department head made it difficult for him to get a permanent academic advisor. He did not want to see him change his major. Carlos was advised by a series of graduate students, one of whom had him bypass a course he needed; another had him take some courses out of sequence. By the time Carlos got his advisory errors corrected so that he might graduate, he was a twenty-three-year-old junior with a marginal record for getting into medical school.

Carlos thought about giving up, but he felt stuck. He had relinquished many of the connections and performances that would advance his career if he were going to stay in music other than as a hobby. Advancement and success were never guaranteed, and if he went on with music his fortune was not all that certain. Medicine was his surest route to success since he was at least connected to it. He had been very happy and optimistic until he failed two courses. He was singing often enough to support himself after having received a small package of financial aid.

He was concerned about his chemistry deficiencies but managed to register the first semester of his junior year without including chemistry in his course load. When it was discovered at the end of the first semester that he had not taken one of the chemistry courses, the dean was irritated and insisted that he take both of them at the same time in the spring semester.

Carlos protested that he had taken what was advised, but the dean rejected this argument and placed the responsibility on Carlos. He had already planned a long singing engagement for the summer so he could take most of the coming year off and devote his time fully to his studies. The dean said the chemistry knowledge was essential to his fourth year, and it was imperative that he take the classes before registering for senior-level courses. It was therefore important that he take the chemistry courses during the spring or over the summer. The dean felt that whatever Carlos did about the singing engagement was his own problem.

Advising Carlos. Carlos appeared to have problems with setting *long-term goals,* particularly his career goals, with *handling the system,* and with his *support system.* His conflict between music and medicine seemed irresolvable. The training career counselors receive would suggest that music and medicine are not compatible (see Holland, 1985). However, Carlos's chemistry professor didn't know that, and he gave Carlos the advising that eventually helped him out of his dilemma.

The Outcome. First, the advisor looked for ways to help him see medicine and music as two components of the same career. Carlos began to perform in local hospitals and work with physicians in seeing music as part of the healing process. He was successful in this, and he began to consider a career that would involve both areas. The advisor worked things out with the dean to be able to make up the chemistry courses. The advisor also worked with Carlos to help him see that all his goals needed to be interconnected, and that he couldn't be successful in negotiating the system unless he saw that.

The advisor also helped the dean and Carlos see that he needed to continue performing with his family. He received financial and other kinds of support from this activity; his family was an important *community* for him. Carlos completed his medical education and is known as "the singing doc" in his area.

Althea Williams

Althea Williams is a forty-year-old African American who has not taken a college course in about twenty years. She is a single mother with four children. In a typical day she is up at 5:00 A.M. and prepares meals for her three children who are still in the public school system, and then she does some housework. She has a part-time job three days a week as a clerk in a retail store in the small town in which she lives. She also works as a part-time teacher's assistant in a local elementary school two days a week. Most of her evenings are spent with her children.

Althea attends church regularly and is a member of the choir. She is a quiet person who does her work, takes care of her family, and prays that she can keep things going.

She has been given the chance to finish her bachelor's degree and become a teacher. She is not sure she can do it, although she has not shared this with anyone. Even though there are many people in her life, there are none with whom she feels comfortable discussing her concerns. She plans to continue calling upon her considerable resolve and pray harder that she will be able to complete her education and handle everything else.

Advising Althea. Althea needs both a *support person* and a *community*. She also needs some help with her *self-concept* and probably on her *long-term goals*. She has gotten some help from one of the teachers for whom she was doing aide work. The teacher noticed that she seemed distracted and asked her if there was anything she wanted to discuss. The advisor was acting assertively in asking, because Althea was unlikely to bring up any issues herself.

The Outcome. They discussed teaching and education courses, and the teacher got Althea to go to a college nearby that is offering the program and get more advice. Althea's confidence was boosted, and with the support and information she successfully completed her degree and is currently an elementary school teacher.

Thelma Jackson

Thelma Jackson is African American, married with two children, and considers herself one of the leaders in her community. She does not have a job where she earns a salary, but her husband makes enough to provide them with a comfortable lifestyle.

She is president of a garden club, the PTA president at the school of one of her children, and president of the women's auxiliary of her husband's lodge. She also belongs to groups concerned with cleaning up city parks, improving the library system, civic improvement, and child abuse.

She has some college credits taken at various times in her life, but she has never had a clear focus or major. Her friends have told her about a new program to train students to teach who have had prior college experience. She feels that people would expect her to take the lead and be in the program. She has applied and is waiting to hear of her acceptance.

Advising Thelma. Thelma appears to have problems with her *goals* and her *self-concept*. She does not appear to have any particular interest in teaching and has made no attempt to find out anything about it. She appears to be a leader, but her roles have been more as a formal head of a group than showing influence on others that is developmental for her. She is under social pressure to be good at everything rather than to pursue her own interests; hence she does not have a good career self-concept. Even though she is in many groups, she does not get the kind of *support* from them that would help her in her current situation.

The Outcome. Thelma entered the program but did not seek assistance with any of these problems. She lasted one semester, withdrawing from her courses and reporting that she had too many other commitments to make a go of it. This is probably true, but Thelma might have been successful in the program had she received some help with the noncognitive dimensions noted earlier. The people connected with the program she entered should have done a better job of assessing Thelma's needs and working with her.

Chapter Summary

Noncognitive variables can be used effectively in advising and counseling programs. Case studies of institutions that have used NCVs in advising or counseling have been discussed in this chapter. Individual student cases have shown how NCVs can be used in working with them. The next chapter discusses how noncognitive variables might be used in evaluating campus programs and services.

CHAPTER EIGHT

EVALUATING AND DESIGNING CAMPUS PROGRAMS WITH NONCOGNITIVE VARIABLES

Noncognitive variables can be employed in evaluating programs and services, including diversity programs for faculty, resident life programs for students, student union services, or any other function that may occur in support of the mission of a college or university. Including NCVs in an evaluation allows the program planner to link program outcomes to student success, and to ensure applicability across nontraditional groups. A number of examples are discussed in this chapter.

Developing Community: Planning and Evaluation

On one campus, the importance of developing community was particularly strong. After administering the NCQ (see Appendix 2), the administration saw that its students had low scores on the community scale, using the norms in Appendix 3. The school implemented a series of programs to strengthen opportunities for students to develop community, on and off campus. The program had three objectives:

1. To make the campus environment more comfortable for students of color, who were 8 percent of the student body

2. To train faculty and student services staff to assist students in finding a community on campus with which they were comfortable
3. To provide volunteer opportunities for students in a variety of situations off campus

To achieve the first objective (groups for students of color), the school increased funding for a number of student organizations that were focused on race and culture. Invitations were extended to faculty, staff, and students to talk to one another, and to prepare the necessary applications for funding. Many groups came forward, and by using campus funds the institution showed its support. Once the groups were funded, the campus sponsored a series of open houses and campuswide events that allowed students to become acquainted with student groups old and new.

The second objective (training in helping students locate community) was addressed by holding for faculty and staff a series of workshops and programs emphasizing their role in helping students find a place on campus. Previously, few faculty members saw this as a relevant function for them, and the student activities staff was more focused on campuswide events than on development of smaller communities.

Off-campus opportunities were developed for students as the administration took the lead in developing better relationships with employers and agencies in the area. In recent years, town-gown relations had deteriorated. One of the most successful programs aimed at this objective was to sponsor a college-community day where employers and campus departments would set up displays; everyone from on and off campus was invited. Many new opportunities were developed for students, and the long-term positive effects for the college seemed to be good.

To evaluate the effectiveness of the programs, the school developed a short questionnaire with face validity of its scores, documenting the community-related behaviors of students, faculty, and staff. The school also readministered the NCQ to students after one year. Results showed that the community-related behaviors of all groups had increased. Additionally, students scored higher on several NCQ scales (community, self-concept, leadership, and goals).

Religion and Multiple Communities

A small Southern college sought to unite students, faculty, and staff around campuswide meetings on topics ranging from the curriculum to social problems in the larger society. The town meeting approach seemed to fit the goals of the institution in involving everyone in presenting their views. The college had a

Christian religious tradition, although it had not been closely affiliated with any religious group for many years. Each meeting was held in the largest auditorium on the campus, which contained many paintings, windows, and other artifacts that were Christian-related, and each meeting was begun with a Christian prayer.

Many campuses have students, faculty, and staff who are not Christian. By planning programs to bring people together, some may be excluded. Schlosser (2003) has called this "Christian privilege," in that the assumption is made—often without even thinking about it—that everyone is Christian. Hence programs that do not consider this point can be divisive, rather than community building (Schlosser & Sedlacek, 2001, 2003). The single-community campus is unusual, whatever it says in the catalogue.

At this particular college, many students and faculty objected to the Christian context of the meetings; the administration was defensive and stunned at the reaction to what they considered a campus tradition. Building community can be difficult, and it may not be possible without considering religious diversity. A truly diverse multicultural campus is one in which multiple communities have the opportunity to express their backgrounds and interests, while respecting the rights of others to do so as well. Diverse groups may never really come together to see or appreciate things in the same way. The school in this example was not allowing different communities to develop on their campus, which some individuals felt was necessary to meet their needs.

Helping Students Set Goals

The special programs office staff of a large Midwestern university was frustrated with their inability to change some of the planning behavior of their clients. Most of the students were receiving some form of financial aid, the bulk of which was given to the students at the beginning of each semester. However, the staff felt that this policy worked against the ability of their clients to set long-term goals and take advantage of the services the school offered.

The staff decided to award students money for accomplishing short-term goals and gradually help their clients set long-term goals. For example, a student might get ten dollars for attending a class, twenty dollars for getting a date, fifty dollars for passing a quiz, and so on, depending on the particular needs of the student. The goals could be academic or nonacademic; the staff worked to make each successive goal for a student more long-term. At the end of the semester the students received all their aid, but it was tied to setting and accomplishing goals. What had been a problem became a proactive solution based on noncognitive variables. The staff needed to bend some rules, but 86 percent of the staff and

73 percent of the students felt the new procedures helped the students negotiate the system and experience success with long-term goals.

Evaluating the Community Off Campus

Noncognitive variables can be used by individuals as well as by institutions in making evaluations. An African American candidate for a top administrative position would arrive unannounced several days before his formal interview and walk the neighborhoods in the area around the campus. He would talk to people, go into stores, visit real estate offices, and check how he was treated by people. He was testing his self-concept as to whether this was a town in which he would be comfortable. He was also assessing how he would handle any racism that came up, and how supportive the community would be for him and his family. He rejected several offers on the basis of his preliminary assessments.

Residence Hall Problems

Some schools have found that a residence hall program intended to be positive or neutral actually produced negative results. NCVs can be used to interpret the reasons for those results.

In the first situation, the resident life office of one Midwestern college offered rooms with built-in computers at a small extra fee for interested students. African American students, who more often than White students felt they could not afford the extra charge, found themselves grouped in certain halls with fewer of the desirable features of the newer rooms. The African American students felt "ghettoized" and victims of racism. Certain halls became known as "Black dorms"—not by choice, which might have been a positive way to develop community, but by economic consequences, which turned out to cause problems for all concerned.

On another campus, as a new residence hall was built no one paid attention to the implications of race relations issues arising in the hall, particularly as the campus was stressing awareness of diversity issues. The hall director had no particular training in race relations, and one insensitive resident assistant was involved in a number of interracial incidents and was asked to resign. White residents refused to allow African American residents into their rooms, and there was no program to discuss these issues among residents. Thus, by not evaluating possible effects of racism or the opportunities to develop a multicultural community, the climate in the residence hall deteriorated and negatively affected all involved.

Evaluating Student Affairs Staff Attitudes Toward Asian Americans

In recent years, administrators have begun to understand that increased enrollment of students of color alone is not enough to create a positive multicultural environment. As such, higher education has been experiencing a shift in its work on multiculturalism. Institutions are moving from merely increasing the number of students of diverse background to implementing programs and services aimed at changing the campus environment (Valverde, 1998). Student affairs professionals have also expanded their roles to include developing services and programs that are sensitive to the developmental needs of all students.

Many look to student affairs staff to develop and encourage inclusive activities and events, promote opportunities for interracial dialogue, and create an environment where all students can achieve academically, develop as culturally sensitive individuals, and feel safe (Pope & Reynolds, 1997; Reynolds & Pope, 1994). Key professional and ethical documents stress the importance of developing environments that are diverse, where students can learn from differences (American College Personnel Association, 1993; National Association of Student Personnel Administrators, 1987). However, evaluations of multicultural preparedness—defined as knowledge, skills, behavior, comfort, and experiences or racial attitudes of student affairs professionals—are limited (Hoover, 1994).

McEwen and Roper (1994) suggested that student affairs professionals may not have sufficient knowledge to work effectively with a diverse population. Hoover's study (1994) lent some support to this by finding a lower level of multicultural preparedness among student affairs professionals in working with racial minority or gay, lesbian, and bisexual students than with women and nontraditional-aged students. The preparation of student affairs professionals in the area of diversity is important in creating an environment where the needs of racial/cultural groups are met (Pope, 1993, 1995; Pope & Reynolds, 1997; Reynolds & Pope, 1994).

Understanding the feelings of one group toward another (Schuman, Steeh, Bobo, & Krysan, 1997) is also crucial in understanding group interactions (Sedlacek & Brooks, 1970). Given the role of student affairs professionals as facilitators of multiculturalism on a college campus, it is important to understand their attitudes toward students of diverse backgrounds. In one specific evaluation, researchers set out primarily to examine the attitudes of White student affairs professionals toward Asian Americans (Liang & Sedlacek, 2003a). Asian Americans were selected because they are growing in number in higher education. Furthermore, Asian

Americans as a group are not well represented in the higher education research literature.

White student affairs professionals were chosen as the target sample for several reasons. The number of student affairs professionals of color is growing, but their White counterparts represent an overwhelming majority of professionals in the field. For instance, as of May 2000 the American College Personnel Association's membership was 73.3 percent Caucasian, 10.7 percent African American, 2.8 percent Asian American or Pacific Islander, 3.4 percent Hispanic or Latino, 1.1 percent multiracial, 0.3 percent Native American, 1.5 percent other, and 6.9 percent unreported (L. Mihalik, personal communication, May 15, 2000). Second, the attitudes, feelings, and behaviors of White individuals, by virtue of their majority status, have more of an effect on minority populations than the attitudes of racial minorities have on Whites or on other racial groups (Sedlacek & Brooks, 1976). Fifty-nine White student affairs staff members (46 percent male) employed at an Eastern university were administered either the control or the experimental form of a version of the Situational Attitude Scale (SAS; Sedlacek, 1996a; see Chapter Three).

Members of a focus group felt that "Asian American" was the term most commonly used by the student affairs professionals at this particular university. (The group referent employed should be the term most commonly used by the respondents, rather than what is preferred by the researcher; see Sedlacek, 1996a.) The focus group then decided on situations thought to engender positive or negative stereotypes of Asian Americans. Situations were related to both the stereotypes that people of Asian descent encounter and the field of student affairs. Twelve situations were developed and used for this study. An example of the situations on the control form (the "race unspecified" scale) is "A student offers to fix your computer." Experimental forms differed in the introduction of the trigger word; the same situation on the experimental form would therefore read, "An Asian American student offers to fix your computer." Reliability coefficients (Cronbach alpha) for scores from the situations on the SAS ranged from .62 to .95, with a median of .79.

Student affairs professionals indicated more positive responses on the Asian American form than on the neutral form for three situations: a student offers to fix your computer; you see a group of young men loitering by your car; and the university's president has just announced the selection of a new vice president of student affairs. Student affairs professionals did not indicate more negative responses to Asian Americans in any of the twelve situations.

That student affairs professionals may have more positive attitudes toward Asian Americans than when race is not considered has important implications for how one engages in student affairs activities. At first glance, an attitude in the positive direction may be construed as good, or harmless. However, Hune and Chan (1997) suggested that attitudes based on a stereotype depicting Americans of Asian descent as well adjusted and without academic or mental health needs have hurt many Asian Americans, particularly Southeast Asians. Similarly, the assumption that Asian Americans are financially stable overlooks the economic difficulties that many Southeast Asians, particularly refugees, are experiencing (Liang, Ting, & Teraguchi, 2001).

Ancis, Bennett-Choney, and Sedlacek (1996) noted that differences in an apparently positive direction do not necessarily suggest that prejudicial attitudes are absent. It may seem positive to want an Asian American to fix your computer, but it supports a stereotype that Asian Americans are experts in technical subjects (the case example of Eric Loo in Chapter Seven illustrated this point). Forcing an expectation on people from other races is a form of racism, even if the expectation appears to be positive (Sedlacek & Brooks, 1976). Having a positive self-concept and being able to handle racism have been shown to be predictors of success for Asian American students (Fuertes, Sedlacek, & Liu, 1994).

Results of past studies using the SAS methodology have yielded significant differential attitudes among participants in the situation where one sees a group of young men loitering (Minatoya & Sedlacek, 1984; Sedlacek & Brooks, 1970; White & Sedlacek, 1987). This study showed similar results. However, even though the results of previous studies indicated that respondents held more negative attitudes toward a group where race was specified, it was found in this study that respondents felt safer and more relaxed around a group of young Asian American men loitering near their car than when race was not specified. Thus it appeared that Asian American men were perceived to be less of a threat to one's personal safety than when an individual's race was not specified.

This result could be based on a perception of Asian Americans as peaceful, docile, or perhaps less intimidating physically and therefore less of a physical threat. Another interpretation could be that Asian Americans are academically and financially successful and thus less likely to engage in criminal behavior. Attitudes of student affairs professionals toward Asian Americans may differ according to the region of the country. For instance, stereotypes of Asian Americans as being in gangs, or skilled in martial arts, may be common in California or New York City. Student affairs professionals in these areas may report more negative attitudes toward Asian Americans in this situation.

The tendency for positive responses toward an Asian American vice president of student affairs may be an indication that student affairs professionals are embracing diversity, and that Asian Americans are becoming more accepted in roles of leadership. However, to date few Asian Americans have occupied high-level positions on college campuses.

Information regarding the experiences and stereotypes of Asian Americans can also be gleaned from scenarios where no significant differences were found, as reported for situations where a student is worried about how her parents will react to her decision to switch majors, and where a student is upset about a B+ he or she received on an exam.

The strong influence of parents on an Asian American's career decisions and academic performance has been documented (Leong, 1998). A practitioner who does not understand the impact of parental influence on Asian American college students and decides to treat academic or career issues the same for all students may not completely understand the stress and anxiety that the student could be experiencing.

In an example outside this study, the tragic story of Elizabeth Shin, an Asian American college student who committed suicide—apparently over stresses in her environment that were not addressed—should remind us all of the importance of this topic (Sontag, 2002). In high school, she seemed to feel pressure to be perfect; she cut her wrists superficially as she learned that she would be salutatorian of her class, rather than valedictorian. She was dropped to second in her class over missing a physics test. Her father threatened to sue the high school because of racism.

Elizabeth did not receive the counseling she seemed to need as she moved onto college at MIT. With the added pressures of the competitive environment, she was unable to share her problems with her parents, and though she sought help from the psychiatric services at the school she was unable to handle the situation. She was showing many signs of stress at a number of points before and during college.

She might have been better understood had people around her been aware of the relevance of noncognitive variables for Asian Americans. For example, Elizabeth's self-concept might not have been as positive as was supposed. Her appraisal of her abilities might not have been realistic, abetted by the pressure to be perfect. Additionally, she apparently had not developed an adequate support person or community, on- or off-campus. Although racism was raised as an issue in her situation, that might not have been done constructively so as to reduce the pressure on her.

Recommendations for Practice for Asian Americans

The Liang and Sedlacek study (2003a) indicates the value for the institution in providing training for staff so that they can better understand their own individual attitude, and how that may affect Asian American students. Without increased attention to what kind of campus environment is created through these held stereotypes, students will continue to feel the powerful impact of prejudice. With the large number of Asian American students on the campus studied (14 percent), the ultimate effect on the campus environment could be substantial.

Improved programs for Asian American students on handling prejudice can also be developed. The Liang and Sedlacek (2003a) study presents some information on what may be included as part of such training. Dealing with apparently positive stereotypes is not a typical way for Asian American students, or student affairs professionals who are developing programs, to think of diversity issues.

Interracial and Intraracial Experiences

The University of Maryland had an enrollment of about one-third students of color and many programs designed to facilitate interactions among students of different racial groups. The university was interested in the effect of its diversity programs on students, and so a study of the nature of different-race and same-race interactions among students was undertaken (Cotton, Kelley, & Sedlacek, 1999).

To interpret the students' college experiences within a larger context, their off-campus experiences were examined and interpreted using NCVs. Undergraduate students from each major racial group on campus (African American, Asian American, Latino, White) were randomly selected, and the critical incidents technique (Flanagan, 1954) was used to obtain the answers to a series of questions (see Appendix 11) requesting a description of specific experiences on and off campus with various racial groups.

Following the questioning phase, response themes were identified and characteristics of negative and positive situations were analyzed. This method allowed analysis of the characteristics of situations that foster a supportive, multicultural environment. Interviews were conducted by White master's-level counseling students as part of a course on multicultural counseling. The study was funded by a grant from the National Association of Student Personnel Administrators and the Ford Foundation.

Four themes emerged from the data:

1. Peer communication in academic environments
2. Campus employment interaction
3. Experiences of residential life
4. Opportunities for social interaction

Noncognitive Variables and Intraracial and Interracial Experiences

The situations described by the students at the University of Maryland varied from structured environments with significant institutional oversight (for instance, classwork) to unstructured situations in which they were free to choose with whom and how they would associate. Here it is useful to consider the noncognitive variable of community (see Table 4.1). Students need to develop a sense of community in groups smaller than the whole campus. These groups are likely to form around a single race, gender, sexual orientation, and so on, unless some attempt is made to create multicultural opportunities for interaction. Many nontraditional students need opportunities to form community within their own group to process the -isms they face that lead to a higher level of success in negotiating the campus systems.

Same-race communities can also help students of color develop the racial identity that is so important for their development. White students tend to have an easier time finding same-race experiences that do not serve the same need as same-race experiences for students of other races. Same-race experiences for Whites can lead to more racism, and multiracial experiences become critical for White students to learn of others, develop their racial identities in a positive way, and improve the campus climate for diversity. Helping students deal with their racial identity is a key part of the self-concept NCV. Higher education professionals should recognize the characteristics of these situations that foster positive community development across races and adopt strategies accordingly.

Many of the incidents described by students concerned their self-appraisal, another of the NCVs. Both same-race and multirace situations can help students learn who they are, and how they are doing in a variety of settings. As with all the noncognitive variables, students can profit from processing their intraracial and interracial experiences with fellow students as well as informed faculty and staff. Some training of faculty and staff in recognizing and processing the NCVs with students could enhance the climate for diversity on campus (Sedlacek, Troy and Chapman, 1976). Processing race-related interactions with students can help faculty and staff become support persons for students, another of the NCVs.

Structured and Unstructured Environments

More structured academic and work environments are a particularly fertile opportunity to foster interaction. Research has shown that it is not sufficient to simply put different people together and expect relationships to improve (Amir, 1969, 1976; Dovidio & Gaertner, 1986). As reported earlier, this is most successful when the members have equal status, are interdependent, and are given ample opportunity to interact. Both the classroom and the work settings create opportunities for faculty and administrators alike to positively affect these interactions. The classroom should be considered a proactive opportunity for different-race peer learning and dialogue: "Rather than leaving cross-racial interactions among students to chance, educators should make peer groups a deliberate and positive part of the educational process in colleges and universities" (Hurtado, Milem, Clayton-Pedersen, & Allen, 1998, p. 292). The work environment is also a prime opportunity to purposefully create cross-racial work teams that can foster better understanding.

A less structured environment, on the other hand, entails both positive opportunity and negative risk. There was a natural tendency for students to interact with people like themselves. When groups of different-race students encountered each other in certain situations, there seemed to be a greater potential for problems. Aggravating factors included alcohol and physical competition. Physical activities are to be encouraged, but one needs to be sensitive to situations in which groups of different-race students are competing, and the ease with which comments or behaviors can cross the line and create negative conflict and increase the need to handle racism.

The NCV of leadership was evident in several of the situations described. Leadership development programs that consider how leadership may differ across races could be an effective strategy in developing a positive multicultural climate.

In a less structured environment, students did not seem to view the administration as the catalyst for bringing different students together; rather, it seems that they saw themselves as the initiators of positive contact. For example, there was little mention of explicit diversity programming as the vehicle of interaction. This does not mean that such programming is unnecessary; it may imply, however, that administrators need to help students work the system by distinguishing between the planning function, which may have a strongly intentional focus on assisting diversity goals, and how these events and activities are publicly presented.

The best strategy may be to help create potentially positive situations and reduce potentially negative ones, without directly labeling activities as diversity-related. An underlying strategy to promote diverse interaction sounds fine, but students may simply want to participate in an interesting activity; if they are able to have a pleasant experience with people they consider different, so much the better.

After having discussed many examples and case studies earlier in the book, I turn in the final chapter to an overview and summary of key concepts in this book.

CHAPTER NINE

CONCLUSIONS AND RECOMMENDATIONS

Now that a great deal of information about noncognitive variables (NCVs) has been presented and discussed, this chapter can deal with the implications of that information. Summary comments and recommendations that can be made for institutions, students, faculty, staff, trustees, off-campus community members, or anyone else interested in improving higher education are included.

A Change Is Needed

The first two chapters of this book discussed the reasons a new approach is needed. Books on assessment do not offer a comprehensive model to approach measurement. Current assessment measures available are inadequate to meet the demands made upon them. They measure limited kinds of abilities and potentials for limited groups. Traditional tests do not give us information on a range of attributes that are crucial to those who have not been socialized in traditional ways. The most common alternatives to standardized tests, such as grades and letters of recommendation, also have problems and give us information similar to what one gets from tests.

Noncognitive Variables

Noncognitive variables have been shown to be useful in many contexts, including admissions, scholarship selection, teaching, and program evaluation. They appear to be fairer to people from all racial, culture, and gender groups than any alternatives. NCVs can also provide for the developmental needs of those evaluated in a way that other evaluation methods cannot. In other words, individuals, groups, and organizations can be worked with in practical terms to increase their progress on the noncognitive dimensions.

Measures Available

The Appendices contain numerous examples of how to measure the NCVs recommended in this book. Questionnaires, short-answer questions, essays, portfolios, interviews, and a review of application materials can all be employed successfully. The materials presented in this book can be used as they are or modified to suit a particular situation. They are available at no cost to you as a reader of this book.

Give Noncognitive Variables a Try

This book is designed to make it easy, inexpensive, and practical to use NCVs in higher education. They can be added to whatever system is currently being employed by an institution or individual. Whether noncognitive variables are used in work with individual students or in attempting to alter the climate of a campus, the examples and evidence throughout this book demonstrate that they have immediate, practical applications. Start small and evaluate how NCVs can increase the success of a function or service. Be creative and employ some of Sternberg's concepts (1996) of the kinds of experiential and contextual intelligence to come up with ideas for noncognitive variables that were not discussed in this book. Here are a number of recommendations that may facilitate the process.

Assessing Campus Climate for Diversity

Noncognitive variables can be employed to conduct a thorough appraisal of an institution's current status on multicultural issues. Basic questions need to be raised during this appraisal, and realistic, unvarnished answers are critical. The questions in this list are basic to realistic appraisal of a school's diversity climate:

- Where does the school stand on each of the eight noncognitive dimensions shown in Table 4.1?
  - Positive self-concept
  - Realistic self-appraisal
  - Successfully handling the system
  - Preference for long-term goals
  - Availability of strong support person
  - Leadership experience
  - Community involvement
  - Knowledge acquired in a field
- Is the school ready for the kind of program being considered?
  - Are there differences among subgroups on the campus on each of noncognitive dimensions?
  - Where does the school stand on issues such as:
    - administrative support
    - hiring policies that favor nontraditional faculty
    - programs for nontraditional students
    - curricular reform
    - attitudes toward gay, lesbian, bisexual, and transgender students
    - recruiting and retaining nontraditional students

These and similar questions should be raised and examined before an appropriate diversity program is planned for a particular school. See Appendix 12 for a sample assessment instrument.

The exact activities that relate to diversity can vary by size, type of governance, budget, geography, teaching or research focus, nature of mission of the institution, the diversity experience of an institution, and many other dimensions (M. García et al., 2001; Sedlacek, 2000).

The Noncognitive Questionnaire or NCQ (Sedlacek, 2003a), Hale's Inventory (1991), the Situational Attitude Scale or SAS (Sedlacek, 1996a), the Universal-Diverse Orientation Scale or UDO (Fuertes, Miville, Mohr, Sedlacek, & Gretchen, 2000), and the models for eliminating racism discussed in Chapter Three (Sedlacek & Brooks, 1976; Helms, 1995) could be useful during the appraisal. See the Appendices for sample instruments.

A formal needs assessment should be conducted to highlight local issues that may not be specifically covered in the general models. For example, is there a specific program, office, group of students, department, or off-campus agency it is particularly important to include while planning a diversity initiative? In addition to involving everyone on campus who is knowledgeable about multicultural issues, seeking assistance from outside consultants is recommended to help ensure that the initial appraisal is as thorough as possible.

Stating Program Goals

On the basis of initial assessment with noncognitive variables, goals could be set for any program as a whole, and for each of its components. These goals should be clearly stated and as operational as possible. Each goal should focus on one or more of the NCVs in the areas of information, attitude, or behavior.

To maximize the chances for success, program goals should be stated in practical, achievable, terms. Nothing helps morale or energizes program participants more than seeing something accomplished. Publicizing program accomplishments is also an important part of any successful program. As one college noted, the form this takes varies with the audience. Students may be reached best through the campus paper; faculty may be most receptive to information presented in department meetings.

Short-term goals make an excellent beginning, but there should be clear links with longer-term goals. Short-term goals should be accomplishable separately, but their value is enhanced if they are tied to future activity.

For example, an honors program decided to focus on the goal of improving the realistic self-appraisals of its students one semester. Faculty evaluated student essays on a variety of topics to determine if students had a better grasp of their strengths and weaknesses at the end of the semester than at the beginning. The essays were a behavioral measure. Program administrators planned to focus on improving community in the next semester by measuring attitudes with the SAS. Each semester was an opportunity for a short-term goal that would eventually be part of the long-term goal of improving students on all the noncognitive dimensions.

As discussed in Chapter Six, if a higher-order goal is attempted before all parties in the group are prepared, overall program goals may not be met. Highly focused goals usually work better than broad ones. Program administrators often try to do too much in one step. Accomplishing a series of smaller goals in certain parts of the campus one at a time may ultimately have more impact on a campus than a diffuse higher-order goals approach. In the uncommon situation where a school has already implemented several successful programs, then a variety of simultaneous new initiatives may work. Situations where programming is concentrated in one or two areas generally produce more success than those with more ambitious broad-based initiatives.

Developing Strategies

When planning an initiative, it is important to distinguish goals from strategies. Strategies are the process through which goals are accomplished. If the process becomes an end in itself, one stresses techniques, rather than outcomes. NCVs can be employed in deciding on program strategies; diversity programming offers some useful examples. Any time one loses sight of program goals in this area, institutional racism is a possible result. For example, if the goal is to retain a course on diversity regardless of what students are learning in the course, the course may come to seem politically correct and the content trivial. This could have a negative effect on intergroup relations on campus.

After a goal has been stated, one can begin to strategize by identifying as many ways as possible to accomplish that goal. Ideas should not be limited to the practical, or even the possible at first. An attempt should be made to get a variety of approaches on the table: the outrageous, the timid, and the logical. The possibilities associated with each can then be discussed.

One school wanted to increase the diversity-related publications of its faculty—a behavioral goal. The school decided to use the knowledge acquired in a field variable as a strategy by exposing its faculty to diversity research presented at professional meetings. Diversity planners from the school contacted presenters beforehand and arranged meetings or discussions. They reported getting good advice and ideas from these contacts, and they also identified potential diversity consultants in this way.

One must be willing to adjust, or abandon, any strategy that does not work. Many of us get attached to a strategy and keep using it over and over again, independent of outcome. The only test of a strategy is whether or not it works.

Another principle to employ is to develop strategies that can be implemented in a realistic amount of time. Patience is required for success; this is a hard lesson for anyone who wants to see change occur. It is often most difficult for students who have a different time frame, due sometimes to their age and tenure at the school. This patience should be tempered with activity: goal setting, feedback, and so forth. It does not suggest a passive, wait-and-see style, or giving up.

In the Sedlacek and Brooks (1976) model, six linear stages need to be worked through before racism is eliminated. Being able to see progress along the way is useful. Perhaps the current students or employees will not be able to see the school move as far as they would like, but they can help pass it on in better shape to the next generation.

One should expect uneven progress. Setbacks, backlash, and frustration occur in any system of change. Not all participants in the process are at the same place or see it the same way. Some actively oppose the best efforts of others. Because there is a jagged curve of progress, one should try to put it in the context of the larger plan and see progress over a longer period of time. For example, the irregular progress in reducing racism at the University of Maryland has been analyzed and interpreted (Sedlacek, 1995a); without stepping back for a longer-term view from time to time, it is difficult to get perspective on changes taking place there.

The models for diversity introduced earlier (Helms, 1995; Sedlacek & Brooks, 1976) allow groups to get a chance to express their cultures positively in their own way while respecting the rights of others to do likewise. The groups may never come together in an overall community that has a single perspective or set of needs. Even agreeing on a conception of diversity is unlikely. One should set goals and design programs to meet the needs of different groups, ensuring that no group is left behind or not considered in the process.

Involving Students

For academic and nonacademic efforts to be successful, schools must involve both traditional and nontraditional students. Efforts to involve nontraditional students can backfire unless a carefully planned needs assessment is conducted to determine how best to reach them on a given campus. It is also important to recognize that the attitudes and behaviors of traditional students have a direct effect on nontraditional students. Traditional students usually determine the overall nature of the campus climate, owing to their larger number and greater power. NCVs can be used to measure and interpret the needs of traditional and nontraditional students.

Faculty Programs

It appears to be particularly difficult to implement faculty programs at many campuses. A thorough needs analysis should include faculty, but they often see themselves as detached from organizational or student issues that they feel don't affect them or their classes directly.

A good principle to use in appealing to any group is self-interest. Rather than trying to make faculty see this process from a program developer's perspective, the approach should be in terms relevant to faculty. As noted earlier, faculty members tend to see themselves as scholars who respond with intellect, rather than emotion, on social issues. Presenting issues in terms of research and scholarship is likely to appeal to faculty. The literature cited throughout this book refers to research findings that support the recommendations made here.

Murray Bowen's theories (1978), and the attitude scaling work that has been done on the SAS (Engstrom, Sedlacek, & McEwen, 1995; Sedlacek, 1996a), suggest that many faculty are uncomfortable dealing with nontraditional students. Offering faculty information about alternative teaching styles (such as interactive teaching) that appeal to the varied learning styles of both traditional and nontraditional students can be an effective way of improving the climate for diversity in the classroom (K. K. Johnson & Sedlacek, 1997). This also helps faculty feel more in control. When faculty realize they can do something that does not compromise their scholarly integrity, that makes their work easier, and that also contributes to diversity, they are likely to embrace the opportunity. Presenting the noncognitive variables and their basis in alternative forms of intelligence as a system to use in teaching and advising, as discussed earlier in this book, can also be useful to faculty.

There appear to be three groups of faculty on any campus. The first group is committed to doing something to improve diversity; the members of this group need approaches, ideas, models, and information to proceed. They should be reinforced and encouraged. K. K. Johnson and Sedlacek (1997) discussed activities that faculty who are active on diversity issues tended to engage in and how they might be encouraged. These incentives included released time from teaching, salary raises, research support, awards of recognition, travel money, and consultation on areas in which they felt they needed it.

The second group of faculty is fair-minded and committed to equality; however, they are busy with many other issues and need some convincing and motivating to take serious action. This is frequently the largest group on any campus.

The third group of faculty is opposed to the ideas in diversity programming and may be direct or indirect about stating their opposition. Such faculty members are unlikely to change regardless of the training or programmatic ideas offered to them. Sometimes program planners become overly concerned with this group. Programming should not totally ignore them or the disruptions that may occur in their classes, but concentrating on the first two groups is frequently sufficient to move the campus forward. This may be a matter of numbers, since usually there are few recalcitrant faculty. However, positive energy in the system often carries the most weight if it is given direction.

Multicultural Program Staff

NCVs can serve as the basis for recruiting, training, and retaining staff of color. The institutions whose programs were most successful in the Lilly study (Sedlacek, 1995a) tended to hire full-time staff knowledgeable of diversity issues with experience in higher education. Part-time arrangements or attempting to involve people who are well intended but who lack knowledge and experience in the area generally did not work well. Although it can be helpful to hire diversity staff from nontraditional groups, that element alone does not ensure the success of a program.

Effective diversity staff members must have positive identity around diversity issues (Helms, 1995; Ossana, Helms, & Leonard, 1992; Suthakaran & Sedlacek, 2001; Tatum, 1992), awareness of how their own socialization affects their behavior (Bowen, 1978), and a positive orientation toward diversity (Fuertes et al., 2001). They should also be aware of prejudices and privileges they may have (Schlosser, 2003). They need as well to be aware of how they are perceived by others, according to their race, culture, gender, and so on, and how to use those perceptions to be constructive and create change. Some diversity issues can be presented effectively by White male staff members; individuals of other races, cultures, and genders can more effectively address other issues, and still others require a team of people from differing backgrounds.

As discussed earlier, the goal in the more advanced stages of the Sedlacek and Brooks (1976) and Helms (1995) models is for all individuals to take responsibility for ending racism, not to be dependent on any one race, gender, or cultural group for answers. Schools can build an effective diversity staff by hiring from the outside—or, as is often more practical, by training current faculty, staff, or students to use established methods for initiating change on racial and cultural issues (Sedlacek, Troy, & Chapman, 1976).

Diversity Training

Noncognitive variables can be key components in any diversity training program. To substantially improve the campus climate for diversity, most schools need to develop a comprehensive program of diversity training (Sedlacek, Troy, & Chapman, 1976). There are many training models available, several of which have been mentioned here. Any effective diversity training program should include developmental stages and provide feedback and evaluation to participants at each stage. Participants enter diversity training at different stages, and they are capable of reaching varying levels of knowledge, insight, and activity during a program for recognizing and working with those differences. Regular evaluations based on noncognitive variables can yield an evaluation system that monitors progress in individuals, groups, and campuswide efforts.

Offering levels of diversity training, as in progressively more advanced academic courses, is often a good idea. Another effective approach is to offer the entire campus a general introductory training and follow it up with a more advanced program that focuses on the needs of a specific group. For example, faculty might receive training on teaching and advising nontraditional students, student affairs staff might receive training on counseling and multicultural programming, and students might receive training on roommate conflicts and issues related to interracial dating.

Diversity training can be expensive. Consultants can be hired to conduct all the training sessions, but a train-the-trainers model should be considered. This approach can make use of the extensive literature available on diversity issues in higher education, some of which has been mentioned in this book (M. García et al., 2001; McEwen & Roper, 1994; McTighe Musil et al., 1999; Ponterotto & Pedersen, 1993; Pope & Reynolds, 1997).

Admissions and Retention

Perhaps the most obvious application of noncognitive variables is in admissions and retention programs. One can expect to admit a more diverse class and show a higher degree of success (such as in completing a program) using NCVs than by not considering them. The value of NCV assessment in retention programs is particularly noteworthy. The legality of using NCVs has been demonstrated in several court cases. They can increase the range of attributes assessed in admissions for greater flexibility and utility of the measures employed.

Student Scholarships

Several scholarship programs that employed NCVs (notably the Gates Millennium Scholars program) were discussed. If scholarships are assigned on the basis of traditional componential intelligence measures such as grades and test scores, many talented and deserving students are denied financial support. Nontraditional students tend to show their potential nontraditionally. Since financial considerations prohibit the matriculation and success of so many students of color, using NCVs can be a primary way to reduce racism in higher education.

Student Services

Noncognitive variables can be employed in planning programs in counseling, student activities, resident life, or other nonacademic areas serving students. A common problem in delivering student services is a lack of time to adequately plan, coordinate, and evaluate programs. Noncognitive variables are a way to incorporate perspective and feedback throughout a program. By using them in different programs, it is possible to coordinate services to examine cumulative or joint effects of those offerings.

The NCVs discussed in this book were chosen to be dimensions with which student affairs professionals are familiar. Most campuses employ people who are comfortable working with some or all of the dimensions covered by the NCVs discussed here. Student service professionals should be able to take the lead in using the variables on campus.

I recommend starting with those NCVs that seem to fit particular programs and personnel. Although the dimensions presented in Table 4.1 are comprehensive, some variables may appear to be more relevant to some situations than others.

A Comprehensive Student Services Program

On the basis of the experience (as discussed in Chapter Seven) of the school that used NCV techniques to advise and counsel nontraditional students with high test scores, here is a model for employing NCVs in delivering overall student services.

Common ways of organizing student services resources in higher education include resident life, counseling, student activities, food services, career services, judicial programs, and so on. These separate units appear functional, and professionals identify with each one. However, a rather constant theme in student affairs literature is how student affairs functions can work better with academic units (Boyer Commission on Educating Undergraduates in the Research University, 1998; C. S. Johnson & Cheatham, 1999; K. K. Johnson & Sedlacek, 1997; Lenning & Ebbers, 1999; Roper & Sedlacek, 1988). Noncognitive variables suggest a way of facilitating that process. This book documents how dimensions that are essentially in the student affairs domain also can have a strong relationship to what happens to students academically. Students with better self-concepts, long-term goals, and ways to work the system get better grades and stay in school longer, among other things. What better way to demonstrate the value of student affairs to the academic enterprise than to say "We can help students work on those things that correlate with their success in school"?

I am reminded of what one of my mentors, Tom Magoon, did on several occasions. He would ask students how many academic credits it was worth to spend a year in a residence hall, or in a series of counseling sessions. Students usually reported that what they gained was equivalent to about three credits. Tom was translating student services into the academic coin of the realm—credit hours, something understood by all. NCVs are attributes that student service people can help students with that pay off in the ultimate values in the academy: grades, retention, and graduation.

Specifically, I suggest that student services be organized around each of the NCVs. In doing so, one student services unit could concentrate on developing student self-concepts and more realistic self-appraisals. Another office might focus upon helping students set better short-term and long-term goals. Yet another might deal with helping students work the maze of our on-campus and off-campus systems. With good referrals, and through efforts to develop better relationships with faculty, there could be a more direct concentration on what students need to succeed than what is usually done.

Of course, someone would have to attend to food, parking, and campus residences, but each of these might be done better in the context of noncognitive variables as well. Recently, my campus held a student affairs employee awards function. No one was recognized for serving good food, enhancing the comfort of residence hall beds, or putting in hours in the counseling center. Outstanding employees helped students deal with parking entanglements, career plans, and their relationships to peers—all noncognitive variables.

Even if the organizational structure were changed very little while concentrating on NCVs, the chances that students are helped would increase. On many campuses, including my own, some people and offices are particularly good at working on one noncognitive variable, but not so good at others. For example, one of my colleagues can do a really good job of helping students develop long-term goals. He employs a series of exercises he enjoys that seem to help students. On the other hand, he is uncomfortable and impatient in assisting students with self-concept issues. Therefore I am careful about which students I refer to him for help.

If designated units concentrate on one or more of the noncognitive dimensions, their staff can be trained to deal with those dimensions. With a good referral system in place, services can be coordinated at a conceptual level in a way that is not possible under a traditional arrangement.

Areas for Research

More research on noncognitive variables that can be employed in higher education is needed. Research on how to better measure each NCV discussed in this book should be conducted. In particular, more studies on NCVs with graduate and professional students are needed. Postbaccalaureate student research, however, presents unique problems, with the restriction of range of scores and getting adequate samples to study (Sedlacek, 2001).

More research is needed on such aspects of diversity as learning disabilities, sexual orientation, and differences among racial groups. For example, it has been found that students with learning disabilities are similar to other students on some dimensions but differ on others. Students with learning disabilities did not differ from other students in their reaction to computers (Suthakaran & Sedlacek, 1999), but they did tend to be aware of their limitations in learning areas (Mitchell & Sedlacek, 1995).

Bisexual clients may present issues to counselors that differ from those of gay, lesbian, transsexual, and heterosexual persons seeking counseling (Mohr & Rochlen, 1999; Ochs, 1996). For example, if sexual orientation is viewed as dichotomous (that is, either heterosexual or homosexual), it renders bisexuality as invisible or abnormal. Counselors with negative attitudes about bisexuality were likely to have negative reactions to a bisexual client (Mohr, Israel, & Sedlacek, 2001).

Another area for possible research is career issues. For example, Sheu and Sedlacek (forthcoming) found differences among Asian American groups regarding their interest in career counseling. They found that Korean American students were more likely to seek career counseling than were Asian Indian American students. Liang, Ting, and Teraguchi (2001) reported on great differences among Asian American groups in their history, cultures, needs, and expectations in higher education, suggesting some important career issues that varied by race.

Creativity Sternberg (1985, 1986, 1996) stressed creativity as one of the key elements of experiential intelligence. However, creativity appears to have been understudied considering its potential importance in understanding human behavior. Guilford, in his American Psychological Association presidential address of 1950, called for more research on creativity. However, relatively little work in the area has been done since.

Sternberg and Lubart (1996) identified a number of reasons creativity has not been studied more. One was that creativity is often seen as a mystical power rather than a measurable attribute. Another reason was a focus on pragmatic approaches to generating creative ideas without understanding how creativity works. Brainstorming was suggested as an example.

Sternberg and Lubart also discussed the marginalizing of creativity research through considering it as a special case of a more general phenomenon rather than a potentially unique area. Additionally, considering creativity as the province of a single discipline within psychology has made its study rather obscure. The authors called for a multidisciplinary study of creativity within psychology. The concept of multidisciplinary research should be expanded to include researchers in many areas, especially those concerned with higher education and test development. Racial, cultural, and gender-related variables should also be included in the research program.

Sternberg and Lubart noted the difficulties in measuring creativity and felt that confluence theory was a potentially fruitful area for research on creativity. The basis of confluence theory is that a combination of cognitive and personality elements is required to have creativity—elements such as "connects ideas," "sees similarities and differences," has "flexibility," and is "unorthodox." All of these elements would seem to be relevant to one or more of the NCVs shown in Table 4.1.

Emotional Intelligence A number of researchers have studied emotional intelligence, but the concept has not been researched often in applied higher education settings (Mayer, 2001). Attempts to improve the measurement of the less empirical conceptions of Gardner (1983) and Goleman (1998) should be made. The work of Mayer and his colleagues (Mayer, 1999, 2001; Mayer, Salovey, & Caruso, 2000) could be studied as well in admissions, scholarship, teaching, advising, and student service situations. Cultural, racial, and gender variables should be included in this line of research. As noted in Chapter Three, Mayer has tried to study aspects of emotional intelligence that are uniform across all persons. This logic is counter to the major thesis of this book—that aspects of ability vary by race, culture, gender, and other aspects of experience. Whether Mayer's work exemplifies the Three Musketeers Problem (Sedlacek, 1994a) or there are measurable attributes of ability that work the same for all should be studied. It may be that Mayer's conceptions can be assessed but scores derived from them do not have validity for applied purposes in higher education.

The "Big Five" Researchers have identified five basic personality variables that exist in all people:

1. Extraversion
2. Agreeableness
3. Conscientiousness
4. Emotional stability
5. Intellect and imagination

Scores on assessments of the "big five" have been shown to have validity in predicting employee and military performance, but they have not been studied in education (Goldberg, 2001). As with emotional intelligence, scores from most of the measures of big-five attributes do not appear to vary by ethnic group (Goldberg, Sweeney, Merenda, & Hughes, 1998). However, Reeve and Hakel (2001) noted the importance of basing validity studies on criteria predicted for specific groups. Therefore, scores on the big five might correlate one way for one group and the opposite way for another, or have no correlation for another.

Epps (1969) noted just this situation for internal and external control measures. He found that Blacks who scored low on external control got better grades than those who got higher scores, while the opposite was true for Whites according to the logic of the scales. Pfeifer and Sedlacek (1974) found that Blacks who had atypical career interests compared to Whites, and who felt the university cared about them, got higher grades than those who felt otherwise. Whites with the highest grades tended to select more traditional careers, while their feelings about whether the university cared about them was not related to their grades. However, against a retention criterion these results may differ. Therefore studies of the big five as they relate to success measures for different groups might prove fruitful.

The Future

A great many challenges lie ahead for those of us interested in improving diversity in all aspects of higher education. We must find better ways to admit and fund students than we have done so far. We must do a better job of teaching and delivering services to students whose demography and needs have changed and will continue to change. While implementing these changes, we must find better methods of evaluating our progress. Noncognitive variables can help with all of these issues. If noncognitive variables are widely employed in colleges and universities, they could make a significant positive difference in how we provide higher education in the United States.

APPENDICES

APPENDIX 1

Examples of the Situational Attitude Scale

Prejudice Against Blacks Version*

Situational Attitude Scale

This questionnaire measures how people think and feel about a number of social and personal incidents and situations. It is not a test, so there are no right or wrong answers. The questionnaire is anonymous, so PLEASE DO NOT SIGN YOUR NAME.

Each item or situation is followed by ten descriptive word scales. Your task is to select, for each descriptive scale, the rating that best describes *your* feelings toward the item.

Sample item:

Going out on a date.

happy o o o o o sad

You indicate the direction and extent of your feelings (for example, you might select the second bubble and indicate your choice on your response sheet by darkening in the appropriate space for that word scale). DO NOT MARK ON THE BOOKLET. PLEASE RESPOND TO ALL WORD SCALES.

---

*Form A is neutral, with no mention of the parenthetic stimulus words connected to *Black*.
Form B is identical to Form A but contains the parenthetic stimulus words connected to *Black* shown in **Bold.**

Sometimes you may feel as though you had the same item before on the questionnaire. This will not be the case, so DO NOT LOOK BACK AND FORTH through the items. Do not try to remember how you checked similar items earlier in the questionnaire. Make EACH ITEM A SEPARATE AND INDEPENDENT JUDGMENT. Respond as honestly as possible without puzzling over individual items. Respond with your first impression wherever possible.

I. A new **(Black)** family moves in next door to you.

good	o	o	o	o	o	bad
safe	o	o	o	o	o	unsafe
angry	o	o	o	o	o	not angry
friendly	o	o	o	o	o	unfriendly
sympathetic	o	o	o	o	o	not sympathetic
nervous	o	o	o	o	o	calm
happy	o	o	o	o	o	sad
objectionable	o	o	o	o	o	acceptable
desirable	o	o	o	o	o	undesirable
suspicious	o	o	o	o	o	trusting

II. You read in the paper that a **(Black)** man has raped a woman.

good	o	o	o	o	o	bad
safe	o	o	o	o	o	unsafe
angry	o	o	o	o	o	not angry
friendly	o	o	o	o	o	unfriendly
sympathetic	o	o	o	o	o	not sympathetic
nervous	o	o	o	o	o	calm
happy	o	o	o	o	o	sad
objectionable	o	o	o	o	o	acceptable
desirable	o	o	o	o	o	undesirable
suspicious	o	o	o	o	o	trusting

III. It is evening and a **(Black)** man appears at your door saying he is selling magazines.

relaxed	o	o	o	o	o	startled
receptive	o	o	o	o	o	cautious
excited	o	o	o	o	o	unexcited
glad	o	o	o	o	o	angered
pleased	o	o	o	o	o	annoyed
indifferent	o	o	o	o	o	suspicious

tolerable	o	o	o	o	o	intolerable
afraid	o	o	o	o	o	secure
friend	o	o	o	o	o	enemy
unprotected	o	o	o	o	o	protected

IV. You are walking down the street alone and must pass a corner where a group of five young **(Black)** men are loitering.

relaxed	o	o	o	o	o	tense
pleased	o	o	o	o	o	angered
superior	o	o	o	o	o	inferior
smarter	o	o	o	o	o	dumber
whiter	o	o	o	o	o	blacker
aggressive	o	o	o	o	o	passive
safe	o	o	o	o	o	unsafe
friendly	o	o	o	o	o	unfriendly
excited	o	o	o	o	o	unexcited
trivial	o	o	o	o	o	important

V. Your best friend has just become engaged **(to a Black person)**.

aggressive	o	o	o	o	o	passive
happy	o	o	o	o	o	sad
tolerable	o	o	o	o	o	intolerable
complimented	o	o	o	o	o	insulted
angered	o	o	o	o	o	overjoyed
secure	o	o	o	o	o	fearful
hopeful	o	o	o	o	o	hopeless
excited	o	o	o	o	o	unexcited
right	o	o	o	o	o	wrong
disgusting	o	o	o	o	o	pleasing

VI. You are stopped for speeding by a **(Black)** policeman.

calm	o	o	o	o	o	nervous
trusting	o	o	o	o	o	suspicious
afraid	o	o	o	o	o	safe
friendly	o	o	o	o	o	unfriendly
tolerant	o	o	o	o	o	intolerant
bitter	o	o	o	o	o	pleasant
cooperative	o	o	o	o	o	uncooperative

VI. You are stopped for speeding by a **(Black)** policeman, *continued.*

acceptive	o	o	o	o	o	belligerent
inferior	o	o	o	o	o	superior
smarter	o	o	o	o	o	dumber

VII. A new **(Black)** person joins your social group.

warm	o	o	o	o	o	cold
sad	o	o	o	o	o	happy
superior	o	o	o	o	o	inferior
threatened	o	o	o	o	o	neutral
pleased	o	o	o	o	o	displeased
understanding	o	o	o	o	o	indifferent
suspicious	o	o	o	o	o	trusting
disappointed	o	o	o	o	o	elated
favorable	o	o	o	o	o	unfavorable
uncomfortable	o	o	o	o	o	comfortable

VIII. You see a **(Black)** youngster steal something in a dimestore.

surprising	o	o	o	o	o	not surprising
sad	o	o	o	o	o	happy
disinterested	o	o	o	o	o	interested
close	o	o	o	o	o	distant
understandable	o	o	o	o	o	baffling
responsible	o	o	o	o	o	not responsible
concerned	o	o	o	o	o	unconcerned
sympathy	o	o	o	o	o	indifference
expected	o	o	o	o	o	unexpected
hopeful	o	o	o	o	o	hopeless

IX. Some **(Black)** students on campus stage a demonstration.

bad	o	o	o	o	o	good
understanding	o	o	o	o	o	indifferent
suspicious	o	o	o	o	o	trusting
safe	o	o	o	o	o	unsafe
disturbed	o	o	o	o	o	undisturbed
justified	o	o	o	o	o	unjustified
tense	o	o	o	o	o	calm

hate						love
wrong	o	o	o	o	o	right
humorous	o	o	o	o	o	serious

X. You get on a bus **(with all Black people on board)** and you are the only person who has to stand.

fearful	o	o	o	o	o	secure
tolerable	o	o	o	o	o	intolerable
hostile	o	o	o	o	o	indifferent
important	o	o	o	o	o	trivial
conspicuous	o	o	o	o	o	inconspicuous
calm	o	o	o	o	o	anxious
indignant	o	o	o	o	o	understanding
comfortable	o	o	o	o	o	uncomfortable
hate	o	o	o	o	o	love
not resentful	o	o	o	o	o	resentful

Prejudice Toward Arabs Measure**

Situational Attitude Scale

This questionnaire measures how people think and feel about a number of social and personal incidents and situations. It is not a test, so there are no right or wrong answers. The questionnaire is anonymous, so please DO NOT SIGN YOUR NAME.

Each item or situation is followed by ten descriptive word scales. Your task is to select, for each descriptive scale, the rating that best describes YOUR feelings toward the item.

Sample item:

Going out on a date.

happy	o	o	o	o	o	sad

You indicate the direction and extent of your feelings (for example, you might select the second bubble and indicate your choice on your response sheet by darkening the appropriate space for that word scale). DO NOT MARK ON THE BOOKLET. PLEASE RESPOND TO ALL WORD SCALES.

** Form A is neutral with no mention of the parenthetic stimulus words connected to *Arab*.
Form B is identical to Form A but contains the parenthetic stimulus words connected to *Arab* shown in **Bold.**

Sometimes you may feel as though you had the same item before on the questionnaire. This will not be the case, so DO NOT LOOK BACK AND FORTH through the items. Do not try to remember how you checked similar items earlier in the questionnaire. Make EACH ITEM A SEPARATE AND INDEPENDENT JUDGMENT. Respond as honestly as possible without puzzling over individual items. Respond with your first impression wherever possible.

I. You are standing on a very crowded bus surrounded by many **(Arab)** people.

fearful	o	o	o	o	o	secure
tolerable	o	o	o	o	o	intolerable
hostile	o	o	o	o	o	indifferent
important	o	o	o	o	o	trivial
conspicuous	o	o	o	o	o	inconspicuous
calm	o	o	o	o	o	anxious
indignant	o	o	o	o	o	understanding
comfortable	o	o	o	o	o	uncomfortable
hate	o	o	o	o	o	love
not resentful	o	o	o	o	o	resentful

II. You are going on vacation with your best friend and his or her **(Arab)** friend of the opposite sex.

aggressive	o	o	o	o	o	passive
happy	o	o	o	o	o	sad
tolerable	o	o	o	o	o	intolerable
complimented	o	o	o	o	o	insulted
angered	o	o	o	o	o	overjoyed
secure	o	o	o	o	o	fearful
hopeful	o	o	o	o	o	hopeless
excited	o	o	o	o	o	unexcited
right	o	o	o	o	o	wrong
disgusting	o	o	o	o	o	pleasing

III. You are boarding a plane for vacation in Florida, and two young **(Arab)** men are boarding immediately behind you.

calm	o	o	o	o	o	fear
bad	o	o	o	o	o	good
safe	o	o	o	o	o	unsafe
happy	o	o	o	o	o	sad

tense	o	o	o	o	o	relaxed
fair	o	o	o	o	o	unfair
love	o	o	o	o	o	hate
trivial	o	o	o	o	o	important
suspicious	o	o	o	o	o	trusting
angry	o	o	o	o	o	not angry

IV. You are buying a used car from a **(an Arab)** salesman.

trust	o	o	o	o	o	mistrust
tense	o	o	o	o	o	relaxed
fair	o	o	o	o	o	unfair
bad	o	o	o	o	o	good
happy	o	o	o	o	o	sad
comfortable	o	o	o	o	o	uncomfortable
clean	o	o	o	o	o	dirty
angry	o	o	o	o	o	not angry
appropriate	o	o	o	o	o	inappropriate
surprised	o	o	o	o	o	not surprised

V. You are watching a television news program about divorced **(Arab)** fathers being given custody of their children.

empathy	o	o	o	o	o	empathy
happy	o	o	o	o	o	sad
fear	o	o	o	o	o	calm
trivial	o	o	o	o	o	important
logical	o	o	o	o	o	illogical
comfortable	o	o	o	o	o	uncomfortable
love	o	o	o	o	o	hate
shocked	o	o	o	o	o	expected
safe	o	o	o	o	o	unsafe
good	o	o	o	o	o	bad

VI. You are required to attend a **(an Islamic)** religious service for a school project.

fear	o	o	o	o	o	calm
strange	o	o	o	o	o	natural
sad	o	o	o	o	o	happy
good	o	o	o	o	o	bad

VI. You are required to attend a **(an Islamic)** religious service for a school project, *continued.*

interesting	o	o	o	o	o	uninteresting
logical	o	o	o	o	o	illogical
suspicious	o	o	o	o	o	not suspicious
bizarre	o	o	o	o	o	normal
reasonable	o	o	o	o	o	unreasonable
love	o	o	o	o	o	hate

VII. You notice a **(an Arab)** student cheating on an exam.

expected	o	o	o	o	o	unexpected
disgusting	o	o	o	o	o	not disgusting
fair	o	o	o	o	o	unfair
calm	o	o	o	o	o	fear
negative	o	o	o	o	o	positive
happy	o	o	o	o	o	sad
angry	o	o	o	o	o	not angry
normal	o	o	o	o	o	not normal
hope	o	o	o	o	o	hopeless
shocked	o	o	o	o	o	not shocked

VIII. You see a group of **(Arab)** students staging an on-campus demonstration about discrimination.

bad	o	o	o	o	o	good
understanding	o	o	o	o	o	indifferent
suspicious	o	o	o	o	o	trusting
safe	o	o	o	o	o	unsafe
disturbed	o	o	o	o	o	undisturbed
justified	o	o	o	o	o	unjustified
tense	o	o	o	o	o	calm
hate	o	o	o	o	o	love
wrong	o	o	o	o	o	right
humorous	o	o	o	o	o	serious

IX. You hear of a **(an Arab)** student getting financial aid.

surprise	o	o	o	o	o	no surprise
fair	o	o	o	o	o	unfair
reasonable	o	o	o	o	o	unreasonable
good	o	o	o	o	o	bad

sad	o	o	o	o	o	happy
angry	o	o	o	o	o	calm
not shocked	o	o	o	o	o	shocked
unexpected	o	o	o	o	o	expected
positive	o	o	o	o	o	negative
serious	o	o	o	o	o	not serious

X. A new **(Arab)** person joins your social group.

warm	o	o	o	o	o	cold
sad	o	o	o	o	o	happy
superior	o	o	o	o	o	inferior
threatened	o	o	o	o	o	neutral
pleased	o	o	o	o	o	displeased
understanding	o	o	o	o	o	indifferent
suspicious	o	o	o	o	o	trusting
disappointed	o	o	o	o	o	elated
favorable	o	o	o	o	o	unfavorable
uncomfortable	o	o	o	o	o	comfortable

APPENDIX 2

Basic Noncognitive Questionnaire with Scoring and Administration Information

Administration

The Noncognitive Questionnaire (NCQ) can be administered individually, in large groups, or online. In either case, it requires very little effort on the part of the administrator. Brief instructions should be given to respondents along the order of:

> You're being asked to complete a brief questionnaire which is mostly about your thoughts and feelings. In addition, some demographic information is requested. There are no right or wrong answers, so try to answer as honestly as you can. It is also important that you not skip items; please attempt all of them. All information you provide will be kept confidential.

At this point, respondents can be left to complete the questionnaire, which typically takes about twenty minutes. The instructions can be adapted as the setting and purpose of administration require (for example, if administration is part of a research project, participants will require additional information as to the purpose of the study, and so on).

Scoring

Scoring the NCQ is a relatively easy procedure; it can be done by hand or computer. The only labor-intensive component is the coding of three open-ended items, which must be done by hand. However, once interrater reliability is established, this process moves quickly as well.

Scoring Open-Ended Items

There are three NCQ items that are open-ended; students write in their own responses as opposed to choosing an option already listed on the questionnaire. Raters must make a decision as to the category in which the response best fits. Given that the three open-ended items must be coded prior to scoring the rest of the instrument, those instructions are given first. The three open-ended items are numbers 8, 10, and 29, and the coding criteria for each are found below.

Establishing Interrater Reliability

When a large number of NCQs need to be scored and more than one rater is coding open-ended items, interrater reliability must be established to ensure that all raters are using the coding system in the same way. To establish acceptable interrater reliability, raters should initially be trained on one set of instruments, usually at least twenty; fifty is better. Their ratings must then be compared and correlation coefficients computed. Acceptable interrater reliability can be said to be established when correlation coefficients reach .80. After acceptable interrater reliability has been established, periodic rating checks should be conducted (every fiftieth protocol, for example) to ensure that raters continue to agree on assigned codes.

Scoring Objective Items and Computing Subscales

Once interrater reliability has been established and the open-ended items coded, the objective items should be scored and subscale scores computed. This can be done either by hand or by computer. One advantage to the computer approach (aside from saving time in scoring a large number of questionnaires) is that scores can be analyzed easily in a variety of ways.

Noncognitive Questionnaire

Please fill in the blank or circle the appropriate answers.

1. Your social security number: ______________________________

2. Your sex is: ______________ 1. Male 2. Female

3. Your age is: ____________ years

4. Your father's occupation: ____

5. Your mother's occupation: ____

6. Your race is:
   1. Black (African American)
   2. White (not of Hispanic origin)
   3. Asian American (Pacific Islander)
   4. Hispanic (Latino)
   5. American Indian (Native American, Alaskan native)
   6. Other

7. How much education do you expect to get during your lifetime?
   1. College, but less than a bachelor's degree
   2. B.A. or equivalent
   3. One or two years of graduate or professional study (master's degree)
   4. Doctoral degree such as M.D., Ph.D., and so on

8. Please list three goals that you have for yourself right now:

   1. ____

   2. ____

   3. ____

9. About 50 percent of university students typically leave before receiving a degree. If this should happen to you, what will be the most likely cause?
   1. Absolutely certain that I will obtain a degree
   2. To accept a good job
   3. To enter military service
   4. It will cost more than my family can afford
   5. Marriage
   6. Disinterest in study
   7. Lack of academic ability
   8. Insufficient reading or study skills
   9. Other

10. Please list three things that you are proud of having done:

   1. ____

   2. ____

   3. ____

Please indicate the extent to which you agree or disagree with each of the following items. Respond to the statements below with your feelings at present or your expectation of how things will be. Write in your answer to the left of each item.

1	2	3	4	5
Strongly agree	**Agree**	**Neutral**	**Disagree**	**Strongly disagree**

_______ 11. The university should use its influence to improve social conditions in the state.

_______ 12. It should **not** be very hard to get a B (3.0) average at this school.

_______ 13. I get easily discouraged when I try to do something and it doesn't work.

_______ 14. I am sometimes looked up to by others.

_______ 15. If I run into problems concerning school, I have someone who would listen to me and help me.

_______ 16. There is no use in doing things for people; you only find that you get it in the neck in the long run.

_______ 17. In groups where I am comfortable, I am often looked to as leader.

_______ 18. I expect to have a harder time than most students at this school.

_______ 19. Once I start something, I finish it.

_______ 20. When I believe strongly in something, I act on it.

_______ 21. I am as skilled academically as the average applicant to this school.

_______ 22. I expect I will encounter racism at this school.

_______ 23. People can pretty easily change me even though I thought my mind was already made up on the subject.

_______ 24. My friends and relatives **don't** feel I should go to college.

_______ 25. My family has always wanted me to go to college.

_______ 26. If course tutoring is made available on campus at no cost, I would attend regularly.

_______ 27. I want a chance to prove myself academically.

_______ 28. My high school grades **don't** really reflect what I can do.

_______ 29. Please list offices held and/or groups belonged to in high school or in your community.

____

____

____

Scoring Key for Noncognitive Questionnaire

Questionnaire Item	*Variable Name (Number)*
7	Use to score for *Self-Concept* (I) Option 1 = 1; 2 = 2; 3 = 3; 4 = 4; no response = 2
8	A. *Options for Long Range Goals* (IV) Each goal is coded according to this scheme: 1 = a vague and/or immediate, short-term goal (for example, "to meet people," "to get a good schedule," "to gain self confidence") 2 = a specific goal with a stated future orientation that could be accomplished during undergraduate study (for example, "to join a sorority so I can meet more people," "to get a good schedule so I can get good grades in the fall," "to run for a student government office") 3 = a specific goal with a stated future orientation that would occur after undergraduate study (for example, "to get a good schedule so I can get the classes I need for graduate school," "to become president of a Fortune 500 company") B. *Options for Knowledge Acquired in a Field* (VIII) Each goal is coded according to this scheme: 1 = not at all academic or school-related; vague or unclear (for example, "to get married," "to do better," "to become a better person") 2 = school related, but not necessarily or primarily education-oriented (for example, "to join a fraternity," "to become student body president") 3 = directly related to education (for example, "to get a 3.5 GPA," "to get to know my teachers") Find the mean for each dimension (for example, *long-range goals)* and round to the nearest whole number.
9	Use to score for *Self-Concept* (I) and *Self-Appraisal* (II) Option 1 = 4; 2 through 9 = 2; no response = 2

Questionnaire Item	*Variable Name (Number)*
10	Use to score *for Self=Concept* (I) Each accomplishment is coded according to this scheme: 1 = at least 75 percent of applicants to your school could have accomplished it (for example, "graduated from high school," "held a part-time summer job") 2 = at least 50 percent of applicants to your school could have accomplished it (for example, "played on an intramural sports team," "was a member of a school club") 3 = only the top 25 percent of applicants to your school could have accomplished it (for example, "won an academic award," "was captain of football team") Find the mean code for this dimension and round to the nearest whole number.

For items 11 through 29, positive (+) items are scored as they are. Negative (–) items are reversed, so that 1 = 5, 2 = 4, 3 = 3, 4 = 2, and 5 = 1. A shortcut is to subtract all negative item responses from 6.

Questionnaire Items	*Direction*	*Variable Name (Number)*
11	–	Use to score for *Racism* (III)
12	–	Use to score for *Realistic self-appraisal* (II)
13	+	Use to score for *Long-range goals* (IV)
14	–	Use to score for *Leadership* (VI)
15	–	Use to score for *Availability of strong support* (V)
16	+	Use to score *for Community service* (VII)
17	–	Use to score for *Leadership* (VI)
18	+	Use to score for *Racism* (III)
19	–	Use to score for *Long-range goals* (IV)
20	–	Use to score for *Positive self-concept* (I)
21	–	Use to score for *Realistic self-appraisal* (II)
22	–	Use to score for *Racism* (III)
23	+	Use to score for *Positive self-concept* (I)

Questionnaire Items	*Direction*	*Variable Name (Number)*
24	+	Use to score for *Availability of strong support* (V)
25	–	Use to score for *Availability of strong support* (V)
26	–	Use to score for *Racism* (III)
27	–	Use to score for *Racism* (III)
28	–	Use to score for *Positive self-concept* (I)
29		Use to score for *Leadership* (VI), *Community service* (VII) and *Knowledge acquired in a field* (VIII). Each organization is given a code for A, B, and C below. Find the mean for each dimension (for example, *Leadership)* and round to the nearest whole number.

A. Leadership (VI)

1 = ambiguous group or no clear reference to activity performed (for example, "helped in school")

2 = membership but no formal or implied leadership role; it has to be clear that it's a functioning group and, unless the criteria are met for a score of 3 as described below, all groups should be coded as 2 even if you, as the rater, are not familiar with the group (for example, "Fashionettes," "was part of a group that worked on community service projects through my church")

3 = leadership was required to fulfill role in group (for example, officer or implied initiator, organizer, or founder) or entrance into the group was dependent upon prior leadership (for example, "organized a tutoring group for underprivileged children in my community," "student council")

B. Community service relatedness (VII)

1 = no community service performed by group, or vague or unclear in relation to community service (for example, "basketball team)

2 = some community service involved, but it is not the primary purpose of the group (for example, "Scouts")

3 = group's main purpose is community service (for example, "Big Brothers/Big Sisters")

C. Knowledge acquired in a field (VIII) same coding criteria as used for item 8B

Noncognitive Questionnaire

Worksheet for Scoring

1. Positive self-concept or confidence

   item 7* + item 9* + item 10* + (6 – item 20) + item 23 + (6 – item 28)

2. Realistic self-appraisal

   item 9* + (6 – item 12) + (6 – item 21)

3. Understands and deals with racism

   (6 – item 11) + item 18 + (6 – item 22) + (6 – item 26) + (6 – item 27)

4. Prefers long-range goals to short-term or immediate needs

   item 8A* + item 13 + (6 – item 19)

5. Availability of a strong support person

   (6 – item 15) + item 24 + (6 – item 25)

6. Successful leadership experience

   (6 – item 14) + (6 – item 17) + item 29A*

7. Demonstrated community service

   item 16 + item 29B*

8. Knowledge acquired in a field

   item 8B* + item 29C*

---

* Recoded item. See scoring instructions for these items above.

APPENDIX 3

Norms Using Noncognitive Questionnaire Scoring Key

Raw Score	Factor 1 (Self-Concept)	Factor 2 (Realistic Self-Appraisal)	Factor 3 (Under-stands Racism)	Factor 4 (Long-Range Goals)	Factor 5 (Support Person)	Factor 6 (Leader-ship)	Factor 7 (Community Service)	Factor 8 (Knowledge Acquired)
2							17	38
3				13		16	26	49
4		19		19	−7	22	36	59
5		24		25	−1	28	45	70
6		30		31	5	35	54	81
7		36		37	11	41	63	
8	9	42	4	43	17	47	72	
9	13	48	9	49	24	54		
10	17	54	14	55	30	60		
11	21	60	19	61	36	66		
12	25	66	24	67	42	73		
13	29	72	28	73	48	79		
14	33	78	33		54			
15	37		38		61			
16	41		43					
17	45		48					
18	49		53					
19	53		58					
20	57		63					
21	61		68					
22	65		72					
23	69		77					
24	73		82					
25	77		87					
26	81							

Notes: Whites (N = 2,144); see Tracey and Sedlacek (1984, 1985).

T score** equivalents; T scores have a mean of 50 and a standard deviation of 10. Enter the table with a raw score and determine the T score equivalent, or vice-versa.

TABLE A.2. NCQ FACTOR NORMS FOR BLACKS, USING SCORING KEY.

Raw Score	Factor 1 (Self-Concept)	Factor 2 (Realistic Self-Appraisal)	Factor 3 (Understands Racism)	Factor 4 (Long-Range Goals)	Factor 5 (Support Person)	Factor 6 (Leadership)	Factor 7 (Community Service)	Factor 8 (Knowledge Acquired)
2							19	37
3				12		18	28	48
4		19		18		24	37	59
5		25		23	3	30	45	70
6		31		29	8	36	54	80
7		37		35	14	42	62	
8	4	43		41	20	48	71	
9	8	49	4	47	25	53		
10	12	54	8	52	31	59		
11	17	60	13	58	36	65		
12	21	66	18	64	42	71		
13	25	72	22	70	47	77		
14	29	78	27		53			
15	33		31		59			
16	37		36					
17	41		41					
18	45		45					
19	49		50					
20	53		54					
21	57		59					
22	61		63					
23	65		68					
24	70		73					
25	74		77					
26	78							

Notes: Blacks (N = 442); see Tracey and Sedlacek (1984, 1985).

T score equivalents; T scores have a mean of 50 and a standard deviation of 10. Enter the table with a raw score and determine the T score equivalent, or vice-versa.

TABLE A.3. NCQ SCALE MEANS AND STANDARD DEVIATIONS FOR SELECTED SAMPLES

	Community College (N = 1,435), 90% White, 10% Students of Color; Mostly Latino and Native American, 55% over 25, 80% First-Generation College Students, 65% Female, Open Admissions		Large State University (N = 5,642), 75% White, 10% African American, 8% Asian American, 5% International, 55% Female, Minimally Selective		Small Private College (N = 263), 92% White, 66% Female, 4% International, Moderately Selective		Veterinary College (N = 591), 95% White, 42% Female, Very Selective		Special Undergraduate Program at Medium-Sized University (N = 91), 90% African American, 50% White, 60% Female, for Students with Low GPA and Test Scores		Historically Black College (N = 212), 70% African American, 10% White, 12% International, 63% Female, Moderately Selective		Small Nonreligious Private College (N = 375), 74% White, 5% Latino, 5% African American, 5% International, 4% Native American, 61% Female, Selective	
NCQ Scale	**Mean**	**SD**	**Mean**	**SD**	**Mean**	**SD**	**Mean**	**SD**	**Mean**	**SD**	**Mean**	**SD**	**Mean**	**SD**
Self-concept	17.40	1.99	16.80	1.72	18.33	2.23	20.01	1.88	14.13	2.61	19.71	2.13	19.07	2.37
Self-appraisal	9.53	1.74	9.40	1.53	10.16	2.01	9.77	1.79	8.61	3.22	11.22	2.31	10.71	2.41
Racism	17.83	2.69	18.01	2.33	15.47	3.10	16.66	3.65	14.60	3.11	18.86	3.17	16.88	3.11
Goals	9.45	1.52	9.34	1.33	10.71	2.26	11.01	2.33	8.31	1.73	10.13	1.76	11.21	1.19
Support person	12.80	1.91	13.23	1.54	14.05	2.27	13.44	2.07	11.67	2.00	13.88	1.79	13.74	2.03
Leadership	8.84	1.76	8.21	1.45	9.17	3.12	8.61	2.73	7.15	3.37	9.11	2.34	10.37	2.22
Community	5.06	1.34	6.17	1.18	6.03	2.36	7.13	1.89	7.32	1.66	7.65	1.66	5.99	2.71
Knowledge	2.91	.74	2.75	.66	3.12	1.34	4.03	.71	4.62	1.81	3.17	.89	3.87	1.84

Note: NCQ scored by instructions in Appendix 4.1

APPENDIX 4

Two Alternate Forms of the Noncognitive Questionnaire and Scoring Instructions

Alternate Form A: Noncognitive Questionnaire

Please fill in the blank or circle the appropriate answers.

1. Your social security number: ______________________________

2. Your sex is: ________________ 1. Male 2. Female

3. Your race is:
   1. Black (African American, Negro)
   2. White (not of Hispanic origin)
   3. Asian American, Asian-American, Pacific Islander
   4. Hispanic (Latino, Chicano)
   5. American Indian or Alaskan native

4. How much education do you expect to get during your lifetime?
   1. College, but less than a bachelor's degree
   2. B.A. or equivalent
   3. One or two years of graduate or professional study (master's degree)
   4. Doctoral degree such as M.D., Ph.D.

5. About 50 percent of college students typically leave before finishing a program. If this should happen to you, what will be the most likely cause?
   1. Absolutely certain that I will finish
   2. To accept a good job
   3. To enter military service
   4. It would cost more than my family or I could afford
   5. Marriage
   6. Disinterest in study
   7. Lack of academic ability
   8. Insufficient reading or study skills
   9. Other

6. Please list three goals that you have for yourself right now:
   1. ____________________
   2. ____________________
   3. ____________________

7. Please list three things that you are proud of having done:
   1. ____________________
   2. ____________________
   3. ____________________

8. Please list groups belonged to (formal or informal) and offices held (if any) in your high school or community.

   ____

   ____

   ____

Please indicate the extent to which you agree with each of the following items. Respond to the statements below with your feelings at present or your expectation of how things will be. Write in your answer to the left of each item.

1	2	3	4	5
Strongly agree	**Agree**	**Neutral**	**Disagree**	**Strongly disagree**

_______ 9. I was a leader in high school.

_______ 10. The college/university should use its influence to improve social conditions in the state.

_______ 11. It should **not** be very hard to a get a B (3.0) average here.

_______ 12. I get easily discouraged when I try to do something and it doesn't work.

_______ 13. If I run into problems concerning school, I have someone who will listen to me and help me.

_______ 14. In groups where I am comfortable, I am often looked to as a leader.

_______ 15. When I believe strongly in something, I act on it.

_______ 16. My family has always wanted me to go to college.

_______ 17. If course tutoring is made available on campus at no cost, I will attend regularly.

_______ 18. My high school grades *don't* really reflect what I can do.

_______ 19. I find I get more comfortable in a new place as soon as I make some good friends.

_______ 20. My friends are exclusively the same race as I am.

_______ 21. If I encounter racism, I believe it is up to me to always point it out and correct it.

_______ 22. I have a good understanding of my strengths and weaknesses.

_______ 23. When I am treated unfairly, I express my anger in no uncertain terms.

_______ 24. I know the areas where I am weak, and I try to improve them.

_______ 25. Contact with faculty is important to academic success.

_______ 26. I usually come up with the ideas that my friends end up doing.

_______ 27. I have learned more outside of school than in school.

_______ 28. I have talked about my career goal with someone who works in that career.

_______ 29. I expect to find lots of people who are like me here.

_______ 30. I am sometimes looked up to by others.

_______ 31. I know what I want to be doing ten years from now.

_______ 32. I will learn all I need to know about my major field in my courses here.

_______ 33. I enjoy going along with what a group likes to do.

_______ 34. I expect to be involved in many off-campus activities while enrolled here.

_______ 35. I **don't** expect to get to know faculty personally during my first year.

_______ 36. I know how the system works.

_______ 37. I have learned more out of school than in school.

Noncognitive Questionnaire A: Worksheet for Scoring

1. Positive self-concept or confidence
   item 4* + item 5* + (6 – item 10) + (6 – item 15) + (6 – item 18)
2. Realistic self-appraisal
   item 5* + (6 – item 11) + (6 – item 22) + (6 – item 24)
3. Understands and deals with racism
   (6 – item 10) + (6 – item 17) + item 20 + item 23 + (6 – item 36)
4. Prefers long-range goals to short-term or immediate needs
   item 6A* + item 12 + (6 – item 28) + (6 – item 31)
5. Availability of a strong support person
   (6 – item 13) + (6 – item 16) + (6 – item 25) + item 35
6. Successful leadership experience
   item 8A* + (6 – item 14) + (6 – item 17)
7. Demonstrated community service
   item 8B* + (6 – item 19) + (6 – item 24) + (6 – item 29)
8. Knowledge acquired in a field
   item 6B* + item 8C* + (6 – item 27) + (item 32)

---

* Recoded item. See scoring instructions above for equivalent items from the basic NCQ. There are no norms available for NCQ Form A.

Alternate Form B: Noncognitive Questionnaire

Please fill in the blanks or circle the appropriate answer.

1. Your social security number: ______________________
2. Your sex is: ___________ 1. Male 2. Female
3. Your race ________
   1. Black (African American)
   2. White (not of Hispanic origin)
   3. Asian American (Pacific Islander)
   4. Hispanic (Latino)
   5. American Indian (Native American or Alaskan native)

4. How much education do you expect to get during your lifetime?
   1. Associate's degree
   2. College, but less than a bachelor's degree
   3. B.A. or equivalent
   4. One or two years of graduate or professional study (master's degree)
   5. Doctoral degree such as M.D., Ph.D.

5. About 50 percent of college students typically leave before finishing a program. If this should happen to you, what will be the most likely cause?
   1. Absolutely certain that I will finish
   2. To accept a good job
   3. To enter military service
   4. It would cost more than my family or I could afford
   5. Marriage
   6. Disinterest in study
   7. Lack of academic ability
   8. Insufficient reading or study skills
   9. Other

6. Please list three goals that you have for yourself right now:
   1. ______________________________
   2. ______________________________
   3. ______________________________

7. Please list three things that you are proud of having done:
   1. ______________________________
   2. ______________________________
   3. ______________________________

8. Please list groups belonged to (formal or informal) and offices held (if any) in your high school or community.

   ____

   ____

   ____

Please indicate the extent to which you agree with each of the following items. Respond to the statements below with your feelings at present or your expectation of how things will be. Write in your answer to the left of each item.

1	2	3	4	5
Strongly agree	**Agree**	**Neutral**	**Disagree**	**Strongly disagree**

_______ 9. I am sometimes looked up to by others.

_______ 10. There is no use in doing things for people; you only find that you get it in the neck in the long run.

_______ 11. I expect to have a harder time than most students here.

_______ 12. Once I start something, I finish it.

_______ 13. I am as skilled academically as the average applicant here.

_______ 14. I expect I will encounter racism at this school.

_______ 15. People can pretty easily change me even though I thought my mind was already made up on the subject.

_______ 16. My friends and relatives **don't** feel I should go to college.

_______ 17. I want a chance to prove myself academically.

_______ 18. I enjoy working with others.

_______ 19. My background should help me fit in well here.

_______ 20. My friends look at me to make decisions.

_______ 21. I expect the faculty to treat me differently from the average student here.

_______ 22. I am uncomfortable interacting with people from other races or cultures.

_______ 23. I try to find opportunities to learn new things.

_______ 24. I think many people see racism where it doesn't exist.

_______ 25. I expect to get picked on by other students and faculty because of my background.

_______ 26. Everyone must work toward improving social conditions.

_______ 27. I often make lists of things to do.

_______ 28. I keep pretty much to myself.

_______ 29. I sometimes need help from others.

_______ 30. I prefer to be spontaneous rather than to make plans.

_______ 31. I have done work in many community projects.

_______ 32. I have already learned something in my proposed major field outside of high school.

_______ 33. I am **not** good at getting others to go along with me.

_______ 34. It is more important to study than to get involved in campus activities.

_______ 35. I usually note important dates on my calendar.

_______ 36. The best way to avoid problems is to take things one day at a time.

_______ 37. I have studied things about my major field on my own.

_______ 38. I expect to have little contact with students from other races.

_______ 39. I enjoy being a student.

Noncognitive Questionnaire B: Worksheet for Scoring

1. Positive self-concept or confidence
   item 4 + item 7* + item 10 + (6 – item 39)
2. Realistic self-appraisal
   item 4 + item 11 + (6 – item 13)
3. Understands and deals with racism
   (6 – item 14) + (6 – item 17) + item 22 + item 24 + item 25 + (6 – item 26) + item 34 + item 38
4. Prefers long-range goals to short-term or immediate needs
   item 6A* + (6 – item 12) + (6 – item 27) + item 30 + (6 – item 35) + item 36
5. Availability of a strong support person
   item 16 + item 21 + (6 – item 29)
6. Successful leadership experience
   item 8A* + (6 – item 9) + (6 – item 20) + item 33
7. Demonstrated community service
   item 8B* + (6 – item 18) + item 28 + (6 – item 31)
8. Knowledge acquired in a field
   item 6B* + item 8C* + (6 – item 23) + (6 – item 32) + (6 – item 37)

---

* Recoded item. See scoring instructions for equivalent items from the basic NCQ. There are no norms available for NCQ Form B.

APPENDIX 5

Short Answer Noncognitive Assessment Form

1. List the subjects with which you had trouble in high school or previous college work.
   High school:
   College:
2. Why do you feel you did not do well in those subjects? Has anything changed that might cause you to do better in those subjects in the future?
3. Why do you feel you will do well at this college or university?
4. Discuss your positive and negative attributes. How did you deal with them before?
5. Describe a situation where things were working against you and you really handled them well and made them work for you.
6. Describe a situation where things were working against you and you did not handle them well.
7. Compare how you handled the situations in questions 5 and 6 above. What did you learn from the experiences?
8. Discuss your short-term goals.
9. Discuss your long-term goals.
10. Discuss the relationship between questions 8 and 9 above.
11. Describe a time when you were having trouble in school. Where did you go for help?

12. Describe a time when you were having trouble with a personal problem. Where did you go for help?
13. Discuss a situation where you have shown leadership in school.
14. Discuss a situation where you have shown leadership outside of school.
15. Describe at least two examples of your involvement in an organizational or community activity.
16. Describe a situation where you have learned something outside of school.

APPENDIX 6

Principles of Interviewing for Noncognitive Variable Diagnosis*

1. *Establish conditions conducive to good interviews.*

   The school atmosphere should reflect an orientation toward the individual, a flexible curriculum and instructional methods, and general use of grades and data in ways that encourage students to seek personal help.

2. *Assemble and relate to the problem all the facts available.*
   Ideally, a cumulative personnel record should be accessible to student service workers.

3. *Meet the interviewee cordially.*
   The friendly spirit needs to be natural, not condescending or patronizing, and in harmony with the interviewer's personality.

4. *Begin the interview with a topic that is secondary but of interest to the interviewer, and of potential interest to the interviewee.*
   Before the main issue is approached, rapport may be built by encouraging a short period during which the interviewer and interviewee can discuss an issue that is of common interest to them.

5. *Approach the problem as soon as rapport is assumed.*
   Ask the student for a statement of the problem as he or she sees it.

---

* The twenty-one principles of interviewing are from Bingham and Moore (1959).

6. *Uncover the real difficulties.*
   Listen to the obvious problems, but watch for clues pointing to the real problems often existing behind them.

7. *Isolate the central problem by asking interviewees questions that direct their attention to salient issues.*
   Give the student a chance to put several sets of facts together to reach new conclusions about his or her problems.

8. *Do not embarrass the interviewee unnecessarily.*
   To make it easy for the student to disclose essential material, do not pry into matters not related to the problem at hand.

9. *Face the facts professionally.*
   Do not betray, surprise, shock, or show emotional tension at disclosures.

10. *Observe the student's behavior closely.*
    As a natural manifestation of your interest while listening, you may give attention to the student's mannerisms and facial expressions (for instance, the student may be noticed giving poor eye contact).

11. *Avoid putting the student on the defensive.*
    In case of resistance, resulting particularly from a difference of opinion, yield as much as possible.

12. *Alleviate the shock of disillusionment.*
    Identifying the student's misinformation, error, or difficulty as similar to that of many other persons often helps to allay chagrin, shock, embarrassment, or new fear.

13. *Establish a reputation for being helpful and fair and for keeping confidences.*
    Personal information should be kept confidential—without exception.

14. *Give advice sparingly, if at all.*
    If your advice is requested, you may say you would rather not advise; but you can review the relevant circumstances and encourage the student to formulate his or her own conclusions.

15. *Give information as needed.*
    Unless you feel the student would be better served by being required to search out essential information for himself or herself, you may feel free to supply facts about educational or vocational opportunities or requirements.

16. *Make certain that all vital considerations relevant to a decision are brought forward.*
    If you expect to have subsequent interviews, you may need to develop a list of the many essential points to be reviewed.

17. *Present alternatives for the interviewee's consideration.*
Possible courses of action may be proposed, without the implication that you are trying to impose your own views.

18. *Make other services available to interviewees.*
Refer to librarians, professors, clinicians, and any other experts who can help the interviewee gain insight into his or her problems.

19. *Let the interviewees formulate their conclusions or plans of action.*
The interviewee's program of action must grow out of the individual's thinking.

20. *Achieve something definite.*
Do not let the interview close until recognizable progress has been made and agreement reached on at least the next step.

21. *Make subsequent interviews easy.*
Do not attempt to move too fast.

APPENDIX 7

Interview Questions Employed in Campus Site Visits (Lilly Endowment Evaluation)

1. What was the best thing about the program?
2. What was the worst thing about the program?
3. Was the program successful?
   A. Yes No
   B. How can you tell? What was your evidence?
4. What are the long- versus short-term effects?
5. What were the goals of the program?
   A. Information
   B. Attitudes
   C. Behavior
6. Are noncognitive variables relevant?
   A. Self-concept
   B. Realistic self-appraisal
   C. Handling racism
   D. Long-range goals
   E. Leadership
   F. Strong-support person
   G. Community involvement
   H. Nontraditional knowledge

7. Audience for program
   A. Students of color
   B. White students
   C. Faculty of color
   D. White faculty, or faculty in general
   E. Program participants only
   F. Those outside the program
   G. Staff
      1. Of color
      2. White
   H. Off campus
8. Advice for other schools?
9. If you had to do it over?
   A. Would do
   B. Would not do
10. If you had more money?
11. What will happen to the program after the grant term?
12. Were there spin-off programs
13. Who have you left out of the program?
14. How does the Lilly program relate to others you have?
15. How did the Lilly program change after you started?
16. Critical incident
   A. +
   B. –
17. What change at the institution would you directly attribute to the Lilly grant?
   A. Were there indirect changes?
18. What changes are there in the campus climate for diversity now?
   A. +
   B. –
19. Overall impression and anecdotes
20. A way of evaluating I might miss

APPENDIX 8

Example Cases for Training Raters in Evaluating Admissions or Financial Aid Applications

Possible Noncognitive Variable Scoring System

When scoring each of the noncognitive variables for each applicant, be sure to consider the complete application. Following is a description of a five-point system that can be used to assign scores.

Score	*Description*
1 (low score)	There is evidence that the applicant does not do well on the variable. Examples: Not sure of ability Plans to leave school before finishing Avoids seeking help from others Is a loner
2 (minimal evidence)	There is some slight positive evidence on the variable. Examples: Minimal involvement in a community Low-level leadership shown in a group Handles small examples of racism Has medium-range goals

3 (neutral or inconsistent evidence)	Contradictory or no information on the demonstration of success on the variable. This is the default option, if the evidence is unclear. Examples: Some good examples and some bad examples of external learning No information provided on goal setting Ambivalence on the value of a support person
4 (solid evidence)	Clear evidence of success on the variable is presented. Examples: Experience with a cultural or racial group Knowledge of a field that applicant has not formally studied in school Has a mentor Evaluates good and bad experiences
5 (outstanding evidence)	Evidence that is unusually well done or consistent over time on the variable. Examples: Goals that are interconnected in stages over time Leadership at many levels and situations over time Can articulate strengths and weaknesses and what can be done or has been done on them Noncognitive variables are well integrated; for example, long-term goals are tied to leadership, feelings about self, and extramural learning

Application One: Martin Hawk, Eighteen-Year-Old American Indian from the Northwest

1. Positive Self-Concept (Score = 5)

Evidence from the personal statement:

- Although Martin's classes are difficult, he is challenging himself, doing well, and understanding complex concepts.
- He told a teacher that he was determined to bring up his grade, so by the end of the semester Martin had earned a "B." He was proud of himself and felt he deserved the grade.
- Martin felt good about doing something for others, and this influenced his goals in life.
- Martin is persistent and believes he can accomplish any goal he sets for himself.

- Martin has the ability to interact and communicate with other ethnic groups.
- After running a lawn mowing business for four years, Martin is sure he wants to major in business and work in the tribal corporation.

Evidence from the recommendation letter:

- Martin is caring and has a confident demeanor.
- His grades reflect that he is determined to do the best he can.
- Many of the classes Martin chose to take are advanced placement courses, and he excelled in these classes.
- Martin is persistent in daily life and his endeavors.

Evidence from the application:

- Martin has taken many advanced courses.

Summary of the scoring: Martin is confident of his strengths and abilities and gets a 5. He is persistent and takes initiative, as shown in his description of starting his own business. Furthermore, his personal experience in the lawn mowing business and as a worker with his tribe have shaped his career goals to work in his native corporation.

2. Realistic Self-Appraisal (Score = 5)

Evidence from the personal statement:

- After running a lawn mowing business, he was interested in majoring in business.
- Martin challenged himself by selecting difficult courses that would prepare him for college and give him the skills to succeed in the world.
- The most challenging class Martin took in high school was physics. He was not really interested in physics but wanted to keep up with the students planning to go to college.
- Martin tried hard to make an impression on the coach for that year. He played his hardest and did his best, though he did not make the team.
- When Martin was a freshman, he had an idea that would change his life forever. He decided to start a lawn mowing business, and after running the business he decided to major in business.

Evidence from the recommendation letter:

- His grades reflect that he is determined to do his best.
- Martin has taken the most difficult classes available.
- Martin has not slacked off, and I am confident this will make college easier for him.

Evidence from the application:

- Martin is the owner/manager of his own lawn mowing business.
- Martin is enrolled in many honors courses.

Summary of the scoring: Martin shows evidence of realistic self-appraisal by discussing his initiative to start his own business. "Well, I had one more chance to make an impression. . . . I feel I did all that I could do to make the team, but for some reason the coach had thought different. . . . I still continue to be a fan of the team and eventually go to the games to cheer on my friends." He gets a 5.

3. Successfully Handles the System (Score = 2)

Evidence from the personal statement:

- Martin tried to make the team even though he had been turned down previously, and continued to support the team and attend games.

Evidence from the recommendation letter:

- None

Evidence from the application:

- None

Summary of the scoring: Martin did try to work the athletic system at his school, and he started a business, but there is little evidence that he understands the effect of larger systems in his life, so he gets a 2 for minimum positive evidence.

4. Preference for Long-Term Goals (Score = 5)

Evidence from the personal statement:

- Martin's short-term goals are to do well in high school and attend a well-respected college. Once in college he will develop his long-term goals, which include graduate school.
- After completion of graduate school, he would like to come back and work with his native corporation and help native people.
- He started his own lawn mowing business and decided on a career in business.

Evidence from the recommendation letter:

- Martin has set his academic and personal goals early in life.

Evidence from the application:

- Martin is the owner/manager of his own lawn mowing business.
- He is very involved in his native community.

Summary of the scoring: Martin has indicated the experiences and activities that influenced his goals. Also, he has a plan to coordinate his short-term and long-term goals, so he gets a 5.

5. Availability of Strong Support Person (Score = 4)

Evidence from the personal statement:

- His mother and father encouraged him to do his best, and he turned to them often for advice.
- Martin developed a close relationship to a teacher whom he feels will always be there for him.

Evidence from the recommendation letter:

- None

Evidence from the application:

- None

Summary of the scoring: Martin's close relationship with his parents and his relationship with his teacher indicate that he has developed and used individual support persons, so he scores a 4.

6. Leadership Experience (Score = 5)

Evidence from the personal statement:

- Martin is currently on the student advisory board, where he meets monthly with the principal to discuss native issue, how the school is operated, and how it relates to the high school population.
- Martin is a member of the tribal council, where he votes on issues concerning his tribe.
- Martin volunteers with junior sports leagues.

Evidence from the recommendation:

- Martin is one of the founding students of the board.
- Martin serves as a mentor for his peers and younger people.
- Martin is sensitive to others and has leadership abilities with school and community.

Evidence from the application:

- Martin is the owner/manager of his own lawn mowing business.
- He received an Award of Excellence for his extracurricular work on the Native Student Advisory Board and served in several leadership roles.

Summary of the scoring: Martin scores a 5 since he has shown leadership in starting his own business, founding a student advisory board representing his native community, and being a role model whom others look to for leadership. Martin's leadership is interwoven throughout his life.

7. Community Involvement (Score = 5)

Evidence from the personal statement:

- When Martin was a sophomore, he traveled to Alaska to help the local native people, and he felt good about doing something for others. This had a strong effect on his life goals.
- Martin felt he could do good things by changing lives through getting an education and helping his native corporation. His father has always been involved in the native corporation, and he wished to follow in his footsteps.
- Martin also worked with junior sports teams.

Evidence from the recommendation letter:

- Martin is involved in the high school's Alaska Native program, and in his village and regional native corporation.
- Martin volunteers his time during the holidays and the summer to improve the local and native community, and he has coached basketball and baseball for native children.

Evidence from the application:

- Martin is a volunteer coach and also volunteered on a mission with his church.

Summary of the scoring: Martin gets a score of 5 because of his involvement in his community, and because he has directly linked his career goals to helping others in his native corporation.

8. Knowledge Acquired in a Field (Score = 4)

Evidence from the personal statement:

- After his first summer, Martin had three confirmed lawn mowing clients and was doing well. He created his own billing system using his computer and by the end of the summer had a thriving business going.

Evidence from the recommendation:

- One accomplishment that Martin is very proud of is his successful business, which he started when he was fourteen.

Evidence from the application:

- Martin owned and managed his own lawn mowing business.
- Martin has attended summer programs to enhance his skills. An example was the Alaska Native Youth Media Institute.

Summary of the scoring: Martin gained firsthand experience running his own lawn mowing business, which influenced his decision to pursue a career in business, so he gets a 4.
Total score: 35

Application Two: Ben Moreno, Nineteen-Year-Old Latino from the East

1. Positive Self-Concept (Score = 4)

Evidence from the personal statement:

- With his creativity, Ben could be a graphic artist.

Evidence from the recommendation letter:

- Ben meets all of his obligations, in and out of school, with persistence and success.
- Ben has the dedication and skills necessary to follow through with his commitments. This shows a maturity that will serve him well in the future. He has the ability to do a number of things at the same time, and still do well at them.
- He was voted "most likely to succeed" by his fellow students, and he has the ability and motivation to go with it.

Evidence from the application:

- None

Summary of the scoring: Ben shows evidence of confidence, determination, and ability to achieve his goals in his personal statement and his recommendation letter. He gets a 4.

2. Realistic Self-Appraisal (Score = 2)

Evidence from the personal statement:

- I didn't do well in elementary school, but once I figured things out I did better.

Evidence from the recommendation letter:

- None

Evidence from the application:

- None

Summary of the scoring: There seemed to be minimum evidence of self-assessment, so Ben gets a 2.

3. Understands How to Handle Racism (Score = 3)

Evidence from the personal statement:

- None

Evidence from the recommendation letter:

- None

Evidence from the application:

- None

Summary of the scoring: Since there is no evidence provided, Ben gets a 3 as the default option.

4. Prefers Long-Range Goals to Short-Term or Immediate Needs (Score = 1)

Evidence from the personal statement:

- "I have many plans for my career after college. Since 9/11, I've wanted to be a policeman or fireman. I like helping people, so I may consider being a social worker. I also like drawing different things, so with my creativity, I could be a graphic artist. I love music, so I may want to get into the music industry as a performer. I may not settle on any one thing for awhile."

Evidence from the recommendation letter:

- None

Evidence from the application:

- None

Summary of the scoring: Ben scored a 1 because the evidence he provides is negative. Although he states his interest in being a policeman or fireman, he describes a number of other areas he is considering. His long-term goals are not clear, nor is the path he might use to pursue his interests.

5. Availability of Strong Support Person (Score = 3)

Evidence from the personal statement:

- None

Evidence from the recommendation letter:

- None

Evidence from the application:

- None

Summary of the scoring: Since there is no evidence, Ben scored a default option, 3.

6. Successful Leadership Experience (Score = 4)

Evidence from the personal statement:

- Ben was on the student council and was a class vice president. He was a part of the student day conference at his school.

- Ben was on a panel about high school life and talked to students about how he did things.

Evidence from the recommendation letter:

- Ben meets all of his obligations, in and out of school, with persistence and success.
- Ben has the dedication and skills necessary to follow through with his commitments. This shows a maturity that will serve him well in the future. He has the ability to do a number of things at the same time, and still do well at them.
- Quite often he reaches out to other students who might be struggling, not to give them the answers but to help them understand the material.
- Students look up to him as a positive role model in many areas.
- He was voted "most likely to succeed" by his fellow students, and has the ability and motivation to go with it.

Evidence from the application:

- Ben lists numerous leadership positions held.

Summary of the scoring: Leadership is shown in a number of ways in Ben's application materials. However, there is little detail about how that leadership comes together for him, and how it may have affected his development, which would be needed for a 5, so Ben gets a 4.

7. Demonstrated Community Service (Score = 2)

Evidence from the personal statement:

- He was group leader for Service Day. He also helped find things for kids for a community fair.

Evidence from the recommendation letter:

- He is involved in serving his school and community.

Evidence from the application:

- Ben helped four community groups in one year.

Summary of the scoring: Ben described his involvement in various activities, but there is little evidence of a sustained commitment to a community. There is also no information on how Ben benefits from his activities, so he gets a 2.

8. Knowledge Acquired in or About a Field (Score = 4)

Evidence from the personal statement:

- None

Evidence from the recommendation letter:

- Ben has matured into an intelligent reader and a skilled writer. He has learned this from his experiences.

Evidence from the application:

- None

Summary of the scoring: Ben's recommendation letter offers some evidence of his ability to learn from his experiences, so he gets a 4.
Total score: 23

Application Three: Alan Jensen, Eighteen-Year-Old White Student from the Midwest

1. Positive Self-Concept (Score = 5)

Evidence from the personal statement:

- Alan has done well in science and tended to excel in science courses by paying attention and preparing for exams.
- Alan has become really proficient with a computer.
- He has a strong motivation to learn and do well in everything.
- He has shown leadership in developing the class Website.
- Alan realizes his weakest subject is English and that he must work extra hard on it.
- He has earned various awards from the Boy Scouts and community organizations.

Evidence from the recommendation letter:

- Alan spends many hours working on community projects.
- Alan has self-confidence and realizes that his success depends on his ability to complete objectives.
- Alan strives for excellence.
- He has consistently chosen the most difficult course work.
- Alan demands the best from himself at all times.

Evidence from the application:

- None

Summary of the scoring: Alan scores a 5 because he is confident of his strengths and takes initiative to get involved at his school and through various community programs. He makes many positive statements about himself. Alan is clear about what it takes to achieve his objectives and recognizes the importance of doing so.

2. Realistic Self-Appraisal (Score = 5)

Evidence from the personal statement:

- Alan has done well in science and tended to excel in science courses by paying attention and preparing for exams.
- Alan realizes his weakest subject is English and that he must work extra hard on it.
- He feels carelessness, lack of interest, and rushing through assignments are the main factors that have contributed to difficulty in English.
- Since becoming an Eagle Scout, Alan has given time and talent back to the organization that helped him learn those skills. Experience with the Boy Scouts has changed his goals. The organization has broadened his perspective, taught him to be a just leader and an understanding follower, and helped him mature.

Evidence from the recommendation letter:

- Alan's persistence led to the school system's initial Website venture, created entirely by Alan and a group of students that he recruited and trained.
- Alan has self-confidence and realizes his success depends on his ability to complete objectives.
- He is serious about learning, which has allowed him to excel in all academic areas.

Evidence from the application:

- Alan has participated in numerous scouting and community activities.

Summary of the scoring: Alan gets a 5 since he shows evidence of realistic self-appraisal by expressing his abilities in his coursework and with computers. He is also aware of his weakness in English, his need to work on it, and why he is weak in that subject. In addition, he knows his participation in the scouts program has had an important effect on his life. He is able to work through difficult situations productively.

3. Understands How to Handle Racism (Score = 3)

Evidence from the personal statement:

- None

Evidence from the recommendation letter:

- None

Evidence from the application:

- None

Summary of the scoring: No evidence is provided on whether Alan can work the system to his advantage, so he scores the default option of 3.

4. Prefers Long-Range Goals to Short-Term or Immediate Needs (Score = 5)

Evidence from the personal statement:

- Once he has completed college, Alan plans to attend medical school and specialize in ophthalmology. After becoming an ophthalmologist, he hopes to join a practice or set up his own.
- Alan says he is going to base most of his short-term goals five years into the future, and long-term goals fifteen years ahead.
- Alan will set up his short-term goals and will always have an eye on his long-term goals.
- Alan has laid out a road map so he can stay on track. He expects difficulties and side trips, but he will maintain his focus.

Evidence from the recommendation letter:

- Alan has made his coursework fit his objectives.
- Alan is persistent.

Evidence from the application:

- Alan maintains a high GPA, which is one of his stated short-term goals.

Summary of the scoring: Alan has coordinated his short-term and long-term goals. He is also specific about stating his goals, so he scores a 5.

5. Availability of Strong Support Person (Score = 1)

Evidence from the personal statement:

- Alan does his best on his own.

Evidence from the recommendation letter:

- Concern is expressed that Alan operates as a loner too often.

Evidence from the application:

- None

Summary of the scoring: Alan sees himself doing his best alone, as does his recommender. There is no evidence that Alan has ever had a strong supporting relationship, so he scores a 1 for negative evidence.

6. Successful Leadership Experience (Score = 5)

Evidence from the personal statement:

- Alan showed leadership in developing the class Website.

Evidence from the recommendation letter:

- Alan led others in creating the class Website. His classmates look to him for advice and guidance.

Evidence from the application:

- Alan shows leadership in a number of community and school areas.

Summary of the scoring: Alan has shown leadership in a number of activities in his community and school, including the scouts and his class Website. His peers have looked to him for advice and guidance. Therefore he gets a 5.

7. Demonstrated Community Service (Score = 4)

Evidence from the personal statement:

- His extensive work with the Boy Scouts and many of their community projects speaks to his community involvement.

Evidence from the recommendation letter:

- None

Evidence from the application:

- Alan has been involved with the Boy Scouts for four years.
- Alan has more than two hundred hours of community service.

Summary of the scoring: Alan has shown a great deal of activity and noted that scouting changed his goals, but we do not have details on how or why he changed, which would have been needed to score a 5; he gets a 4.

8. Knowledge Acquired in or About a Field (Score = 4)

Evidence from the personal statement:

- Alan learned to be a public speaker by trial and error. He was not taught by anyone and gradually improved to be an effective speaker.
- He learned about developing a Website pretty much on his own.

Evidence from the recommendation letter:

- Alan learned a great deal about computers on his own.

Evidence from the application:

- Alan participated in the scouts and was Webmaster of the school Website.

Summary of the scoring: Alan learned on his own about public speaking and computers, so he scores a 4.

Total score: 32

Application Four: Lisa Bradley, Eighteen-Year-Old African American from the East

1. Positive Self-Concept (Score = 3)

Evidence from the personal statement:

- None

Evidence from the recommendation letter:

- None

Evidence from the application:

- None

Summary of the scoring: Since there is no evidence provided, the applicant scored a 3.

2. Realistic Self-Appraisal (Score = 2)

Evidence from the personal statement:

- No one from Lisa's family has ever graduated from college.

Evidence from the recommendation letter:

- Last year she worked extremely hard and toured Asia with a high school group. She got some financial help from the school, and with some part-time work she was able to go on the tour.

Evidence from the application:

- None

Summary of the scoring: Lisa mentions being the first in her family to attend college, and the recommendation notes Lisa's effort to pay for her trip to Asia. However, little detail is given about how she has evaluated the experiences, so she receives a 2 for minimum evidence.

3. Understands How to Handle Racism (Score = 3)

Evidence from the personal statement:

- None

Evidence from the recommendation letter:

- None

Evidence from the application:

- None

Summary of the scoring: Since there is no evidence, the score is a 3.

4. Prefers Long-Range Goals to Short-Term or Immediate Needs (Score = 2)

Evidence from the applicant's essay:

- Lisa is going to major in engineering and hopes to graduate with a bachelor's degree and then get a master's.
- She wants to work for a big engineering company to repair hardware or fix software. She feels this is the field of the future.

Evidence from the applicant's recommendation letter:

- None

Evidence from the application:

- Lisa took a one-semester computer course at a community college.

Summary of the scoring: Lisa expresses a sense of her long-term goal of working with computers but offers minimum evidence of her way of achieving that goal, so she receives a 2.

5. Availability of Strong Support Person (Score = 2)

Evidence from the personal statement:

- Her mother was both mother and father to her, and Lisa admired her for that.

Evidence from the recommendation letter:

- None

Evidence from the application:

- None

Summary of the scoring: Lisa notes her mother's role in her life; however, she does not actively discuss how she depends or relies on her mother. Thus, she rates a 2 for minimal evidence.

6. Successful Leadership Experience (Score = 2)

Evidence from the personal statement:

- When Lisa was a freshman she was treasurer of her class. As a sophomore, she was co-captain of the pep squad.

Evidence from the recommendation letter:

- Lisa is sought out by other students for her advice.
- She works very well with other students, and she is a wonderful leader.

Evidence from the application:

- Lisa was class secretary and co-captain of the pep squad and was given responsibilities at work.

Summary of the scoring: Although Lisa lists her involvement in formal leadership positions, there is no evidence of how she exercised her leadership. Though her recommendation letter says she is sought out by other students for her advice, she gets a 2 for evidence containing little detail.

7. Demonstrated Community Service (Score = 2)

Evidence from the applicant's essay:

- Lisa collected bottles and cans for her school to help the environment.

Evidence from the recommendation letter:

- None

Evidence from the application:

- Lisa worked at her father's restaurant and did some cleanup work for another business.

Summary of the scoring: Lisa mentions a can-and-bottle drive and lists community service hours, but she presents little information about involvement, commitment, or connection to her community. There is also no information on a cultural community to which she relates. Thus, she gets a 2 for minimal evidence.

8. Knowledge Acquired in or About a Field (Score = 2)

Evidence from the personal statement:

- She has taken a class at a community college in microcomputers.

Evidence from the applicant's recommendation letter:

- None

Evidence from the application:

- Lisa attended a community college for one semester and studied computers.

Summary of the scoring: Lisa mentions her enrollment in a computer course at a community college while she was still a high school student but provides no details on how this has benefited her. The application lacks details, and she gets a 2 for minimum evidence.

Total score: 18

Application Five: Lourdes Ranjel, Nineteen-Year-Old Latina from the Southwest

1. Positive Self-Concept (Score = 4)

Evidence from the personal statement:

- Lourdes refers to her own abilities often.

Evidence from the recommendation letter:

- She knows when to make decisions herself, but she is not afraid to take an unpopular stand. I have seen her choose her own values over popularity.
- She approaches challenging tasks with resolve to complete assignments and have in-depth understanding.

Evidence from the application:

- Lourdes worked fifteen to twenty hours a week during the school year.

Summary of the scoring: Lourdes's self-assessment can be found in her essay and in the recommendation and nomination letters, which assert that she is willing to express her own values despite peer pressure.

2. Realistic Self-Appraisal (Score = 4)

Evidence from the personal statement:

- Lourdes states some things she can do well, and others she would like to improve upon.

Evidence from the recommendation letter:

- She communicates well with her family and has worked outside of school to contribute to family income.

Evidence from the application:

- She worked fifteen to twenty hours a week during the school year.

Summary of the scoring: Lourdes has some sense of her strengths and weaknesses and has recognized her family's financial need by working a significant number of hours.

3. Understands How to Handle Racism (Score = 3)

Evidence from the personal statement:

- With Spanish spoken in her home, she understands the difficulty of learning English.
- She is frustrated at not being able to communicate, and she sometimes gives up.

Evidence from the recommendation letter:

- She helps her family communicate with others, but sometimes she resents it.

Evidence from the application:

- None

Summary of the scoring: Lourdes expresses an understanding of the challenges that a Spanish speaker faces in communicating with those who speak only English, but sometimes she does not handle it well and expresses her frustration with the role that is placed upon her.

4. Prefers Long-Range Goals to Short-Term or Immediate Needs (Score = 5)

Evidence from the personal statement:

- Lourdes wants to be a community worker.
- She is going to attend College X; she is going to major in English, with a minor in education.
- She plans to go to two countries, where she plans to be a missionary.

Evidence from the recommendation letter:

- In the future I know Lourdes will make wonderful contributions and service to her community.
- Her commitment to her faith sets her apart from her peers.
- Her commitment to helping others is indicative of her desire to become a community worker.

Evidence from the application:

- Lourdes was president of the English Club in her school.

Summary of the scoring: Lourdes expresses a clear sense of her long-term goal to be a missionary teacher. More significantly, she details a clear and realistic pathway to achieving this goal: serving as president of the English Club, going to college, majoring in an appropriate field, gaining experience, and then applying to two specific missionary sites. Lourdes received a 5 because there were multiple sources of evidence on this dimension. The nominator discusses the applicant's commitment to her moral code as evidence of her willingness to stay focused. Furthermore, she has participated in a variety of volunteer and leadership activities related to her goals of being a missionary and community worker.

5. Availability of Strong Support Person (Score = 2)

Evidence from the personal statement:

- Lourdes believes God will show the true path.

Evidence from the recommendation letter:

- None

Evidence from the application:

- None

Summary of the scoring: Lourdes expresses a strong sense of spiritual support and has significant involvement in her spiritual community. She says she will seek help if needed but currently lacks a clear support person.

6. Successful Leadership Experience (Score = 4)

Evidence from the personal statement:

- Lourdes is president of the English Club.
- She was the president of *Mujeres Jovenes* and is currently the treasurer.

Evidence from the recommendation letter:

- Since arriving in the United States with her family, Lourdes has taken on family responsibilities. She helps her family communicate with others and has worked outside of school to contribute to the family income.
- Lourdes is president of the English Club.

Evidence from the application:

- Lourdes is president of the English Club.

Summary of the scoring: Lourdes notes leadership positions but does not give much evidence of how she applies her leadership skills to other areas. However, since her leadership roles are connected with her future goals, she scores a 4.

7. Demonstrated Community Service (Score = 4)

Evidence from the personal statement:

- Lourdes has helped in the local rodeo and will help this year.
- She also helps in translating for Latinos who do not know the English language. She helped in a clinic translating for Latino patients who do not speak much English. During the school year, she was called upon several times to translate for a new student who did not speak English well. She has also worked on the local rodeo.

Evidence from the recommendation letter:

- She has always been active in her community.
- Lourdes takes an active role in several high school clubs and church groups.

Evidence from the application:

- Lourdes works in the local rodeo and translates for Latinos.

Summary of the scoring: Lourdes mentioned, but did not provide much detail on, her involvement with the rodeo. She scored a 4 because of her work as a translator at the clinic. As previously noted, Lourdes discussed the challenges that non-English speakers face. Her concerns go beyond words to action, through commitment to a professional career as a missionary and her experience as a translator for Latino families. Lourdes takes her commitments and interests seriously and expresses them through community action.

8. Knowledge Acquired in or About a Field (Score = 2)

Evidence from the personal statement:

- She is president of the English Club.

Evidence from the recommendation letter:

- Lourdes has been an outstanding student in my classes for three years, studying several languages.

Evidence from the application:

- Lourdes is president of the English Club.

Summary of the scoring: Lourdes shows her interest in community work through involvement in the local rodeo, and her commitment to language study. There is little direct evidence of her learning extramurally.
Total score: 28

Applicant Six: Sue Chan, Seventeen-Year-Old Asian American from the West

1. Positive Self-Concept (Score = 2)

Evidence from the personal statement:

- None

Evidence from the recommendation letter:

- Sue is very conscientious and sets high standards for herself.
- She can be successful in whatever she chooses to do.

Evidence from the application:

- None

Summary of the scoring: There is some information provided, but it is minimal and lacks detail; Sue gets a 2.

2. Realistic Self-Appraisal (Score = 4)

Evidence from the personal statement:

- Sue really likes to help others, and nothing gives her more satisfaction than to see the good she may have done.

Evidence from the recommendation letter:

- I have seen Sue excel in her schoolwork and athletics.
- Sue has demonstrated the ability to succeed in all areas of high school life.
- In each of these areas, Sue has demonstrated her ability to handle problems effectively.

Evidence from the application:

- None

Summary of the scoring: Sue's interest in helping others, and her awareness of its effect on her, is evidence of realistic self-appraisal. This is supported in her recommendation letter, so she gets a 4.

3. Understands How to Handle Racism (Score = 3)

Evidence from the personal statement:

- None

Evidence from the recommendation letter:

- None

Evidence from the application:

- None

Summary of the scoring: Since there is no evidence, Sue gets a 3.

4. Prefers Long-Range Goals to Short-Term or Immediate Needs (Score = 4)

Evidence from the personal statement:

- In fall, Sue will be attending school at "X" University, with a major in anthropology and a minor in mathematics.

Evidence from the recommendation letter:

- Sue intends to study anthropology in college, and I believe she will be successful in her endeavors.

Evidence from the application:

- Sue is on the gymnastics team, and she is a member of the student volunteers and the math club.

Summary of the scoring: The evidence does suggest some interconnection between Sue's intended major and other parts of the application, so Sue scores a 4.

5. Availability of Strong Support Person (Score = 3)

Evidence from the personal statement:

- None

Evidence from the recommendation letter:

- None

Evidence from the application:

- None

Summary of the scoring: Since there is no evidence, Sue is scored a 3.

6. Successful Leadership Experience (Score = 4)

Evidence from the personal statement:

- "The Air Force Junior ROTC has been so enjoyable and informative for the three years with which I have been affiliated. I enjoyed having the opportunity to be in leadership positions and to help volunteer my services to this corp. While in JROTC I received the Military Order Purple Heart Leadership Award, which they give for outstanding leadership."
- "As an active member of my church youth group I have served as vice president."

Evidence from the recommendation letter:

- This year, Sue has served as captain of the girls' gymnastic team. As a coach, I can always trust Sue to help out in practice by setting a positive example for the younger athletes. Sue has also distinguished herself as a leader by reaching the rank of first lieutenant in the ROTC.
- Her record of her leadership is outstanding.
- She will make great contributions to her community.

Evidence from the application:

- Sue was treasurer and member of the runners for many years, held a position in AFJROTC for three years, and was co-captain of the gymnastics team for four years.

Summary of the scoring: Sue has had leadership experience over time with the JROTC program. She has attained the rank of first lieutenant and has been recognized for her leadership abilities. Her recommender also verifies her leadership in several ways. She gets a 4.

7. Demonstrated Community Service (Score = 4)

Evidence from the personal statement:

- Sue was in leadership positions and helped a student volunteer group.
- During the summer Sue worked with the "Community Defenders" and with the local schools on preventing violence.
- Sue worked in a summer camp that helped first-year cadets coming into AFJROTC better understand the procedures and policies of the Air Force.

Evidence from the recommendation letter:

- Sue is very involved in her church.
- Sue has also been active in extracurricular activities at school.

Evidence from the application:

- During the summer Sue worked with the "Community Defenders" and with the local schools on preventing violence.

Summary of the scoring: Sue's activities are related to her leadership situations, and she has spent time on community service, so she gets a 4.

8. Knowledge Acquired in or About a Field (Score = 4)

Evidence from the personal statement:

- Sue worked in a summer camp that helped first-year cadets coming into AFJROTC better understand the procedures and policies of the Air Force.

Evidence from the recommendation letter:

- Sue showed her ability by attaining the rank of first lieutenant.

Evidence from the application:

- During the summer Sue worked with the "Community Defenders" and with the local schools on preventing violence.

Summary of the scoring: Sue shows experience and participation in the AFJROTC program as a leader, which gave her information about the military. She is scored a 4.
Total score: 28

Application Seven: Alan Howard, Eighteen-Year-Old African American from the Midwest

1. Positive Self-Concept (Score = 4)

Evidence from the personal statement:

- None

Evidence from the recommendation letter:

- Alan has the potential to accomplish anything he sets his mind to, and he certainly has the vision and perseverance to do just that. May it be college or the world of work, I have no question in my mind that Alan will be a successful individual in many of his future endeavors.
- Alan demonstrates the combination of hard work, ability, and motivation that should make him a good college student.

Evidence from the application:

- None

Summary of the scoring: The recommendation letter offers information on Alan's confidence, determination, and ability to achieve his goals.

2. Realistic Self-Appraisal (Score = 4)

Evidence from the personal statement:

- Alan felt that everyone has problems and choices. Attending college was an important choice for him and his family. He would be the first in his family to go to college, and there is a lot he wants to accomplish.
- He played football because he liked it, not just because it was a way to achieve recognition in school.

Evidence from the recommendation letter:

- He was new to football and had a hard time understanding plays, as well as techniques used at his position. However, Alan showed the tenacity and drive to become better. He worked hard and earned a starting position on our offensive line.

Evidence from the application:

- None

Summary of the scoring: The statements Alan makes about the choice to attend college and pursue his goals show his realistic self-appraisal. He realizes he will be limited if he does not get a college degree. The recommender also addresses Alan's realistic self-appraisal when commenting on his ability and desire to overcome a challenge and accomplish his goals playing football.

3. Understands How to Handle Racism (Score = 3)

Evidence from the personal statement:

- "Computers are everything. I need to learn about them to succeed."

Evidence from the recommendation letter:

- None

Evidence from the application:

- None

Summary of the scoring: Alan has some sense that he needs to know about computers to succeed in the system, but he presents no details or corroborating evidence on this dimension. Therefore he gets a 3.

4. Prefers Long-Range Goals to Short-Term or Immediate Needs (Score = 3)

Evidence from the personal statement:

- The main reason why Alan wants to go to college is that it is the only way to succeed. Currently, he is a government and politics major, but he may change to business.

Evidence from the recommendation letter:

- Alan has a great deal of potential to accomplish anything he wishes. Alan will be successful in his future endeavors.
- Alan has the combination of hard work, ability, and motivation that should make him successful.

Evidence from the application:

- None

Summary of the scoring: Alan has vague long-term goals, and he does not know what he wants to pursue. His lack of focus on a major is some evidence of this, particularly since his major does not seem to be tied to his goals in any specific way. Alan feels a degree is important but does not necessarily know why; however, his recommender and nominator express their sense of his ability to succeed in college and achieve long-term goals. This combination of positive and negative evidence along with vague goal statements gets a score of 3.

5. Availability of Strong Support Person (Score = 3)

Evidence from the personal statement:

- "There are three in my family, although my brother has recently moved to another town. My mother works two jobs, but is there when I need her."

Evidence from the recommendation letter:

- None

Evidence from the application:

- None

Summary of the scoring: There is limited information about Alan's family. It does not indicate how he depends on his mother or brother, or if he can go to either one for support. He gets a 3.

6. Successful Leadership Experience (Score = 3)

Evidence from the personal statement:

- Alan had a chance to be the lineman of the week on his team on two occasions.

Evidence from the recommendation letter:

- Alan became a role model for other students, working hard on his grades as well as in my computer lab. Currently, he is a student in my class and is often the leader in group discussions, as well as helping other students with understand the material.

Evidence from the application:

- Alan was lineman of the week twice.

Summary of the scoring: Although he helped in some group discussion in class and was lineman of the week on two occasions, there is little about the quality of his leadership experiences. Therefore, Alan receives a score of 3.

7. Demonstrated Community Service (Score = 3)

Evidence from the personal statement:

- "In these clubs all I do is community service."

Evidence from the recommendation letter:

- Alan has been active in the boy's club and often does service projects for the club.

Evidence from the application:

- Alan volunteered at a community center and a food bank last year.

Summary of the scoring: This is not very specific or detailed information about Alan's community involvement, or involvement in any cultural community; therefore, he receives a 3 for neutral evidence.

8. Knowledge Acquired in or About a Field (Score = 3)

Evidence from the personal statement:

- None

Evidence from the recommendation letter:

- None

Evidence from the application:

- None

Summary of the scoring: Since there is no evidence, Alan scored a 3 as the default option.
Total score: 26

Application Eight: Soon Park, Seventeen-Year-Old, Recently Arrived in United States from an Asian Country

1. Positive Self-Concept (Score = 5)

Evidence from the personal statement:

- He excelled at chemistry and math; he has excelled in computer programming mainly because of his interest in it.
- Soon helped others because he had shown the teacher some advanced knowledge.
- He gained additional skills in computer programming due to the wide selection of tutorials on the Internet as well as his own personal study.

Evidence from the recommendation letter:

- One of the most amazing qualities about Soon is his ability to teach himself new material. . . . He is quite resourceful and willing to help others with his skills.
- Soon is a self-motivated young man who uses many resources to teach himself new technology concepts.

Evidence from the application:

- Soon was a project leader at a computer firm.

Summary of the scoring: Evidence of Soon's positive self-concept shows in that he takes the initiative to teach himself and create computer programs to meet his needs and assist others. His interests, volunteer work, and academic strengths are coordinated with his goals, so he gets a 5.

2. Realistic Self-Appraisal (Score = 4)

Evidence from the personal statement:

- Soon has excelled at chemistry and math, and at computer programming mainly because of his interest in it.
- Soon became a project leader because of his knowledge of HTML and other Webpage-related code languages.
- This happened because of the school systems and the styles they use to teach. Although his situation hasn't improved, it has taught him a lesson.

Evidence from the recommendation letter:

- Soon can always handle a new situation calmly and evaluate all factors involved before he makes a decision.
- Soon uses his errors to make him a stronger math student. He works hard and spends time perfecting his math skills.
- The many hardships Soon faced in the transition to the United States have created a strong drive in him to be successful and work hard to get a good education at any sacrifice.

Evidence from the application:

- None

Summary of the scoring: Soon shows evidence of realistic self-appraisal by expressing his abilities and interests in math and computer programming. Soon's letter of recommendation says he can work through difficult situations well, so he gets a 4.

3. Understands How to Handle Racism (Score = 4)

Evidence from the personal statement:

- When Soon moved to the United States, all of his honors courses were counted as regular ones. He talked to his counselor but could not get the situation changed. He believes it has taught him a lesson.

Evidence from the recommendation letter:

- The many hardships Soon faced in the transition to the United States have created a strong drive in him to be successful and work hard to get a good education at any sacrifice.

Evidence from the application:

- None

Summary of the scoring: Soon receives a 4. Although he demonstrates that he is aware of the effect of the different educational systems on his academic record and made attempts to better the situation by talking to his counselor, he was unsuccessful. Had he specifically mentioned the lesson he learned or revealed ways of overcoming obstacles, he might have received a 5.

4. Prefers Long-Range Goals to Short-Term or Immediate Needs (Score = 4)

Evidence from the personal statement:

- His short-term goal is to learn about machinery. He has always been fascinated by machines and wants to know more about how they work.
- His long-term goal, however, is to work in the technology industry to satisfy his yearning to do programming.

Evidence from the recommendation letter:

- He has repaired many computers for his teachers and friends. Soon has extensive knowledge of computer technology.
- Setting goals is a strength for Soon. He has always aimed high and pushes himself to excel. . . . Soon would like to attend Stanford or Michigan.
- Soon is currently a member of a selected honors course for information technology. . . . This is designed for college-bound students who plan a career in information technology.
- Evidence from the application:
- Soon was a project leader at a computer firm.

Summary of the scoring: Soon expresses an interest in machines and technology, but he is not specific about his goals; so he gets a 4.

5. Availability of Strong Support Person (Score = 2)

Evidence from the personal statement:

- When Soon moved to the United States, all of his honors courses were counted as regular, and he talked with the counselor about that.

Evidence from the recommendation letter:

- His parents are physicians and provide a strong family support structure for their children.

Evidence from the application:

- None

Summary of the scoring: There is only vague and minimal evidence of having a support person, so Soon gets a 2.

6. Successful Leadership Experience (Score = 4)

Evidence from the personal statement:

- Soon became a project leader because of his knowledge of HTML and other Webpage-related code languages.
- Soon was given the opportunity to teach other students.

Evidence from the recommendation letter:

- Soon is a leader by personal example. Classmates come to him for assistance in coursework and computer help.
- Soon is selected to be a group leader in many informal projects. He provides leadership by example; he can influence other students with sound decisions and expression of commonsense ideas.
- His classmates look to him for his knowledge and leadership.

Evidence from the application:

- Soon was a project leader for a computer firm.
- He was selected to help students solve conflicts in a nonviolent manner.

Summary of the scoring: Soon shows leadership by being a project leader and teaching others. He is seen by others as a leader, so he receives a 4.

7. Demonstrated Community Service (Score = 4)

Evidence from the personal statement:

- Soon has been unable to participate in many community activities since he moved to the United States and had to take summer classes to meet the graduation requirements at his new school.
- He has been involved in his community through a group that designs Webpages for local small businesses and nonprofit organizations at no cost.

Evidence from the recommendation letter:

- Soon is the lead Web developer for a small business operated by a technology class that provides service free to the community.

Evidence from the application:

- Soon has devoted nearly one hundred hours to community service.

Summary of the scoring: Soon gets a 4, even though his move prevented him from being involved in many community activities. What he has shown indicates his community involvement.

8. Knowledge Acquired in or About a Field (Score = 5)

Evidence from the personal statement:

- Soon has excelled at computer programming mainly because of his interest in it. He has shown interest in machines and technology for some time.
- Soon has developed additional skills in computer programming due to the wide selection of tutorials on the Internet, as well as his own personal study. He spent a majority of his free time studying aspects of computer programming and has undertaken several projects to test his knowledge.

Evidence from the recommendation letter:

- Soon will be successful because of his drive to excel and learn new materials.
- Soon is self-motivated and uses many resources to teach himself new technology concepts.

Evidence from the application:

- Soon was a project leader at a computer firm.
- He manages computers and a network in a law firm.
- He took a computer programming course.

Summary of the scoring: Soon shows am interest and knowledge in computer technology through his coursework, his community service, his employment, and his personal time. He has worked independently to acquire applicable knowledge in this field and has tested it on his own, through his service and through teaching other students, so he gets a 5.
Total score: 32

APPENDIX 9

Online References for Racism Class

Class Website: www.inform.umd.edu/EDCP/courses/420
Contains course syllabus and information on evaluating information from the Web.

Diversity Web: http://www.diversityweb.org
Provides information on campus diversity programs nationwide.

Diversity database: www.inform.umd.edu/diversity
Provides research and database information on diversity.

Website evaluation: www.trochim.human.cornell.edu/webeval/webeval.html
Information on evaluating Websites, from Cornell University.

Learning principles and collaborative action: www.acpa.nche.edu
Part of report on "Powerful Partnerships: A Shared Responsibility for Learning" (1998) from the Joint Task Force on Student Learning of the American Association for Higher Education, the American College Personnel Association, and the National Association of Student Personnel Administrators.

APPENDIX 10

Racism Course Rating Form

Categories for weekly record comments:

1. Expresses awareness of own power to have an effect on racism
2. Sees it as an unsolvable (overwhelming) problem
3. Expresses feelings about own racist attitudes or behaviors
4. Denies the existence of racism
5. Expresses helplessness against racism
6. Expresses belief that racism can be eliminated
7. Expresses feelings that racism is a broad social problem
8. Expresses having no feelings or thoughts about racism, or inability to describe feelings
9. Expresses satisfaction with progress in race relations
10. Expresses feelings about impact of racism on own life
11. Expresses avoidance of thinking about or looking for racism
12. Expresses feelings of anger about racism
13. Expresses optimism concerning efforts to deal with racism
14. Expresses awareness of the existence of racism
15. Expresses own growth or knowledge relative to racism
16. No change in feelings

APPENDIX 11

Protocol for Interracial Interaction Study

This protocol is from Cotton, Kelley, and Sedlacek (1999).

Interview Guide

- Think of an occasion where you had a *positive experience* about being in a group with *people of different races on* the University of Maryland Campus.
- Think of an occasion where you had a *positive experience* about being in a group with *people of different races off* the University of Maryland Campus.
- Think of an occasion where you had a *negative experience* about being in a group of *people of different races on* the University of Maryland Campus.
- Think of an experience where you had a *negative experience* about being in a group of *people of different races off* the University of Maryland Campus.

Descriptions of Experiences

- What precise aspect of the experience was positive or negative?
- What led you to become involved in the experience?
- How many people were involved in the experience?
- Are you able to tell me the racial or ethnic background of the members involved in the experience?

Degree of Time Spent in the Interaction

- How long were you involved in the experience?

Location of the Activities

- Are you able to tell me where the experience occurred?

APPENDIX 12

Campus Climate Survey*
(University of Maryland Diversity Survey)

Letter Accompanying the Survey

The following is the letter accompanying the survey, from the president of the University of Maryland at College Park and from the president of the Student Government Association (SGA).

FROM THE OFFICE OF THE PRESIDENT

Dear Student:

The University of Maryland at College Park continually explores ways to improve its diversity and campus climate. We like to know how well our students think we are doing to promote diversity, especially as it pertains to race and ethnicity. In order to do this, from time to time, we seek student assistance. You have been chosen, as part of a random sample of newer students (freshmen) and students who have been on campus for several years (juniors), to participate in our survey. Please take 10 minutes to complete the attached survey,

* See Helm, Sedlacek, and Prieto (1998); and Ancis, Sedlacek, and Mohr (2000) for reliability and validity information.

"Cultural Attitudes and Climate at UMCP." It is important that you know your name will not be associated with your response: therefore, we ask that you do not include it on the survey.

Your responses are very important to us. To show our appreciation for taking the time to share your opinion, we are enclosing a ticket which will enter you in a drawing for CASH PRIZES (one $100 prize, two $50 prizes, five $20 prizes) or free movie passes.

To help us improve the racial and ethnic climate at the University of Maryland and to be entered into the drawing, we ask that you:

- Complete the enclosed survey by [date] and return it in the postage-paid pre-addressed envelope enclosed; and
- Write your phone number on the raffle ticket/postage-paid postcard (so we can call you if you win a prize) and mail it back separately.

Cultural Attitudes and Climate Survey

This questionnaire examines attitudes and beliefs about issues important to racial and ethnic diversity at your institution. Your honest responses are very important in studying these issues on the campus. All responses are anonymous. Thank you for your participation.

General instructions: Read each item carefully and circle or check your response.

Racial and Ethnic Climate

1. Please indicate to what extent you agree with the following statements (strongly disagree = 1, disagree = 2, neutral = 3, agree = 4, strongly agree = 5, not applicable = NA).

   A. My experiences since coming to school here have led me to become more understanding of racial and ethnic differences.

   1 2 3 4 5 NA

   B. Getting to know people with racial or ethnic backgrounds different from my own has been easy on this campus.

   1 2 3 4 5 NA

   C. My social interactions on this campus are largely confined to students of my race or ethnicity.

   1 2 3 4 5 NA

D. I feel there are expectations about my academic performance because of my race or ethnicity.

1 2 3 4 5 NA

E. I feel pressured to participate in ethnic activities at this school.

1 2 3 4 5 NA

F. I feel I need to minimize various characteristics of my racial or ethnic culture (for example, language, dress) to be able to fit in here.

1 2 3 4 5 NA

G. My experiences since coming to this school have strengthened my own sense of ethnic identity.

1 2 3 4 5 NA

2. Think about the faculty whose courses you have taken here. How many of them (none = 1, few = 2, some = 3, most = 4, all = 5, not applicable = NA) would you describe as:

A. Approachable outside of the classroom?

1 2 3 4 5 NA

B. Fair to all students regardless of their racial or ethnic background?

1 2 3 4 5 NA

3. Think about your experiences in the classroom. Please indicate to what extent you agree with the following statements (strongly disagree = 1, disagree = 2, neutral = 3, agree = 4, strongly agree = 5, not applicable = NA):

A. In my experience, students of different racial and ethnic backgrounds participate equally in classroom discussion and learning.

1 2 3 4 5 NA

B. I feel I am expected to represent my race or ethnic group in discussions in class.

1 2 3 4 5 NA

C. Faculty use examples relevant to people of my race or ethnic group in their lectures.

1 2 3 4 5 NA

D. In my classes I feel that my professors ignore my comments or questions.

1 2 3 4 5 NA

4. Please indicate how comfortable you feel (very uncomfortable = 1, uncomfortable = 2, neutral = 3, comfortable 4, very comfortable 5, not applicable NA) in the following situations at this school:

   A. Going to see a faculty member of my own race or ethnicity

      1 2 3 4 5 NA

   B. Speaking with others about my racial or ethnic background

      1 2 3 4 5 NA

   C. Being in situations where I am the only person of my racial or ethnic group

      1 2 3 4 5 NA

   D. Saying what I think about racial and ethnic issues

      1 2 3 4 5 NA

   E. Being with people whose racial or ethnic backgrounds are different from my own

      1 2 3 4 5 NA

   F. Participating in class

      1 2 3 4 5 NA

   G. Going to see a faculty member of a race or ethnicity different from my own

      1 2 3 4 5 NA

   H. Being with people whose racial or ethnic backgrounds are the same as my own

      1 2 3 4 5 NA

How Well Is This School Doing on Diversity?

1. The effort made by your school to improve relations and understanding between people of different racial or ethnic backgrounds is:

   Too little About right Too much Don't know

2. Please indicate to what extent (strongly disagree 1, disagree 2, neutral 3, agree 4, strongly agree 5, not applicable NA) you agree with the following statements:

   A. The campus has done a good job of providing programs and activities that promote multicultural understanding.

      1 2 3 4 5 NA

B. At this school students are resentful of others whose race or ethnicity is different from their own.

1 2 3 4 5 NA

C. There should be a requirement, for graduation, that students take at least one course on the role of ethnicity and race in society.

1 2 3 4 5 NA

D. This school does not promote respect for diversity.

1 2 3 4 5 NA

E. The student newspaper's coverage of racial and ethnic events and issues is balanced.

1 2 3 4 5 NA

F. Diversity is was one of the reasons I chose to come here.

1 2 3 4 5 NA

3. Which racial or ethnic groups should the school make special efforts to recruit as students and as faculty? (please check all that apply)

   A. Hispanic Americans

   B. Native Americans

   C. Asian Americans

   D. African Americans

   E. None; no special efforts should be taken to recruit any particular racial or ethnic group members

General Experience on Campus

1. Please indicate to what extent you agree (strongly disagree 1, disagree 2, neutral 3, agree 4, strongly agree 5, not applicable NA) with the following statements:

A. The school provides an environment for free and open expression of ideas opinions and beliefs.

1 2 3 4 5 NA

B. Overall, my educational experience here has been a rewarding one.

1 2 3 4 5 NA

C. The atmosphere in my classes does not make me feel as if I belong.

1 2 3 4 5 NA

D. I would recommend this school to siblings or friends as a good place to go to college.

1 2 3 4 5 NA

E. The overall quality of academic programs here is excellent.

1 2 3 4 5 NA

F. I feel as though I belong in the campus community

1 2 3 4 5 NA

Your Experiences on Campus

1. Please use the scale below to indicate the extent to which you believe each of the following is present at your school.

Little or none 1, some 2, quite a bit 3, a great deal 4, not applicable NA

A. Racial conflict on campus

1 2 3 4 5 NA

B. Respect by faculty for students of different racial and ethnic groups

1 2 3 4 5 NA

C. Respect by students for other students of different racial and ethnic groups

1 2 3 4 5 NA

D. Racial and ethnic separation on campus

1 2 3 4 5 NA

E. The school's commitment to the success of students of different racial and ethnic groups

1 2 3 4 5 NA

F. Friendship between students of different racial and ethnic groups

1 2 3 4 5 NA

G. Interracial tensions in the residence halls

1 2 3 4 5 NA

H. Interracial tensions in the classroom

1 2 3 4 5 NA

2. How fairly (very unfairly 1, unfairly 2, neutral 3, fairly 4, very fairly 5, no interaction NA) do you believe you have been treated by the following:

   A. University police

      1 2 3 4 5 NA

   B. Residence hall personnel

      1 2 3 4 5 NA

   C. Faculty

      1 2 3 4 5 NA

   D. Teaching assistants

      1 2 3 4 5 NA

   E. Students

      1 2 3 4 5 NA

3. In each of these settings, to what extent (not at all 1, a little 2, some 3, quite a bit 4, a great deal 5, not applicable NA) have you been exposed to information about the history, culture, and social issues of racial and ethnic groups other than whites?

   A. In course readings, lectures, and discussions

      1 2 3 4 5 NA

   B. In activities and programs in the residence halls

      1 2 3 4 5 NA

   C. In other school programs or activities

      1 2 3 4 5 NA

   D. In informal interactions and conversations with friends

      1 2 3 4 5 NA

4. How many for-credit courses have you taken from faculty members of the following racial and ethnic groups on this campus?
   A. Hispanic Americans
   B. Native Americans
   C. Asian Americans
   D. African Americans
   E. Not sure of race or ethnicity of faculty member

5. How many courses have you taken here that focused primarily on the culture, history, or social concerns of:

   A. Racial and ethnic groups (other than whites) in the United States?
   (Number of courses: _____)

   B. Non-Western racial and ethnic groups outside the United States?
   (Number of courses: _____)

6. How often (never 1, seldom 2, sometimes 3, often 4, not applicable NA) do you have difficulty getting help or support from:

   A. Faculty?

   1 2 3 4 5 NA

   B. Students?

   1 2 3 4 5 NA

   C. Teaching assistants?

   1 2 3 4 5 NA

7. How often (never 1, seldom 2, sometimes 3, often 4, not applicable NA) have you been exposed to a racist atmosphere created by the faculty:

   A. In the classroom?

   1 2 3 4 5 NA

   B. Outside the classroom?

   1 2 3 4 5 NA

8. How often (never 1, seldom 2, sometimes 3, often 4, not applicable NA) have you been exposed to a racist atmosphere created by other students:

   A. In the classroom?

   1 2 3 4 5 NA

   B. Outside the classroom?

   1 2 3 4 5 NA

9. Please indicate whether your experience here has changed your behavior in any of the following ways (yes or no):

   A. I now recognize culturally biased behavior I had not previously identified.
   B. I now discuss topics related to cultural awareness with friends.

C. I now stop myself from using language that may be offensive to others.
D. I now handle negative language used by another in such a way as to try to educate the other person.
E. I now initiate contact with people who are not of my culture or ethnic background.

Diversity Programs

1. Have you attended or participated in any diversity programs on campus this year?

   Yes No Don't Know

2. To what extent do you agree (strongly disagree, disagree, neutral, agree, strongly agree, not applicable) that attending programs on diversity contributes to the goal of building community?

Your Intentions for the Future

1. Do you plan to return to school here next semester?

   Yes No Don't Know

2. If you do not return to school here, do you think you will transfer to another college or university?

   Yes No Don't Know

3. Please indicate your current major: ______________________________

4. Please indicate your cumulative GPA:
   3.5–4.0
   3.0–3.4
   2.5–2.99
   2.0–3.49
   below 2.0

5. Please indicate your current place of residence:
   Residence hall
   Fraternity or sorority house
   Off-campus rental housing or apartment
   Home of parents or relatives
   Own home
   Other (please specify)

Please tell us what you think the school could do differently to improve campus climate with regard to diversity.

Thank you very much for completing this survey. Your cooperation will help the school in its efforts to provide a quality education to students.

REFERENCES

Adarand Constructors v. *Peña,* 93–1841, 515 US 200 (1995).

Adelman, C. (1997). Diversity: Walk the walk and drop the talk. *Change, 29*(4), 34–45.

Adelman, C. (1999). *Answers in the tool box: Academic intensity, attendance patterns, and bachelor's degree attainment.* (U.S. Department of Education, Office of Educational Research and Improvement.) Washington, DC: U.S. Government Printing Office.

Adelstein, S. M., Sedlacek, W. E., & Martinez, A. C. (1983). Dimensions underlying the characteristics and needs of returning women students. *Journal of the National Association for Women Deans, Administrators, and Counselors, 46*(4), 32–37.

Advisory Committee on Student Financial Assistance. (2001). *Access denied.* Washington, DC: U.S. Department of Education.

Allen, W. R. (1992). The color of success: African American college student outcomes at predominantly white and historically black public colleges and universities. *Harvard Educational Review, 62*(1), 26–44.

Allen, W. R., Bobo, L., & Fleuranges, P. (1984). *Preliminary report: 1982 undergraduate students attending a predominantly white state-supported university.* Ann Arbor, MI: Center for Afro-American and African Studies.

Allport, G. W. (1954). *The nature of prejudice.* Reading, Mass.: Addison-Wesley.

Altman, J. H., & Sedlacek, W. E. (1991). Differences in volunteer interest by level of career orientation. *Journal of Employment Counseling, 28*(3), 121–128.

American College Personnel Association. (1993). Statement of ethical principles and standards. *Journal of College Student Development, 34,* 89–92.

Amir, Y. (1969). Contact hypothesis in ethnic relations. *Psychological Bulletin, 71,* 319-342.

Amir, Y. (1976). The role of intergroup contact in change of prejudice and ethnic relations. In P. A. Katz (Ed.), *Toward the elimination of racism* (pp. 245–308). New York: Pergamon Press.

Anastasi, A., & Urbina, S. (1997). *Psychological testing* (7th Ed.). Upper Saddle River, NJ: Prentice Hall.

Ancis, J. R., Bennett-Choney, S. K., & Sedlacek, W. E. (1996). University student attitudes toward American Indians. *Journal of Multicultural Counseling and Development, 24,* 26–36.

Ancis, J. R., & Phillips, S. D. (1996). Academic gender bias and women's behavioral agency and self-efficacy. *Journal of Counseling and Development, 75,* 131–137.

Ancis, J. R., & Sedlacek, W. E. (1997). Predicting the academic achievement of female students using the SAT and noncognitive variables. *College and University, 72*(3), 1–8.

Ancis, J. R., Sedlacek, W. E., & Mohr, J. J. (2000). Student perceptions of the campus cultural climate by race. *Journal of Counseling and Development, 78*(2), 180–185.

Angoff, W. H. (1971). *The College Board admissions testing program.* New York: College Entrance Examination Board.

Arbona, C., Sedlacek, W. E., & Carstens, S. P. (1987). *Noncognitive variables in predicting counseling center use by race.* Counseling Center Research Report no. 3–87. College Park: University of Maryland.

Astin, A. W. (1975). *Preventing students from dropping out.* San Francisco: Jossey-Bass.

Astin, A. W. (1977). *Four critical years.* San Francisco: Jossey-Bass.

Astin, A. W. (1993). *What matters in college?: Four critical years revisited.* San Francisco: Jossey-Bass.

Astin, A. W., Tsui, L., & Avalos, J. (1996). Degree attainment rates at American colleges and universities: Effects of race, gender, and institutional type. Los Angeles: Higher Education Research Institute, University of California, Los Angeles.

Bakeman, R., & Gottman, J. M. (1986). *Observing interaction: An introduction to sequential analysis.* Cambridge, England: Cambridge University Press.

Balenger, V. J., Hoffman, M. A., & Sedlacek, W. E. (1992). Racial attitudes among incoming white students: A study of ten-year trends. *Journal of College Student Development, 33*(3), 245–252.

Balenger, V. J., & Sedlacek, W. E. (1993). Black and white student differences in volunteer interests at a predominantly white university. *National Association of Student Personnel Administrators Journal, 30,* 203–208.

Bandalos, D., & Sedlacek, W. (1989). Predicting success of pharmacy students using traditional and nontraditional measures by race. *American Journal of Pharmaceutical Education, 53,* 145–148.

Barbarin, O. A. (Ed.). (1981). *Institutional racism and community competence.* Bethesda, MD: National Institute of Mental Health.

Beckenstein, L. (1992). Success rate of transfer students enrolled in a program for the underprepared at a senior college. *Journal of College Student Development, 33,* 56–60.

Bennett, C. I. (2002). Enhancing ethnic diversity at a Big Ten university through project TEAM: A case study in teacher education. *Educational Researcher, 31,* 21–29.

Bennett, C., & Okinaka, A. M. (1990). Factors related to persistence among Asian, black, Hispanic, and white undergraduates at a predominantly white university: Comparison between first and fourth year cohorts. *Urban Review, 22,* 33–60.

Berger, J., & Milem, J. (2000). Exploring the impact of historically black colleges in promoting the development of undergraduates' self-concept. *Journal of College Student Development, 41,* 381–393.

Berk, R. A. (1982) *Handbook of methods for detecting test bias.* Baltimore: Johns Hopkins University Press.

Betz, N. E., & Fitzgerald, L. F. (1987). *The career psychology of women.* San Diego: Academic Press.

Bingham, W.V.D., & Moore, B. V. (1959). *How to interview.* New York: HarperCollins.

Bohn, M. J., Jr. (1973). Personality variables in successful work study performance. *Journal of College Student Development, 14,* 135–140.

Bowen, M. (1978). *Family practice in clinical practice.* New York: Aronson.

Bowen, W. G., & Bok, D. (1998). *The shape of the river: Long-term consequences of considering race in college and university admissions.* Princeton, NJ: Princeton University Press.

Boyer Commission on Educating Undergraduates in the Research University. (1998). *Reinventing undergraduate education: A blueprint for America's research universities.* Stony Brook: State University of New York.

Boyer, E. (1987). *The undergraduate experience in America.* New York: HarperCollins.

Boyer, S. P., & Sedlacek, W. E. (1988). Noncognitive predictors of academic success for international students: A longitudinal study. *Journal of College Student Development, 29,* 218–222.

Bridgeman, B., McCamley-Jenkins, L., & Ervin, N. (2000). *Predictions of freshman grade point average from the revised and recentered SAT-I: Reasoning Test* (RR 2000–1). New York: College Board.

Brigham, C. C. (1926). The Scholastic Aptitude Test of the College Entrance Examination Board. In T. S. Fiske (Ed.), *The work of the College Entrance Examination Board, 1901–1925.* New York: Ginn.

Brooks, G. C., Jr., Sedlacek, W. E., & Chaples, E. A. (1974). A cross-cultural comparison of Danish and U.S. attitudes toward minority groups. *Research in Higher Education, 2,* 207–220.

Brown, S. E., & Marenco, E., Jr. (1980). *Law school admissions study.* San Francisco: Mexican American Legal Defense and Educational Fund.

Brush, S. G. (1991). Women in science and engineering. *American Scientist, 79,* 404–419.

Burton, N. W., & Ramist, L. (2001). *Predicting success in college: SAT studies of classes graduating since 1980* (RR2001–2). New York: College Board.

Camara, W. (1997, March 3). *Inter-office memorandum to Donald Stewart* [President. College Board]. New York: College Board.

Campbell, D. T., & Fiske, D. W. (1959). Convergent and discriminant validation by the multitrait-multimethod matrix. *Psychological Bulletin, 56,* 81–105.

Carnavale, A. P., Haghighat, E., & Kimmel, E. W. (1998). *Role of tests in college admissions: Evaluating skills for higher education.* Princeton, NJ: Educational Testing Service.

Carney, P. I., & Sedlacek, W. E. (1985). *Attitudes of young adults toward children.* Counseling Center Research Report no. 4–85. College Park: University of Maryland.

Carstens, S. P. (1993). *Use of noncognitive variables to predict the academic persistence and graduation of students who are admitted using special admission standards.* Unpublished doctoral dissertation, State University of New York at Buffalo.

Carter, S. L. (1996). *Integrity.* New York: HarperCollins.

Carter, R. T., & Cook, D. A. (1992). A culturally relevant perspective for understanding the career paths of visible racial/ethnic group people. In H. D. Lea & Z. B. Leibowitz (Eds.), *Adult career development: Concepts, issues and practices* (pp. 192–217). Washington, DC: National Career Development Association.

Carter, R. T., White, T. J., & Sedlacek, W. E. (1987). White student attitudes toward blacks: Implications for black student recruitment and retention. *Journal of Social and Behavioral Science, 33,* 165–175.

Castañeda et al. v. *The Regents of the University of California,* U.S. District Court for the Northern District of California, Civil Action no. C. 99–0525 (1999).

Chaples, E. A., Sedlacek, W. E., & Brooks, G. C., Jr. (1972). Measuring prejudicial attitudes in a situational context: A report on a Danish experiment. *Scandinavian Political Studies, 7,* 235–247.

Chaples, E. A., Sedlacek, W. E., & Miyares, J. (1978). The attitudes of tertiary students to aborigines and New Australians. *Politics, 13*(1), 167–174.

Chen, H. L., & Mazow, C. (2002). *Electronic learning portfolios and student affairs.* Washington, DC: National Association of Student Personnel Administrators. (www.netresults@naspa.org/NetResults/article.cfm?ID=825)

Chernin, J. M., Miner-Holden, J., & Chandler, C. (1997). Bias in psychological assessment: Heterosexism. *Measurement and Evaluation in Counseling and Development, 30,* 68–76.

Christensen, K. C., & Sedlacek, W. E. (1974). Differential faculty attitudes toward blacks, females and students in general. *Journal of the National Association for Women Deans, Administrators, and Counselors, 37,* 78–84.

Chung, B. Y., & Sedlacek, W. E. (1999). Ethnic differences in career, academic, and social self-appraisals among college freshmen. *Journal of College Counseling,* 2(1), 14–24.

Cizek, G. J., & Fitzgerald, S. M. (1999). An introduction to logistic regression. *Measurement and Evaluation in Counseling and Development, 31,* 223–241.

Cofer, J., & Somers, P. (2000). A comparison of the influence of debt load on the persistence of students at public and private colleges. *Journal of Student Financial Aid, 30*(2), 39–58.

Cole, N. S. (1997, March 6–7). *Merit and opportunity: Testing and higher education at the vortex.* Paper presented at conference New Directions in Assessment for Higher Education: Fairness, Access, Multiculturalism and Equity, New Orleans.

College Board. (1998). *High school grading policies.* Research Note no. RN-04. New York: Office of Research and Development, College Board.

College Board. (2000). *Trends in student aid.* Washington, DC: Author.

Connor, K., & Vargyas, E. J. (1992). The legal implications of gender bias in standardized testing. *Berkeley Women's Law Journal, 7,* 13–89.

Cook, S. W. (1985). Experimenting in social issues: The case of school desegregation. *American Psychologist, 40,* 452–460.

Cortina, J. M. (1993). What is coefficient alpha? An examination of theory and applications. *Journal of Applied Psychology, 78,* 98–104.

Cotton, V., Kelley, W., & Sedlacek, W. E. (1999). *Situational characteristics of positive and negative experiences with same race and different race students.* Washington, DC: National Association of Student Personnel Administrators.

Crouse, J., & Trusheim, D. (1988). *The case against the SAT.* Chicago: University of Chicago Press.

Darlington, R. B. (1998). Range restriction and the Graduate Record Examination. *American Psychologist, 53,* 572–573.

D'Augelli, A. R., & Patterson, C. J. (1995). *Lesbian, gay, and bisexual identities over the lifespan: Psychological perspectives.* New York: Oxford University Press.

Davidson, M. N., & Foster-Johnson, L. (2002). Mentoring in the preparation of graduate researchers of color. *Review of Educational Research, 71,* 549–574.

Deslonde, J. L. (1971, February). *Internal-external control beliefs and racial militancy of urban community college students: The "problem" of militancy.* Paper presented at meeting of American Educational Research Association, New York.

DiCesare, A., Sedlacek, W. E., & Brooks, G. C., Jr. (1972). Nonintellectual correlates of black student attrition. *Journal of College Student Personnel, 13,* 319–324.

Diversity and Democracy: The Unfinished Work. [Advertisement]. (July 11, 2003). *Chronicle of Higher Education,* p. A29.

Dovidio, J. F., & Gaertner, S. L. (1986). *Prejudice, discrimination and racism: Historical trends and contemporary approaches.* Orlando, FL: Academic Press.

Education Commission of the States. (1995). *Making quality count in undergraduate education.* Denver, CO: Author. (ERIC Document Reproduction Service no. ED 388 208).

Edwards, A. L. (1957). *Techniques of attitude scale construction.* New York: Appleton Century Crofts.

El-Khawas, E. H. (1980). *Differences in academic development during college.* In *Men and women learning together: A study of college students in the late 70s.* Providence, RI: Office of the Provost, Brown University.

El-Khawas, E. H. (1995). *Campus trends.* Washington, DC: American Council on Education.

Ellingson, J. E., Smith, D. B., & Sackett, P. R. (2001). Investigating the influence of social desirability on personality factor structure. *Journal of Applied Psychology, 86,* 122–133.

Engstrom, C. M., & Sedlacek, W. E. (1991). A study of prejudice toward university student-athletes. *Journal of Counseling and Development, 70,* 189–193.

Engstrom, C. M., & Sedlacek, W. E. (1993). Attitudes of residence hall students toward student-athletes: Implications for training, programming, and advising. *Journal of College and University Student Housing, 23*(1), 8–33.

Engstrom, C. M., & Sedlacek, W. E. (1997). Attitudes of residence life staff toward lesbian, gay, and bisexual students. *Journal of College Student Development, 38*(6), 565–576.

Engstrom, C. M., Sedlacek, W. E., & McEwen, M. K. (1995). Faculty attitudes toward male revenue and nonrevenue student-athletes. *Journal of College Student Development, 36,* 217–227.

Epps, E. G. (1969). Correlates of academic achievement among northern and southern urban Negro students. *Journal of Social Issues, 3,* 5–13.

Evans, C. L. (1997). *A comparison of white male college students attending an urban black university and an urban white university: White racial identity and perceived comfort with blacks.* Unpublished doctoral dissertation, Old Dominion University.

FairTest Examiner. (1997, Spring). Vol. 11, no. 2.

Farmer v. *Ramsay et al.,* U.S. District Court for the District of Maryland, case no. L-98–1585 (1998).

Farver, A. S., Sedlacek, W. E., & Brooks, G. C., Jr. (1975). Longitudinal predictions of university grades for blacks and whites. *Measurement and Evaluation in Guidance, 7,* 243–250.

Faubert, M. (1992). *Cognitive and ego development of successful African American rural youth: Deliberate psychological education.* Unpublished doctoral thesis, North Carolina State University, Raleigh.

Feagin, J. R. (2000). *Racist America.* New York: Routledge.

Feagin, J. R., & Feagin, C. B. (1978). *Discrimination American style: Institutional racism and sexism.* Upper Saddle River, NJ: Prentice Hall.

Feagin, J., & Sikes, M. (1995). How black students cope with racism on white campuses. *Journal of Blacks in Higher Education, 8,* 91–97.

Fitzgerald, L. F., Shullman, S. L., Bailey, N., Richards, M., Swecker, J., Gold, Y., Ormerod, M., & Weitzman, L. (1988). The incidence and dimensions of sexual harassment in academia and the workplace. *Journal of Vocational Behavior, 32,* 152–175.

Flanagan, J. (1954). The critical incident technique. *Psychological Bulletin, 51,* 327–358.

Fleming, J. (1994). *Blacks in college.* San Francisco: Jossey-Bass.

Fogelman, B. S., & Saeger, W. (1985). Examining Sedlacek's nontraditional variables of minority student success in a summer enrichment program for health careers. *Journal of the National Medical Association, 78,* 545–549.

Forrer, S. E., Sedlacek, W. E., & Agarie, N. (1977). Racial attitudes of Japanese university students. *Research in Higher Education, 6,* 125–137.

Foster, M. E., Sedlacek, W. E., Hardwick, M. W., & Silver, A. E. (1977). Student affairs staff attitudes toward commuters. *Journal of College Student Personnel, 18,* 291–297.

Fowler, J. W. (1981) *Stages of faith: The psychology of human development and the quest for meaning.* San Francisco: Harper San Francisco.

Fox, J. W. (1995). *Attitudes of heterosexual African American resident assistants toward lesbian and gay students at historically black universities.* Unpublished master's thesis, University of Maryland, College Park.

Frankenburg, R. (1993). *The social construction of whiteness: White women, race matters.* Minneapolis: University of Minnesota Press.

Fredericksen, N. O. (1954). The evaluation of personal and social qualities. In *College Admissions.* New York: College Entrance Examination Board.

Fries-Britt, S. (2000). Identity development of high-ability black collegians. In M. Baxter Magolda (Ed.), *Teaching to promote intellectual and personal maturity: Incorporating students' worldviews and identities into the learning process.* (New Directions for Teaching and Learning no. 82, pp. 55–65). San Francisco: Jossey-Bass.

Fries-Britt, S., & Turner, B. (2002). Uneven stories: Successful black collegians at a black and a white campus. *Review of Higher Education, 25,* 315–330.

Fuertes, J. N., Miville, M. L., Mohr, J. J., Sedlacek, W. E., & Gretchen, D. (2000). Factor structure and Short Form of the Miville-Guzman Universality-Diversity Scale. *Measurement and Evaluation in Counseling and Development, 33*(3), 157–169.

Fuertes, J. N., & Sedlacek, W. E. (1993). Barriers to the leadership development of Hispanics in higher education. *National Association of Student Personnel Administrators Journal, 30,* 277–283.

Fuertes, J. N., & Sedlacek, W. E. (1994). Predicting the academic success of Hispanic university students using SAT scores. *College Student Journal, 28,* 350–352.

Fuertes, J. N., & Sedlacek, W. E. (1995). Using noncognitive variables to predict the grades and retention of Hispanic students. *College Student Affairs Journal, 14,* 30–36.

Fuertes, J. N., Sedlacek, W. E, & Liu, W. (1994). Using the SAT and noncognitive variables to predict the grades and retention of Asian American university studies. *Measurement and Evaluation in Counseling and Development, 27,* 74–84.

Gaertner, S. L., Dovidio, J. F., & Bachman, B. A. (1996). Revisiting the contact hypothesis: The induction of a common in-group identity. *International Journal of Intercultural Relationships, 20,* 271–290.

Gaertner, S. L., Rust, M. C., Dovidio, J. F., Bachman, B. A., & Anastasio, P. A. (1994). The contact hypothesis: the role of a common in-group identity on reducing intergroup bias. *Small Group Research, 25,* 224–249.

Galligani, D. J., Caloss, D. Jr., Ferri, C. (1995). *The use of socio-economic status in place of ethnicity in undergraduate admissions: A preliminary report on the results of a computer simulation.* Berkeley, CA: University of California.

Gamache, L. M., & Novick, M. R. (1985). Choice of variables and gender differentiated prediction within selected academic programs. *Journal of Educational Measurement, 22,* 53–70.

Garcia, C., & Levenson, H. (1975). Differences between blacks' and whites' expectations of control by chance and powerful others. *Psychological Reports, 37,* 563–566.

García, M., Hudgins, C. A., McTighe Musil, C., Nettles, M. T., Sedlacek, W. E., & Smith, D. G. (2001) *Assessing campus diversity initiatives; A guide for practitioners.* Washington, DC: Association of American Colleges and Universities.

Gardner, H. (1983). *Frames of mind: The theory of multiple intelligences.* New York: Basic Books.

Gardner, H. (1995, November). Reflections on multiple intelligences: Myths and messages. *Phi Delta Kappan,* 201–209.

Garnett, D. T. (1990). Retention strategies for high-risk students at a four-year university. *National Academic Advising Association Journal, 10*(1), 22–25.

Garrod, A., & Larimore, C. (Eds.). (1997). *First person, first peoples: Native American college graduates tell their stories.* Ithaca, NY: Cornell University Press.

Gerson, S. S., & Sedlacek, W. E. (1992). Student attitudes toward "JAPS": The new anti-Semitism. *College Student Affairs Journal, 11*(3), 44–53.

Gill, R. C. (1993). *Public school counselors' attitudes toward aging African-Americans.* Unpublished doctoral dissertation, University of Maryland, College Park.

Gilman, L. J. (1983). *Assisting evangelicals in presenting a positive witness to Mormons.* Unpublished doctoral dissertation no. 94941, Golden Gate Baptist Theological Seminary, Mill Valley, CA.

Gladieux, L. E., & Wolanin, T. (1976). *Congress and the colleges: The national politics of higher education.* Lexington, MA: Lexington Books.

Goldberg, L. R. (2001, June 21). *The big-five factor structure as a framework for the consideration of noncognitive assessments for graduate admissions.* Paper presented at Symposium on Noncognitive Assessments for Graduate Admissions, Graduate Record Examinations Board, Toronto.

Goldberg, L. R., Sweeney, D., Merenda, P. F., & Hughes, J. E., Jr. (1998). Demographic variables and personality: The effects of gender age, education, and ethnic/racial status on self-descriptions of personality attributes. *Personality and Individual Differences, 24,* 393–403.

Goleman, D. (1998). *Working with emotional intelligence.* New York: Bantam.

Gordon, V. N., & Grites, T. J. (1984). The freshman seminar course: Helping students succeed. *Journal of College Student Personnel, 25,* 315–320.

Gratz and Hamacher v. *Bollinger et al.,* U.S. Court of Appeals for the Sixth Circuit, no. 02–516 (2002).

Grimes, S. K., & David, K. C. (1999). Underprepared community college students: Implications of attitudinal and experiential differences. *Community College Review, 27*(2), 73–93.

Grutter v. *Bollinger et al.,* U.S. Court of Appeals for the Sixth Circuit, no. 02-241 (2002).

Guilford, J. P. (1950). Creativity. *American Psychologist,* 5, 444–454.

Gurin, P. G., Gurin, R., Lao, R., & Beattie, M. (1969). Internal-external control in the motivational dynamics of Negro youth. *Journal of Social Issues, 3,* 29–53.

Hale, F. W. (1991). *Inventory for assessing an institution's commitment to multicultural programming.* Columbus, OH: Technical Instructional Professional Support Services.

Hargrove, B., & Sedlacek, W. E. (1997). Counseling interests among entering black university students over a ten year period. *Journal of the Freshman Year Experience and Students in Transition,* 9(2), 83–98.

Harris, S. M., & Nettles, M. T. (1996) Ensuring campus climates that embrace diversity. In L. R. Rendón & R. O. Hope (Eds.), *Educating a new majority: Transforming America's educational system for diversity* (pp. 330–371). San Francisco: Jossey-Bass.

Harvey, C., & Hurtado, A. (1994).The jurisprudence of race and meritocracy: Standardized testing and "race neutral" racism in the workplace. *Law and Human Behavior, 18,* 223–248.

Harvey, W. B. (2002). *Minorities in higher education 2001–2002: Nineteenth annual status report.* Washington DC: American Council on Education.

Hathaway, S. R., & McKinley, J. C. (1943). *The Minnesota Multiphasic Personality Inventory* (Rev. Ed.). Minneapolis: University of Minnesota Press.

Helm, E. G., Prieto, D. O, & Sedlacek, W. E. (1997). Simulated minority admission exercise at Louisiana State University School of Medicine: An evaluation. *Journal of the National Medical Association, 89,* 609–605.

Helm, E., Sedlacek, W. E., & Prieto, D. (1998a). Career advising issues for African American entering students. *Journal of the Freshman Year Experience and Students in Transition, 10*(2), 77–87.

Helm, E. G., Sedlacek, W. E., & Prieto, D. O. (1998b). The relationship between attitudes toward diversity and overall satisfaction of university students by race. *Journal of College Counseling, 1,* 111–120.

Helms, J. E. (1992). Why is there no study of cultural equivalence in standardized cognitive ability testing? *American Psychologist, 47,* 1083–1101.

Helms, J. E. (1995). An update of Helms' white and people of color racial identity models. In J. G. Ponterotto, J. M. Casas, L. A. Suzuki, & C. M. Alexander (Eds.), *Handbook of multicultural counseling* (pp. 181–198). Thousands Oaks, CA: Sage.

Henson, R. K. (2001). Understanding internal consistency reliability estimates: A conceptual primer on coefficient alpha. *Measurement and Evaluation in Counseling and Development, 34,* 177–189.

Herman, M. H., & Sedlacek, W. E. (1973). Sexist attitudes among male university students. *Journal of College Student Personnel, 14,* 544–548.

Herrnstein, R. J., & Murray, C. (1994). *The bell curve: Intelligence and class structure in American life.* New York: Free Press.

Heubert, J. P., & Hauser, R. M. (Eds.). (1998). *High stakes: Testing for tracking, promotion and graduation.* Washington, DC: National Research Council.

Hill, W. (1995). *The academic retention and graduation status of African American students: Factors in a public university.* Doctoral dissertation, North Carolina State University, Raleigh.

Hill, M. D., & Sedlacek, W. E. (1994). *Discrimination on campus: Using a campus newspaper to defend a lawsuit.* Counseling Center Research Report no. 8–94. College Park: University of Maryland.

Hirt, J., Hoffman, M. A., & Sedlacek, W. E. (1983). Attitudes toward changing sex roles of male varsity athletes vs. non-athletes: Developmental perspectives. *Journal of College Student Personnel, 24,* 33–38.

Hoey, J. J. (1997). *Developing a retention risk indicator at North Carolina State University.* Raleigh: North Carolina State University.

Holland, J. (1985). *The Self-directed search.* Lutz, FL: Psychological Assessment Resources.

Hoover, C. K. (1994). *An investigation of the preparedness of student affairs professionals to work effectively with diverse populations on campus.* Unpublished doctoral dissertation, University of Maryland, College Park.

Hopple, G. W. (1976). Protest attitudes and social class: Working class authoritarianism revisited. *Sociology and Social Research, 60,* 229–246.

Hopwood v. *Texas,* 861 F. Supp. 551 (WD Tex. 1994), in no. 94–50664.

Horseman, R. (1981). *Race and manifest destiny: Origin of American Anglo Saxonism.* Cambridge, MA: Harvard University Press.

Houston, L. N. (1980). Predicting academic achievement among specially admitted black female college students. *Educational and Psychological Measurement, 40,* 1189–1195.

Hughey, A. W. (1995). Observed differences in Graduate Record Examination scores and mean undergraduate grade point average by gender and race among students admitted to a master's degree program in college student affairs. *Psychological Reports, 77,* 1315–1321.

Hune, S., & Chan, K. S. (1997). Special focus: Asian Pacific American demographic and educational trends. In D. J. Carter & R. Wilson (Eds.), *Fifteenth annual status report on minorities in higher education* (pp. 39–67). Washington DC: American Council on Education.

Hurtado, S., Milem J. F., Clayton-Pedersen, A. R., & Allen, W. R. (1998). Enhancing campus climates for racial/ethnic diversity: Educational policy and practice. *Review of Higher Education, 21,* 279–302.

Isaac, S., & Michael, W. B. (1995). *Handbook in research and evaluation for education and the behavioral sciences* (3rd Ed.). San Diego: EdITS.

Johnson, C. S., & Cheatham, H. E.(Eds.). (1999). *Higher education trends for the next century: A research agenda for student success.* Washington, DC: American College Personnel Association.

Johnson, E. S. (1993). College women's performance in a math-science curriculum: A case study. *College and University, 68,* 74–78.

Johnson, I. H. (1996). Access and retention: Support programs for graduate and professional students. In I. H. Johnson & A. J. Ottens (Eds.), *Leveling the playing field: Promoting academic success for students of color.* San Francisco: Jossey-Bass.

Johnson, K. K., & Sedlacek, W. E. (1997). *Faculty diversity efforts at UMCP.* Counseling Center Research Report no. 9–97. College Park: University of Maryland.

Joint Task Force on Student Learning (1998).Washington, DC: American College Personnel Association (http://www.aahe.org/teaching/tsk_frce.htm).

Jones, S. R. (1997). Voices of identity and difference: A qualitative exploration of the multiple dimensions of identity development in women college students. *Journal of College Student Development, 38,* 376–385.

Kim, S. H., & Sedlacek,, W. W. (1996). Gender differences among incoming African American freshmen on academic and social expectations. *Journal of the Freshman Year Experience, 8*(2), 25-37.

Knapp, L. G., Kelly, J. E., Whitmore, R. W., Wu, S., & Gallego, L. M. (2002). *Enrollment in postsecondary institutions, fall 2000 and financial statistics, fiscal year 2000.* (No. 2002212.) Washington, DC: National Center for Education Statistics.

Knight, G. D., Seefeldt, C., & Sedlacek, W. E. (1984). *Measuring the attitudes of adults toward children.* Counseling Center Research Report no. 4–84. College Park: University of Maryland.

Koretz, D. (1993). New report of the Vermont project documents challenges. *National Council on Measurement in Education Quarterly Newsletter, 1*(4), 1–2.

Kornhaber, M. (1997). Seeking strengths: Equitable identification for gifted education and the theory of multiple intelligences. Doctoral dissertation, Harvard University.

Krieger, N., & Sidney, S. (1996). Racial discrimination and blood pressure. The CARDIA study of young black and white adults. *American Journal of Public Health, 86,* 1370–1378.

Laanan, F. S. (1996). Making the transition: Understanding the adjustment process of community college transfer students [Abstract]. *Community College Review, 23,* 69–85.

LaMahieu, P. G., Gitomer, D. H., & Eresch, J. T. (1995). Portfolios in large scale assessment: Difficult but not impossible. *Educational Measurement: Issues and Practice, 14,* 11–28.

Latino Eligibility Task Force. (1997). *Latino student eligibility and participation in the University of California: Ya Basta!* Report no. 3. Berkeley, CA: Latino Eligibility Task Force, Institute for the Study of Social Change.

Lea, H. D., Sedlacek, W. E., & Stewart, S. S. (1980). Faculty attitudes toward resident and commuting students. *Southern College Personnel Association Journal, 2,* 23–32.

Leitner, D. L., & Sedlacek, W. E. (1976). Characteristics of successful campus police officers. *Journal of College Student Personnel, 17,* 304–308.

Lemann, N. (2000). *The big test: The secret history of the American meritocracy.* New York: Farrar, Straus & Giroux.

Lenning, O. T., & Ebbers, L. H. (1999). *The powerful potential of learning communities: Improving education for the future* (6th Ed., vol. 26). Washington, DC: Graduate School of Education and Human Development, George Washington University.

Leong, F.T.L. (1998). Career development and vocational behaviors. In L. C. Lee & N.W.S. Zane (Eds.), *Handbook of Asian American psychology* (pp. 359–398). Thousand Oaks, CA: Sage.

Leong, F.T.L., & Schneller, G. (1997). White Americans' attitudes toward Asian Americans in social situations: An empirical examination of potential stereotypes, bias and prejudice. *Journal of Multicultural Counseling and Development, 25,* 68–78.

Leuner, B. (1966). Emotional intelligence and emancipation. *Praxis der Kinderpsychologie und Kinderpsychiatrie, 15,* 193–203.

Liang C.T.H. & Sedlacek W. E. (2003a). Attitudes of White student services practitioners toward Asian Americans. *National Association of Student Personnel Administrators Journal,* 40(3), 30-42. http://publications.naspa.org/naspajournal/vol40/iss3/art2.

Liang, C.T.H., & Sedlacek, W. E. (2003b). Utilizing factor analysis to understand the needs of Asian American Students. *Journal of College Student Development, 44,* 260–266.

Liang, C.T.H., Ting, M. P., & Teraguchi, D. H. (2001, Spring). Access denied: The complexity of Asian Pacific Americans. *Diversity Digest,* p. 3.

Light, R. J. (2001). *Making the most of college: Students speak their minds.* Cambridge, MA.: Harvard University Press.

Linn, M. R. (1993, Summer). College entrance examinations in the United States: A brief history for college admission counselors. *Journal of College Admission, 140,* 6–16.

Linn, R. L., & Gronlund, N. E. (2000). *Measurement and assessment in teaching.* Upper Saddle River, NJ: Prentice Hall.

Linnell, D. (2001). *College students' attitudes toward two disability populations: Crime victims and police officers.* Unpublished doctoral dissertation, University of Maryland.

Liu, W. M., & Sedlacek, W. E. (1999). Differences in leadership and co-curricular perception among male and female Asian Pacific American college students. *Journal of the Freshman Year Experience, 11,* 93–114.

Lockett, G. C. (1980). *A study of traditional measures and nontraditional measures used to predict the success of black college students.* Unpublished doctoral dissertation, University of Missouri, Columbia.

Longerbeam, S. L., Sedlacek, W. E., & Alatorre, H. A. (forthcoming). In their own voices: Latino student retention. *National Association of Student Personnel Administrators Journal.*

Loo, C. M., & Rolison, G. (1986). Alienation of ethnic minority students at a predominantly white university. *Journal of Higher Education, 57,* 58–77.

Majors, M. S., & Sedlacek, W. E. (2001). Using factor analysis to organize student services. *Journal of College Student Development, 42,* 272–278.

Mallinckrodt, B. (1988). Student retention, social support, and dropout retention: Comparison of black and white students. *Journal of College Student Development, 29,* 60–64.

Mallinckrodt, B., & Sedlacek, W. E. (1987). Student retention and the use of campus facilities by race. *National Association of Student Personnel Administrators Journal, 24*(3), 28–32.

Marshall, D.M.A. (1983). *Attitudes of able-bodied students in integrated and non-integrated residence halls toward blind and wheelchair-bound students.* Unpublished master's thesis, University of Maryland, College Park.

Mayer, J. D. (1999). Emotional intelligence: Popular or scientific psychology? *APA Monitor, 30,* 50.

Mayer, J. D. (2001, June 21). *On new methods of personality assessment.* Paper presented at Symposium on Noncognitive Assessments for Graduate Admissions, Graduate Record Examinations Board, Toronto.

Mayer, J. D., Salovey, P., & Caruso, D. R. (2000). Models of emotional intelligence. In R. J. Sternberg (Ed.), *Handbook of intelligence* (pp. 396–420). Cambridge, England: Cambridge University Press.

McEwen, M. K., & Roper, L. D. (1994). Interracial experiences, knowledge, and skills of master's degree students in graduate programs in student affairs. *Journal of College Student Development, 35,* 81–87.

McNairy, F. G. (1996). The challenge for higher education: Retaining students of color. In I. H. Johnson & A. J. Ottens (Eds.), *Leveling the playing field: Promoting academic success for students of color* (pp. 3–14). San Francisco: Jossey-Bass.

McNeill, J. V. (1992). *Variables related to grade performance of African American freshmen at a predominantly white university.* Unpublished doctoral dissertation, North Carolina State University.

McQuilkin, J. I., Freitag, C. B., & Harris, J. L. (1990). Attitudes of college students toward handicapped persons. *Journal of College Student Development, 31,* 17–22.

McTighe Musil, C., García, M., Hudgins, C. A., Nettles, M. T., Sedlacek, W. E., & Smith, D. G. (1999). *To form a more perfect union: Campus diversity initiatives.* Washington DC: Association of American Colleges and Universities.

Mehrens, W. A., & Lehman, I. J. (1991). *Measurement and evaluation in education and psychology.* Austin, Tex.: Holt, Rinehart and Winston.

Merenda, P. F. (1997). A guide to the proper use of factor analysis in the conduct and reporting of research: Pitfalls to avoid. *Measurement and Evaluation in Counseling and Development, 30,* 156–164.

Michaelson, M. (1996, Summer). Affirmative action: Few easy answers. *Priorities, 7,* 1–15.

Milem, J. F., & Berger, J. B. (1997). A modified model of college student persistence: Exploring the relationship between Astin's theory of involvement and Tinto's theory of student departure. *Journal of College Student Development, 38,* 387–400.

Minatoya, L. Y., & Sedlacek, W. E. (1983). The Situational Attitude Scale toward Women (SASW): A means to measure environmental sexism. *Journal of the National Association for Women Deans, Administrators, and Counselors, 47*(1), 26–30.

Minatoya, L. Y., & Sedlacek, W. E. (1984). Assessing attitudes of white university students toward blacks in a changing context. *Journal of Non-White Concerns in Personnel and Guidance, 12,* 69–79.

Mitchell, A. A., Beardsley, K. P., & Sedlacek, W. E. (1997). Decreasing transfer student hassles: Collaborative research and action. *Journal of College Student Development, 38,* 84–86.

Mitchell, A. A., & Sedlacek, W. E. (1995). Freshmen with learning disabilities: A profile of needs and concerns. *Journal of the Freshman Year Experience, 7*(2), 27–41.

Mitchell, A. A., & Sedlacek, W. E. (1996). Ethnically sensitive messengers: An exploration of racial attitudes of health care workers and organ procurement officers. *Journal of the National Medical Association, 88,* 349–352.

Mitchell, A. A., Sergent, M. T., & Sedlacek, W. E. (1997). Mapping the university learning environment. *National Association of Student Personnel Administrators Journal, 35,* 20–28.

Miville, M. L., Molla, B., & Sedlacek, W. E. (1992). Attitudes of tolerance for diversity among university freshmen. *Journal of the Freshman Year Experience, 4,* 95–110.

Miville, M. L., & Sedlacek, W. E. (1994). Post-war attitudes toward Arab-Americans: A university campus dilemma. *Journal of the Freshman Year Experience, 6*(2), 77–88.

Miville, M. L., & Sedlacek, W. E. (1995). Transfer students and freshmen: Different or parallel experiences? *National Association of Student Personnel Administrators Journal, 32,* 145–152.

Mohr, J. J., Israel, T., & Sedlacek, W. E. (2001). Counselors' attitudes regarding bisexuality as predictors of counselors' clinical responses: An analogue study of a female bisexual client. *Journal of Counseling Psychology, 48,* 212–222.

Mohr, J. J., & Rochlen, A. B. (1999). Measuring attitudes regarding bisexuality in homosexual and heterosexual populations. *Journal of Counseling Psychology, 46,* 353–369.

Mohr, J. J., & Sedlacek, W. E. (2000). Perceived barriers to friendship with lesbians and gay men among university students. *Journal of College Student Development, 41,* 70–79.

Moore, S. K. (1995). *Indicators of academic success and the student characteristics of international students at Santa Monica College.* Unpublished doctoral dissertation, Pepperdine University.

National Association of Student Personnel Administrators. (1987). *Points of view.* Washington, DC: NASPA.

Nettles, M. (1990). *Black, Hispanic and white doctoral students: Before, during and after enrolling in graduate school.* Princeton, NJ: Educational Testing Service.

Neville, H. A., Heppner, P., & Wang, L. (1997). Relations among racial identity attitudes, perceived stressors, and coping styles in African American college students. *Journal of Counseling and Development, 75,* 303–311.

Nisbet, J., Ruble, V. E., & Shurr, K. T. (1982). Predictors of academic success with high risk college students. *Journal of College Student Personnel, 23,* 227–235.

Noble, J., Crouse, J., & Schulz, M. (1996). *Differential prediction/impact in course placement for ethnic and gender groups* (Research Report 96–8). Iowa City, IA: ACT.

Noonan, B., Sedlacek, W. E., & Suthakaran, V. (2001). *Predicting the success of community college students using noncognitive variables.* Counseling Center Research Report no. 5–01. College Park: University of Maryland.

O'Brien, K. M., Sedlacek, W. E., & Kandell, J. J. (1994). Willingness to volunteer among university students. *National Association of Student Personnel Administrators Journal, 33,* 67–73.

O'Callaghan, K. W., & Bryant, C. (1990). Noncognitive variables: A key to black-American academic success at a military academy. *Journal of College Student Development, 31,* 121–126.

Ochs, R. (1996). Biphobia: It goes more than two ways. In B. A. Firestein (Ed.), *Bisexuality: The psychology and politics of an invisible minority* (pp. 217–239). Thousand Oaks, CA: Sage.

Ossana, S. M., Helms, J. E., & Leonard, M. M. (1992). Do "womanist" identity attitudes influence college women's self-esteem and perceptions of environmental bias? *Journal of Counseling and Development, 70,* 402–408.

Pascarella, E. T., Edison, M., Nora, A., Hagedorn, L., & Terenzini, P. T. (1996). Influences on students' openness to diversity and challenge in the first year of college. *Journal of College Student Development, 67,* 174–195.

Pascarella, E., & Terenzini, P. (1991). *How college affects students: Findings and insights from twenty years of research.* San Francisco: Jossey-Bass.

Patterson, A. M., Jr., Sedlacek, W. E., & Perry, F. W. (1984). Perceptions of blacks and Hispanics in two campus environments. *Journal of College Student Personnel, 25,* 513–518.

Patterson, A., Sedlacek, W. E., & Scales, W. R. (1988). The other minority: Disabled student backgrounds and attitudes toward their university and its services. *Journal of Postsecondary Education and Disability, 6,* 86–94.

Peabody, S. A., Metz, J. F., & Sedlacek, W. E. (1983). A survey of academic advising models. *Journal of College Student Personnel, 24,* 83–84.

Peabody, S. A., & Sedlacek, W. E. (1982). Attitudes of younger university students toward older students. *Journal of College Student Personnel, 23,* 140–143.

Perrone, K. M., Sedlacek, W. E., & Alexander, C. M. (2001). Gender and ethnic differences in career goal attainment. *Career Development Quarterly, 50,* 168–178.

Pfeifer, C. M., Jr., & Sedlacek, W. E. (1974). Predicting black student grades with nonintellectual measures. *Journal of Negro Education, 43,* 67–76.

Ponterotto, J. C., & Pedersen, P. B. (1993). *Preventing prejudice: A guide for counselors and educators.* Thousand Oaks, CA: Sage.

Pope, R. L. (1993). Multicultural organizational development in student affairs: An introduction. *Journal of College Student Development, 34,* 201–205.

Pope, R. L. (1995). Multicultural organizational development: Implications and applications in student affairs. In J. Fried (Ed.), *Shifting paradigms in student affairs: A cultural perspective* (pp. 233–249). Washington, DC: ACPA Media.

Pope, R. L., & Reynolds, A. L. (1997). Student affairs core competencies: Integrating multicultural awareness, knowledge, and skills. *Journal of College Student Development, 38,* 266–277.

Prediger, D. J. (1994). Multicultural assessment standards: A compilation for counselors. *Measurement and Evaluation in Counseling and Development, 27,* 68–73.

Prieto, D. O., Bashook, P. G., D'Costa, A. G., Elliot, P. R., Jarecky, R. K., Kahrahrah, B., & Sedlacek, W. E. (1978). *Simulated minority admissions exercise.* Washington, DC: Association of American Medical Colleges.

Reeve, C. L., & Hakel, M. D. (2001, June 21). *Criterion issues and practical considerations concerning noncognitive assessment in graduate admissions.* Paper presented at Symposium on Noncognitive Assessments for Graduate Admissions, Graduate Record Examinations Board, Toronto.

Regents of the University of California v. Bakke. Supreme Court of the United States. 438 U.S. 265 (1978).

Reynolds, A. L., & Pope, R. L. (1994). Perspectives on creating multicultural campuses. *Journal of American College Health, 42,* 223–233.

Rigol, G., & Kimmel, E. (1997). *A picture of admissions in the United States* (unpublished paper). New York: College Entrance Examination Board.

Rojstraczer, S. (2003). *Where all grades are above average* (http://www.gradeinflation.com).

Roper, L. D. (1988). *Relationship among levels of social distance, dogmatism, affective reactions and interracial behaviors in a course on racism.* Unpublished doctoral dissertation, University of Maryland.

Roper, L. D., & McKenzie, A. (1989). Academic advising: A developmental model for black student-athletes. *National Association of Student Personnel Administrators Journal, 26*(2), 91–98.

Roper, L. D., & Sedlacek, W. E. (1988). Student affairs professionals in academic roles: A course on racism. *National Association of Student Personnel Administrators Journal, 26*(1), 27–32.

Rosser, P. (1989). *The SAT gender gap: Identifying the causes.* Washington, DC: Center for Women's Policy Studies.

Russo, N. F., Olmedo, E. L., Stapp, J., & Fulcher, R. (1981). Women and minorities in psychology. *American Psychologist, 36,* 1315–1365.

Sackett, P. R., Schmidt, N., Ellingson, J. E., & Kabin, M. B. (2001). High-stakes testing in employment, credentialing and higher education: Prospects in a post-affirmative-action world. *American Psychologist, 56,* 302–318.

Sandler, B. R. (1987). The classroom climate: Still a chilly one for women. In C. Lasser (Ed.), *Educating men and women together: Co-education in a changing world.* Urbana: University of Illinois Press.

Schlosser, L. Z. (2003). Christian privilege: Breaking a sacred taboo. *Journal of Multicultural Counseling and Development, 31,* 44–51.

Schlosser, L. Z., & Sedlacek, W. E. (2001). Hate on campus: A model for evaluating, understanding, and handling critical incidents. *About Campus, 6*(1), 25–27.

Schlosser, L. Z., & Sedlacek, W. E. (2003). Christian privilege and respect for religious diversity: Religious holidays on campus. *About Campus, 7*(6), 31–32.

Schuman, H., Steeh, C., Bobo, L., & Krysan, M. (1997). *Racial attitudes in America: Trends and interpretations.* Cambridge, MA: Harvard University Press.

Schwalb, S. J., & Sedlacek, W. E. (1990). Have college student attitudes toward older people changed? *Journal, 31,* 127–132.

Sedlacek, W. E. (1974). Issues in predicting black student success in higher education. *Journal of Negro Education, 43,* 512–516.

Sedlacek, W. E. (1983). Teaching minority students. In J. H. Cones III, J. Noonan, and D. Janha (Eds.), *Teaching minority students: New directions for teaching and learning.* (pp. 39–50). San Francisco: Jossey-Bass.

Sedlacek, W. E. (1986). Sources of method bias in test bias research. In *Measures in the college admissions process* (pp. 86–92). New York: College Entrance Examination Board.

Sedlacek, W. E. (1988). Institutional racism and how to handle it. *Health Pathways, 10*(9), 4–6.

Sedlacek, W. E. (1989, Fall). Noncognitive indicators of student success. *Journal of College Admissions,* (No.125), 2–10.

Sedlacek, W. E. (1991). Using noncognitive variables in advising nontraditional students. *National Academic Advising Association Journal, 11*(1), 75–82.

Sedlacek, W. E. (1993). Employing noncognitive variables in the admission and retention of nontraditional students. In *Achieving diversity: Issues in the recruitment and retention of traditionally underrepresented students* (pp. 33–39). Alexandria, VA: National Association of College Admission Counselors.

Sedlacek, W. E. (1994a). Issues in advancing diversity through assessment. *Journal of Counseling and Development, 72,* 549–553.

Sedlacek, W. E. (1994b). Advising nontraditional students: The big bang or another universe? *National Academic Advising Association Journal, 14*(2), 103–104.

Sedlacek, W. E. (1995a). *Improving racial and ethnic diversity and campus climate at four year independent Midwest colleges.* (Evaluation report of the Lilly Endowment Grant Program.) Indianapolis, IN: Lilly Endowment.

Sedlacek, W. E. (1995b). Using research to reduce racism at a university. *Journal of Humanistic Education and Development, 33,* 131–140.

Sedlacek, W. E. (1996a). An empirical method of determining nontraditional group status. *Measurement and Evaluation in Counseling and Development,* 28, 200–210.

Sedlacek, W. E. (1996b). Employing noncognitive variables in admitting students of color. In I. H. Johnson & A. J. Ottens (Eds.), *Leveling the playing field: Promoting academic success for students of color* (pp. 79–91). San Francisco: Jossey-Bass.

Sedlacek, W. E. (1998a). Admissions in higher education: Measuring cognitive and noncognitive variables. In D. J. Wilds & R. Wilson (Eds.), *Minorities in higher education 1997–98: Sixteenth annual status report* (pp. 47–71). Washington, DC: American Council on Education.

Sedlacek, W. E. (1998b, Winter). Multiple choices for standardized tests. *Priorities, 10,* 1–16.

Sedlacek, W. E. (1998c). Strategies for social change research. In C. C. Lee & G. R. Walz (Eds.), *Social action: A mandate for counselors* (pp. 227–239). Alexandria, VA: American Counseling Association.

Sedlacek, W. E. (1999). Blacks on White campuses: 20 years of research. *Journal of College Student Development, 40,* 538–550.

Sedlacek, W. E. (2000, Spring/Summer). A campus climate survey! Where to begin. *Diversity Digest* (Association of American Colleges and Universities), 24–25.

Sedlacek, W. E. (2001, June 21). *Why we should use noncognitive variables with graduate students.* Paper presented at Symposium on Noncognitive Assessments for Graduate Admissions, Graduate Record Examinations Board, Toronto.

Sedlacek, W. E. (2002). *Thurstone equal appearing intervals: The forgotten method.* (Counseling Center Research Report no. 14–02). College Park: University of Maryland.

Sedlacek, W. E. (2003a). Alternative measures in admissions and scholarship selection. *Measurement and Evaluation in Counseling and Development, 35,* 263–272.

Sedlacek, W. E. (2003b). Negotiating admissions to graduate and professional schools. In V. L. Farmer (Ed.), *The black student's guide to graduate and professional school success* (pp. 13–22). Westport, CT: Greenwood.

Sedlacek, W. E. (2004). A multicultural research program. In F. W. Hale (Ed.), *What makes racial diversity work in higher education* (pp. 256–271). Sterling, VA: Stylus.

Sedlacek, W. E. (forthcoming). The case for noncognitive measures. In W. Camara & E. Kimmel (Eds.). *Choosing students: Higher education admission tools for the 21st century.* Mahwah, NJ: Lawrence Erlbaum.

Sedlacek, W. E., & Adams-Gaston, J. (1992). Predicting the academic success of student-athletes using SAT and noncognitive variables. *Journal of Counseling and Development, 70*(6), 724–727.

Sedlacek, W. E., Bailey, B., & Stovall, C. (1984). Following directions: An unobtrusive measure of student success. *Journal of College Student Personnel, 25,* 556.

Sedlacek, W. E., & Brooks, G. C., Jr. (1970). Measuring racial attitudes in a situational context. *Psychological Reports, 27,* 971–980.

Sedlacek, W. E., & Brooks, G. C., Jr. (1972a). Race of experimenter in racial attitude measurement. *Psychological Reports, 30,* 771–774.

Sedlacek, W. E., & Brooks, G. C., Jr. (1972b). Racial attitudes, authoritarianism and dogmatism among university students. *College Student Journal, 6,* 43–44.

Sedlacek, W. E., & Brooks, G. C., Jr. (1973). Racism and research: Using data to initiate change. *Personnel and Guidance Journal, 52,* 184–188.

Sedlacek, W. E., & Brooks, G. C., Jr. (1976). *Racism in American education: A model for change.* Chicago: Nelson-Hall.

Sedlacek, W. E., Brooks, G. C., Jr., & Mindus, L. A. (1973). Racial attitudes of white university students and their parents. *Journal of College Student Personnel, 14,* 517–520.

Sedlacek, W. E., & Hutchins, E. B. (1966). An empirical demonstration of restriction of range artifacts in validity studies of the Medical College Admission Test. *Journal of Medical Education, 41,* 222–229.

Sedlacek, W. E., & Kim, S. H. (1995). *Multicultural assessment.* (ERIC/CASS Digest series on assessment in counseling and therapy, EDO-CG-95–24.) Greensboro, NC.: U.S. Department of Education.

Sedlacek, W. E., & Prieto, D. O. (1982). An evaluation of the Simulated Minority Admissions Exercise (SMAE). *Journal of Medical Education, 57,* 119–120.

Sedlacek, W. E., & Prieto, D. O. (1990). Predicting minority students' success in medical school. *Academic Medicine, 65,* 161–166.

Sedlacek, W. E., & Sheu, H. B. (2003, August 4). *Correlates of early academic behaviors of Washington State Achievers.* Paper presented at Conference on Transition to College in Washington State, Seattle.

Sedlacek, W., E. & Sheu, H. B. (forthcoming, a). Academic success of Gates Millennium Scholars. *Readings on Equal Education.*

Sedlacek, W. E., & Sheu, H. B. (forthcoming, b). Correlates of leadership activities among Gates Millennium Scholars. *Readings on Equal Education.*

Sedlacek, W. E., Troy, W. G., & Chapman, T. H. (1976). An evaluation of three methods of racism-sexism training. *Personnel and Guidance Journal, 55,* 196–198.

Sergent, M. T., & Sedlacek, W. E. (1989). Perceptual mapping: A methodology in the assessment of environmental perceptions. *Journal of College Student Development, 30,* 319–322.

Sergent, M. T., & Sedlacek, W. E. (1990). Volunteer motivations across student organizations: A test of person-environment fit theory. *Journal of College Student Development, 31,* 255–261.

Sergent, M. T., Woods, P. A., & Sedlacek, W. E. (1992). University student attitudes toward Arabs: Intervention implications. *Journal of Multicultural Counseling and Development, 20,* 123–131.

Shanbacher, J. (1980). *A comparison of feminist and nonfeminist therapists' attitudes toward clients.* Unpublished master's thesis, University of Maryland.

Sherif, C. W. (1973). Social distance as categorization of intergroup integration. *Journal of Personality and Social Psychology, 25,* 327–334.

Sheu, H. B., & Sedlacek, W. E. (forthcoming) *Measurement and evaluation in counseling and development.*

Sigelman, L., & Welch, S. (1993). The contact hypothesis revisited: Black-white interaction and positive racial attitudes. *Social Forces, 71,* 781–795.

Sivanandan, A. A. (1983). Challenging racism. *Race and Class, 25*(2), 1–11.

Smith, D. G., García, M., Hudgins, C. A., McTighe Musil, C., Nettles, M. T., & Sedlacek, W. E. (2000). *A diversity research agenda.* Washington DC: Association of American Colleges and Universities.

Smittle, P. (1995). Academic performance predictors for community college student assessment. *Community College Review, 23*(2), 37–47.

Sontag, D. (2002, April 28). Who was responsible for Elizabeth Shin? *New York Times Magazine,* p. 57.

Sowa, C. J., & Gressard, C. F. (1983). Athletic participation: Its relationship to student development. *Journal of College Student Personnel, 24,* 237–239.

Spector, P. E. (1992). *Summated rating scale construction: An introduction.* Thousand Oaks, CA: Sage.

Standards for educational and psychological testing. (1999). Washington, DC: American Educational Research Association, American Psychological Association, National Council on Measurement in Education.

Stanfield, J.H. (1994). *Ethnic modeling in qualitative research.* In N. K. Denzin & Y. S. Lincoln (Eds.), *Handbook of Qualitative Research* (pp. 175-188). Thousand Oaks, CA: Sage.

Stanley, J. C. (1971). Predicting college success of the educationally disadvantaged. *Science, 171,* 640–647.

Steele, C. M. (1997). A threat in the air: How stereotypes shape intellectual identity and performance. *American Psychologist, 52,* 613–629.

Stericker, A. B., & Johnson, J. E. (1977). Sex role identification and self-esteem in college students: Do men and women differ? *Sex Roles, 3,* 19–26.

Sternberg, R. J. (1985). *Beyond IQ.* London: Cambridge University Press.

Sternberg, R. J. (1986). What would better intelligence tests look like? In *Measures in the college admissions process* (pp. 146–150). New York: College Entrance Examination Board.

Sternberg, R. J. (1996). *Successful intelligence.* New York: Plume.

Sternberg, R. J., Lubart, T. I. (1996). Investing in creativity. *American Psychologist, 51,* 667–688.

Sternberg, R. J., & Williams, W. M. (1997). Does the Graduate Record Examination predict meaningful success in graduate training of psychologists? *American Psychologist, 52,* 630–641.

St. John, E. P. (1994). *Prices, productivity and investment: Assessing financial strategies in higher education* (ASHE/ERIC Higher Education Report no. 3). Washington, DC: George Washington University.

St. John, E. P., & Hossler, D. (1998). Higher education desegregation in the post-Fordice legal environment: A critical-empirical perspective. In R. E. Fossey (Ed.), *Readings on equal education, Vol. 15, Race, the courts, and equal education: The limits of the law* (pp. 123–156). New York: AMS Press.

St. John, E. P., & Musoba, G. D. (2001) *Academic access and equal opportunity: Rethinking the foundations for policy on diversity* (Policy Research Report no. 01–05). Bloomington: Indiana Education Policy Center, Indiana University.

Stovall, C. D. (1989). *Development of a measure of white counselor racial attitude toward black male client characteristics: The Counselor Situational Attitude Scale (CSAS).* Unpublished doctoral dissertation, University of Maryland.

Stovall, C., & Sedlacek, W. E. (1983). Attitudes of male and female university students toward students with different physical disabilities. *Journal of College Student Personnel, 24,* 325–330.

Stricker, L. J., Rock, D. A., & Burton, N. W. (1993). Sex differences in predictions of college grades from Scholastic Aptitude Test scores. *Journal of Educational Psychology, 85,* 710–718.

Students who decline to identify their race in college admission. (1996/1997, Winter). *Journal of Blacks in Higher Education, 14,* 58–59.

Sue, D. W., Arredondo, P., & McDavis, R. J. (1992). Multicultural counseling competencies and standards: A call to the profession. *Journal of Counseling and Development, 70,* 477–486.

Suthakaran, V., & Sedlacek, W. E. (1999). Computer aversion among students with and without learning disabilities. *Journal of College Student Development, 40*(4), 428–431.

Suthakaran, V., & Sedlacek, W. E. (2001, April 18). *Developing a model of religious identity.* Presented at Counseling Center Research and Development Meeting, University of Maryland, College Park.

Tapia, R. (1998). *Assessing and evaluating the evaluation tool: The standardized test.* Paper presented at NISE Forum.

Tatum, B. D. (1992). Talking about race, learning about racism: The application of racial identity development theory in the classroom. *Harvard Educational Review, 62*(1), 1–24.

Thomson, G. E. (1995). *A simpler explanation? Comment on Leonard and Jiang's gender bias in the college predictions of the SAT.* University of California.

Thurstone, L. L., & Chave, E. J. (1929). *The measurement of attitude.* Chicago: University of Chicago Press.

Tidball, M. E. (1986). Baccalaureate origins of recent natural science doctorates. *Journal of Higher Education, 57,* 606–620.

Ting, S. R. (1997). Estimating academic success in the first year of college for specially admitted white students: A model combining cognitive and psychosocial predictors. *Journal of College Student Development, 38,* 401–409.

Ting, S. R., & Robinson, T. L. (1998). First-year academic success: A prediction combining cognitive and psychosocial variables for white and African American students. *Journal of College Student Development, 39,* 599–610.

Ting, S. R., & Sedlacek, W. E. (2000). *Validity of the Noncognitive Questionnaire-Revised 2 in predicting the academic success of university freshmen.* Counseling Center Research Report no. 1–00. College Park: University of Maryland.

Tinto, V. (1993). *Leaving college: Rethinking the causes and cures of student attrition* (2nd Ed.). Chicago: University of Chicago Press.

Tinto, V., & Goodsell, A. (1993). *Freshman interest groups and the first year experience: Constructing student communities in a large university.* (ERIC Document Reproduction Service no. ED 358 778) Washington, DC: U.S. Department of Education.

Tipling, A. N. (1993). *Cognitive and noncognitive predictors of academic success in older returning women students.* Unpublished doctoral dissertation, University of Virginia, Charlottesville.

Top colleges look for extracurricular success. (1999). *Career World, 28*(3), 2–3.

Tracey, T. J., & Sedlacek, W. E. (1984a). Noncognitive variables in predicting academic success by race. *Measurement and Evaluation in Guidance, 16,* 172–178.

Tracey, T. J., & Sedlacek, W. E. (1984b). Using ridge regression with noncognitive variables by race in admissions. *College and University, 50,* 345–350.

Tracey, T. J., & Sedlacek, W. E. (1985). The relationship of noncognitive variables to academic success: A longitudinal comparison by race. *Journal of College Student Personnel, 26,* 405–410.

Tracey, T. J., & Sedlacek, W. E. (1987). Prediction of college graduation using noncognitive variable by race. *Measurement and Evaluation in Counseling and Development, 19,* 177–184.

Tracey, T. J., & Sedlacek, W. E. (1988). A comparison of white and black student academic success using noncognitive variables: A LISREL analysis. *Research in Higher Education, 27,* 333–348.

Tracey, T. J., & Sedlacek, W. E. (1989). Factor structure of the Noncognitive Questionnaire-Revised across samples of black and white college students. *Educational and Psychological Measurement, 49,* 637–648.

Tracey, T. J., Sedlacek, W. E., & Miars, R. D. (1983). Applying ridge regression to admissions data by race and sex. *College and University, 58,* 313–318.

Trimble, J. E. (1988). *Stereotypical images, American Indians and prejudice.* In P. A. Katz & D. A. Taylor (Eds.), Eliminating racism: Profiles in controversy (pp. 181–202). New York: Plenum.

Trippi, J., & Cheatham, H. E. (1989). Effects of special counseling programs for black freshmen on a predominantly white campus. *Journal of College Student Development, 30,* 35–40.

Upcraft, M. L., Gardner, J., & Associates. (1989). *The freshman year experience.* San Francisco: Jossey-Bass.

Upcraft, M. L., & Schuh, J. H. (1996). *Assessment in student affairs: A Guide for practitioners.* San Francisco: Jossey-Bass.

U.S. Department of Education, National Center for Education Statistics. (1998). *The condition of education 1998.* Washington, DC: U.S. Government Printing Office.

U.S. Department of Education. (2002). *Digest of education statistics.* Washington, DC: National Center for Education Statistics.

Valverde, L. A. (1998). Future strategies and actions: Creating multicultural higher education campuses. In L. A. Valverde & L. A. Castenell, Jr. (Eds.), *The multicultural campus: Strategies for transforming higher education* (pp. 19–29). Walnut Creek, CA: Alta Mira.

Van Ghent, D. (1961). *The English novel: Form and function.* New York: HarperCollins.

van Rossum, C. F. (2002, April 30). *Applying non-cognitive variables to the selection and admission of students of color.* Paper presented at Fifth Annual Symposium on the Recruitment and Retention of Students of Color, University of Nebraska-Lincoln.

Vars, F. E., & Bowen, W. G. (1998). Scholastic Aptitude Test scores, race, and academic performance in selective colleges and universities. In C. Jencks & M. Phillips (Eds.), *The black-white test score gap* (pp. 457–479). Washington, DC: Brookings Institution Press.

Wainer, H. (1988). How accurately can we assess changes in minority performance on the SAT? *American Psychologist, 43,* 774–778.

Washington, J. E. (1993). *An investigation of attitudes of heterosexual identified resident assistants towards based on the sexual orientation of the student.* Unpublished doctoral dissertation, University of Maryland, College Park.

Wawrzynski, M. R. (1999). *The student in the university: A longitudinal study of the relationship between a first-year student seminar and the student persistence process.* Counseling Center Research Report no. 10–99. University of Maryland, College Park.

Wawrzynski, M. R., & Sedlacek, W. E. (2003). Race and gender differences in the transfer student experience. *Journal of College Student Development, 44*(4), 489–501.

Webb, C. T., Sedlacek, W. E., Cohen, D., Shields, P., Gracely, E., Hawkins, M., & Nieman, L. (1997). The impact of nonacademic variables on performance at two medical schools. *Journal of the National Medical Association, 89*(3), 173–180.

Webster, D. W., & Sedlacek, W. E. (1982). The differential impact of a university student union on campus subgroups. *National Association of Student Personnel Administrators Journal, 19*(2), 48–51.

Webster, D. W., Sedlacek, W. E., & Miyares, J. (1979). A comparison of problems perceived by minority and white students. *Journal of College Student Personnel, 20,* 165–170.

West, C. (1993). *Race matters.* Boston: Beacon Press.

Westbrook, F. D., & Sedlacek, W. E. (1988). Workshop on using noncognitive variables with minority students in higher education. *Journal for Specialists in Group Work, 13,* 82–89.

Westbrook, F. D., & Sedlacek, W. E. (1991). Forty years of using labels to communicate about nontraditional students: Does it help or hurt? *Journal of Counseling and Development,* 70, 20–28.

Whitaker, V. W., & Roberts, F. L. (1990). Applying values and lifestyles psychographics to parental involvement in college and university orientation. *National Academic Advising Association Journal, 10*(1), 41–46.

White, T. J., & Sedlacek, W. E. (1986). Noncognitive predictors of grades and retention for specially admitted students. *Journal of College Admissions, 3,* 20–23.

White, T. J., & Sedlacek, W. E. (1987). White student attitudes toward blacks and Hispanics: Programming implications. *Journal of Multicultural Counseling and Development, 15,* 171–182.

White, C. J., & Shelley, C. (1996). Telling stories: Students and administrators talk about retention. In I. H. Johnson & A. J. Ottens. (Eds.). *Leveling the playing field: Promoting academic success for students of color.* San Francisco: Jossey-Bass. Pp. 15–34.

Wilbur, S. A., & Bonous-Hammarth, M. (1998). Testing a new approach to admissions: The Irvine experience. In *Chilling admissions: The affirmative action crisis and the search for alternatives.* In G. Orfield & E. Miller (Eds.), Cambridge, MA: Harvard Education Publishing Group.

Wilds, D. J., & Wilson, R. (Eds.). (1998). *Minorities in higher education: Sixteenth annual status report.* Washington, DC: American Council on Education.

Wilkshire, D. M. (1989). *Differential attitudes of student affairs professionals toward commuter and resident students.* Unpublished master's thesis, University of Maryland.

Williams, J. B. (1997). *Race discrimination in higher education.* New York: Praeger.

Williams, W. M. (1997, October 10). Reliance on test scores is a conspiracy of lethargy. *Chronicle of Higher Education,* p. A60.

Willingham, W. W. (1985). *Success in college: The role of personal qualities and academic ability.* New York: College Entrance Examination Board.

Willingham, W. W., & Cole, N. S. (1997). *Gender and fair assessment.* Mahwah, NJ: Erlbaum.

Willingham, W. W., Lewis, C., Morgan, R., & Ramist, L. (1990). *Predicting college grades: An analysis of institutional trends over two decades.* Princeton, NJ: Educational Testing Service.

Wilson, E. S. (1955). Sorting by personal factors. In *College Admissions 2.* New York: College Entrance Examination Board.

Wilson, K. K. (1980). *A review of research on the prediction of academic performance after the freshman year* (RR 83–11). Princeton, NJ: Educational Testing Service.

Wilson, K. K. (1983). The performance of minority students beyond the freshman year: Testing a late bloomer hypothesis in one state university setting. *Research in Higher Education, 13,* 23–47.

Woods, P. A., & Sedlacek, W. E. (1988). *Construct and congruent validity of the Noncognitive Questionnaire (NCQ).* Counseling Center Research Report no. 6–88. College Park: University of Maryland.

Wyckoff, S. C. (1998). Retention theories in higher education: Implications for institutional practice. *Recruitment and Retention in Higher Education, 12*(2), pp. 1–2, 7.

Yalof-Garfield, L. Y. (1997). Squaring affirmative action admissions policies with federal judicial guidelines: A model for the twenty-first center. *Higher Education Extension Service.* (www.review.org)

Ziomek, R. L., & Andrews, K. M. (1996). *Predicting the college grade point averages of special-tested students from their ACT assessment score and higher school grades* (Research Report 96–1). Iowa City, IA: ACT.

Ziomek, R. L., & Svec, J. C. (1995). *High school grades and achievement: Evidence of grade inflation* (Research Report 95–3.) Iowa City, IA: ACT.

NAME INDEX

SUBJECT INDEX

U

V

W